Library of
Davidson College

PORTUGAL

WESTVIEW PROFILES • NATIONS OF CONTEMPORARY WESTERN EUROPE

Portugal: From Monarchy to Pluralist Democracy,
Walter C. Opello, Jr.

Ireland: The Challenge of Conflict and Change,
Richard B. Finnegan

Spain: From Repression to Renewal,
E. Ramón Arango

Denmark: A Troubled Welfare State,
Kenneth E. Miller

PORTUGAL

From Monarchy to Pluralist Democracy

Walter C. Opello, Jr.

Westview Press
BOULDER • SAN FRANCISCO • OXFORD

Westview Profiles/Nations of Contemporary Western Europe

All photos not otherwise attributed were taken by the author.

All rights reserved. No part of this publication may be reproduced or transmitted in any form or by any means, electronic or mechanical, including photocopy, recording, or any information storage and retrieval system, without permission in writing from the publisher.

Copyright © 1991 by Westview Press, Inc.

Published in 1991 in the United States of America by Westview Press, Inc., 5500 Central Avenue, Boulder, Colorado 80301, and in the United Kingdom by Westview Press, 36 Lonsdale Road, Summertown, Oxford OX2 7EW

Library of Congress Cataloging-in-Publication Data
Opello, Walter C.
 Portugal : from monarchy to pluralist democracy / Walter C. Opello.
  p. cm.—(Westview profiles. Nations of contemporary Western Europe)
 Includes bibliographical references and index.
 ISBN 0-8133-0488-1
 1. Portugal—Politics and government. 2. Portugal—Social life and customs—20th century. 3. Portugal—Economic conditions—20th century. 4. Portugal—Foreign relations. I. Title. II. Series.
DP556.O64 1991
946.904—dc20   90-27257
                                                                                                          CIP

Printed and bound in the United States of America

∞ The paper used in this publication meets the requirements of the American National Standard for Permanence of Paper for Printed Library Materials Z39.48-1984.

10   9   8   7   6   5   4   3   2   1

For Olivia

Contents

List of Illustrations   ix

1   **Introduction**   1

2   **Topography and Climate**   4
    North, 5
    Center, 7
    South, 15
    Atlantic Islands, 16
    References, 17

3   **Portuguese Society**   18
    People, 18
    Social Cleavages, 20
    Religion, 25
    Education, 28
    The Arts, 29
    References, 36

4   **From Castilian Province to Portuguese Republic**   37
    The Birth of Portugal, 37
    Invasion by Castile, 40
    Voyages of Discovery, 41
    Iberian Union, 44
    Absolutism, 46
    Constitutional Monarchy, 48
    The First Republic, 53
    References, 58

5   **Corporatists and Monarchists Versus Republicans**   59
    Military Dictatorship, 59

Salazar, 61
The Constitution of 1933, 64
The New State, 67
Opposition to the New State, 71
References, 76

6 **Downfall of the New State** 77
Caetano, 77
The Colonial Wars, 80
The Armed Forces Movement, 83
Spínola, 87
The Shift to the Left, 91
The Group of Nine, 93
References, 97

7 **Consolidation of Democracy** 98
The Constitution of 1976, 98
A Freely Elected Government, 102
The Democratic Alliance, 106
Constitutional Revisions, 109
The Central Bloc, 114
A Civilian President, 116
Prospects for Stability, 120
References, 126

8 **The Economy** 127
Economic Life Under Salazar, 127
The Economic Effects of April 25, 1974, 131
Economic Integration with Europe, 135
References, 138

9 **Portugal and the Wider World** 140
Decolonization, 140
Relations with Selected Countries, 144
References, 151

10 **Whither Portugal?** 152
References, 155

List of Acronyms 157
About the Book and Author 160
Index 161

Illustrations

Maps
Portugal	x
2.1 Portugal in its regional setting	5

Photos
Young and old villagers, central Portugal	9
Villagers from Soutocico parading in traditional dress	10
A view of Lisbon from Edward VII Park	11
A street scene in the Alfama, Lisbon	12
The Torre de Belém	13
The Jerónimos Monastery, Belém	14
The Manueline window at the Convento de Cristo, Tomar	35
The Monument of the Discoveries, Belém	42
King Manuel II	55
António de Oliveira Salazar	62
Marcello José das Neves Alves Caetano	78
April 25, 1974, Carmo Square, Lisbon	86
April 25, 1974, Trinity Square, Lisbon	87
The Board of National Salvation, April 28, 1974	88
António dos Santos Ramalho Eanes	104
Aníbal António Cavaco Silva	118
Mário Alberto Nobre Lopes Soares	121

Portugal. *Source:* Eugene K. Keefe et al., *Area Handbook for Portugal* (Washington, D.C.: Government Printing Office, 1977), p. xiv.

1
Introduction

Portugal is one of the oldest countries in Western Europe. Its name is derived from the medieval Latin *Portucalense*, which referred to the territory inland from the Roman town of Portus Cale situated on the mouth of the Douro River. Reconquered from the Moslems in the ninth century, this region was resettled by Christians and administered as a province of the kingdom of Asturias. Because of their country's isolation, the Portucalense developed a strong sense of individuality, unity, and self-reliance. Cut off from the rest of Asturias, the inhabitants of the province of Portugal, as it came to be called in the vernacular, oriented themselves toward the Atlantic Ocean and the south.

By the middle of the thirteenth century the Portuguese kingdom had achieved Portugal's present borders as well as a degree of internal political, economic, social, and cultural unity that was well ahead of other European monarchies of the time. This precocious development imparted to the Portuguese a sense of national purpose and a set of centralized political institutions that led them to embark on the great voyages of discovery and eventually to acquire a vast seaborne empire. Stretching from the Americas to the Far East, this empire made the Portuguese crown the richest and most bureaucratic in Europe at the end of the sixteenth century. An oceanic mission had become central to Portugal's image and definition of its national purpose. Portugal saw itself as a major Atlantic power, as the core of a far-reaching and racially diverse, pan-Lusitanian, global community.

Unlike other European monarchies, the Portuguese crown itself organized and directed the voyages of discovery. This policy retarded the growth of a commercial, entrepreneurial middle class and, at the same time, diverted profits from the overseas trade into sumptuous palaces for the king and aristocracy and cathedrals for the Catholic church. Much of this wealth also flowed through Portugal to northern Europe for the acquisition of manufactures and played no small part in the Industrial Revolution in Great Britain and elsewhere. Thus, early nation-state development and Portugal's oceanic policy not only exaggerated the authority and power of the traditional, artistocratically based monarchical system but kept Portugal marginal to the process of industrialization and accompanying social change taking place in northern Europe.

In the early decades of the nineteenth century, industrialization finally began and a middle class started to emerge. As elsewhere in Europe, as the economic importance of the Portugese middle class grew, its members began to challenge the traditional monarchical system because its political structures prevented middle-class involvement in national affairs commensurate with its sense of economic importance. In Portugal, however, this challenge resulted in an extremely long struggle between the traditional aristocracy and the monarchy that strove to protect the ancien régime and the middle classes that aspired to change it: first, by limiting the crown by a written constitution and, later, by replacing the monarchy with a republic. This struggle waxed and waned for well over 150 years—from the 1820s until the 1970s—during which time the governmental framework of Portugal was structured and restructured as absolute monarchy, constitutional monarchy, republic, and dictatorship. For well over a century, first liberal and then republican political concepts and institutions were in juxtaposition with the traditional values and institutions of monarchical and aristocratic power and privilege.

It can be argued that the *golpe d'estado* of April 25, 1974, which overturned the authoritarian dictatorship established in 1932 by António de Oliveira Salazar, marks the end of Portugal's long transition from absolutist monarchy to pluralist democracy. The final transition to democracy did not, however, take place without turmoil. Between 1974 and 1976 a struggle for control of the state ensued among various factions of Portugal's new political elite. In 1975 Portugal came very close to civil war as these various factions aligned themselves into two camps, each drawing support from regionally based social groups and each mobilized to strike at the other militarily. On November 25, 1975, a group of military officers committed to a Western-European-style pluralist democracy went into action against those who supported a people's democracy of the Eastern European variant. The officers emerged victorious. This paved the way for the promulgation of a new constitution on April 2, 1976. It also brought to an end Portugal's oceanic mission and turned the country toward Western Europe.

The promulgation of a democratic constitution, the election of a civilian government on April 25, 1976, and the turn toward Western Europe did not, however, bring stability to Portugal. Conditioned by the struggles of the first two years of political freedom, the constitution represented a truce among warring political parties who were forced to coexist with one another. This resulted in a decade of political bickering and backbiting, no one party able to form a lasting coalition or win an absolute majority at the polls. The support for each of the parties was remarkably uniform from election to election, and it seemed that Portugal's new democracy was going to follow the Italian pattern. This was not to be: In 1987 the stalemate was broken when a single party won over 50 percent of the vote and an absolute majority of seats in Parliament, which opened a new phase of political stability in Portugal's democratic development.

This book is a survey of Portugal's evolution from an absolute monarchy into a nascent pluralist democracy. I do not follow any particular general explanatory approach such as structural-functionalism, class analysis, or world systems theory. Rather, I simply describe the process of Portugal's political transformation. Yet I do have a point of view: that Portugal, because of its location on the periphery of Western Europe, has historically been *in* but not *of* the continent. That is, although the political, economic, and social change in Portugal recapitulates such change elsewhere in Western Europe, the country's relative isolation, early development as a nation-state, and vast colonial empire retarded the country's transformation into a modern industrial pluralist democracy.

The plan of the book is as follows: Chapters 2 and 3 provide geographical, social, and cultural background material. Chapter 4 presents the historical context from Portugal's founding as a nation-state nearly 900 years ago to the collapse of the First Republic in 1910. Chapter 5 discusses the New State dictatorship established by Salazar in 1932. Chapter 6 deals with the golpe d'estado that overturned the New State dictatorship and Chapter 7 with the consolidation of democracy in subsequent years. Chapter 8 examines Portugal's economic life; Chapter 9 discusses Portugal's foreign policy and place in the wider world. The tenth and concluding chapter speculates briefly about Portugal's future.

I have spared the reader footnotes, instead listing at the end of each chapter important works on various aspects of Portugal's geography, society, history, politics, and foreign policy. Apart from these sources, as well as my own research and periods of residence in Portugal, the book draws on countless conversations with Portuguese, German, British, French, Canadian, and U.S. academics well acquainted with Portugal's history, society, and politics.

2
Topography and Climate

Portugal is a narrow, rectangular country some 350 miles long and between 80 and 140 miles wide. Its 35,516 square miles are not a geographically identifiable portion of the Iberian peninsula, and the frontier with Spain does not, except here and there, follow any distinct geographical feature such as river valley or mountain chain (see Map 2.1). This is so because the border between Spain and Portugal is essentially political, having been defined by Portuguese kings and their Spanish counterparts as they drove southward during the reconquest of the peninsula from the Moslems in the thirteenth and fourteenth centuries. Thus, the various regions of Portugal, although different from one another, correspond to those of Spain: The northeastern part of Portugal is an extension of the Spanish *meseta;* the area to the south of the Tagus River (Tejo in Portuguese, Tajo in Spanish) is an extension of Spain's Estremadura; the Serra da Estrela mountains, which traverse central Portugal, are an arm of Spain's Sierras de Gata, Gredos, and Guardarrama; and Portugal's two major rivers, the Douro (Duero in Spanish) and the Tejo are also two of Spain's principal waterways.

Portugal contains considerable physical and climatic diversity. The most striking contrasts in topography and climate are between the region north of the Tejo and the region to the south. The terrain to the north is generally mountainous and moist; rain falls quite evenly throughout the year. The north is verdant and considerably cooler on average than is the south. The Serra da Estrela, Portugal's highest mountain range (the tallest peak is 6,532 feet), receives quite heavy snows, which frequently block roads and isolate villages. The terrain of the south, except for the extreme south, comprises gently rolling hills and plains. The climate is Mediterranean, with bright sunshine, warm temperatures and low precipitation, except in winter months, when the region is inundated by torrential rains. Summer droughts are common, and water frequently has to be rationed in the major towns. The extreme south has a distinct topography and climate because of its separation from the rest of Portugal by two low ranges of

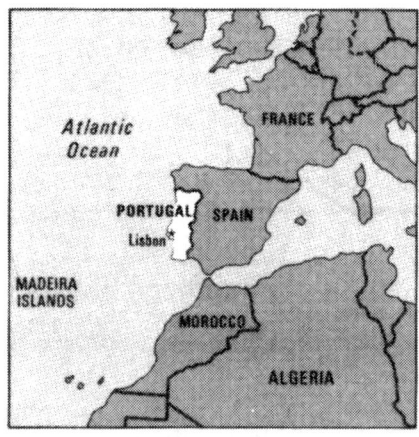

Portugal in its regional setting. *Source:* U.S. Department of State, *Background Notes: Portugal* (Washington, D.C.: Government Printing Office, 1985), p. 1.

mountains, the Serra do Caldeirão in the east and the Serra de Monchique in the west. Sheltered by these mountains, this region faces the sea, which makes its climate similar to that of North Africa.

In order to discuss the various regions in some systematic fashion, it is necessary to say a few words about how Portugal is organized for administrative purposes. Following the French example, Portuguese liberals of the 1830s divided their country into districts (*distritos*) that continue to the present, the twenty-second and last, the district of Setúbal, having been created in 1926. Eighteen of these districts—Aveiro, Beja, Braga, Bragança, Castelo Branco, Coimbra, Évora, Faro, Guarda, Leiria, Lisboa, Portalegre, Porto, Santarém, Setúbal, Viana do Castelo, Vila Real, and Viseu—are on the mainland. The remaining four are on the Atlantic archipelagoes: The district of Funchal encompasses Madeira and the districts of Angra do Heroísmo, Horta, and Ponta Delgada encompass the Azores. As the boundaries of the mainland districts were not drawn in accordance with homogeneous topographies, an administrative code in 1936, superimposed eleven provinces (*províncias*) over these districts in an attempt to reintroduce into official life Portugal's traditional, preliberal administrative regions.

NORTH

The northernmost of these provinces is the Minho, which encompasses the districts of Braga and Viana do Castelo. In the Minho the land rises steeply from a narrow coastal strip, perhaps 5 miles wide, to heights of between 1,000 and 2,000 feet. The eastern boundary of the province is delimited from the province to its west, the Trás-os-Montes, by a series of mountain ranges, the Serras do Gerês, da Cabreira, do Barroso, and do Marão, which form an amphitheater facing the Atlantic Ocean. It was these mountains that isolated the inhabitants of Portucalense from Asturias and oriented them toward the south and the sea, making the Minho the historical cradle of Portugal. The Minho is, as it was in Roman and medieval times, bounded in the north by the Minho River (Miño in Spanish), which for part of its course forms the international frontier between Spain and Portugal. The province receives persistent and copious rainfall (between 80 and 100 inches per year), which makes the region very wet and green and allows it to support the most intensive agriculture in Portugal. The second most densely populated mainland province (503 inhabitants/mi^2), the land of the Minho is excessively fragmented into small, family-owned farms, or *minifúndios*, which are the result of ancient settlement patterns, a strong attachment to the land, and the tradition of subdividing land equally among all family members.

The hamlet is the usual settlement pattern, but most Minhotos, as the inhabitants of this province are called, live in individual houses scattered throughout the countryside. Extreme land fragmentation led to a high level of emigration of young single men to Brazil in the 1960s and Western Europe, especially France, in the 1970s, leaving much of the farm work to old men, women, and children. Despite a strong tradition of familial self-reliance, there is much communal cultivation, neighbors and friends frequently conjoining to tend each other's fields and flocks. Minhotos are the most religious Portuguese, with the rhythm of life turning on the observances of saint's days and pilgrimages (*romarias*). These times of communal celebration involve wearing traditional costumes, vigorous dancing, and singing. The Minho is the home of *caldo verde*, a potato-based soup with shredded kale, a staple of the Portuguese diet, and *vinho verde* (green wine), a light, sparkling white wine of low alcohol content best drunk well chilled. The Minho contains the town of Guimarães, the capital of Portugal when it was still a province of Asturias, and Barcelos, famed for its ceramic roosters, Portugal's national symbol.

To the east of the Minho is the province of Trás-os-Montes (literally, behind the mountains), reportedly the poorest region not only in Portugal but in Western Europe as well. Encompassing the districts of Vila Real and Bragança, the Trás-os-Montes, in contrast to the Minho, is arid, rugged, and brown. The province's aridity is a result of the mountains between the Minho and Trás-os-Montes, which act as a barrier to storms carrying moisture from the west and northeast. The province is sparsely populated (106 inhabitants/mi^2); the main economic activity is animal grazing and cereal cultivation. There is also some mining of coal, iron ore, and tin.

The northern half of the Trás-os-Montes, called the *terrafria* (cold land), has a continental climate of hot summers and extremely cold winters similar to those of the Spanish meseta. The southern half, or *terraquente* (hot land), is characterized by low, protected valleys with a climate much warmer than that of the high plateau of the terrafria. As in neighboring parts of Spain, in the wilder parts of the province in winter, wolves kill livestock and, upon occasion, small children. Trásmontanos, as the inhabitants of the province are called, are not particularly religious, but they are deeply conservative. There is a clan spirit among some of the families, especially among those living in the terrafria.

The southern edge of the terraquente abuts the Alto Douro (Upper Douro), a region especially noted for its intense cultivation of the port wine grape. The grapes, which are grown in the intricately terraced valley of the Douro, are harvested in late September and early October by migrant labor from the Trás-os-Montes and elsewhere in Portugal. After the wine has been made, it is shipped downriver to Vila Nova de Gaia, on the opposite bank from Porto, where it is matured in the cellars of the numerous port wine lodges, or firms, located there, many of which were established over 300 years ago and have much in common with Spain's sherry *bodegas*.

Porto, the industrial and commercial capital of the north, with a population of about 330,000, is Portugal's second largest city after Lisbon. An ancient city that gave Portugal its name, Porto is a conurbation of narrow streets and dull gray, granite structures built on the steep northern bank of the Douro River. The city is dominated by the massive Paço Episcopal (Bishop's Palace), the Romanesque cathedral, and the rococo tower of the Igreja dos Clérigos (Clerics' Church). Since the fifteenth century the city's inhabitants, the Portuenses, have been nicknamed *tripeiros* (tripe eaters); tripe has long been a staple of the local diet, typically prepared with beans and a hearty sauce made from spices such as paprika, cumin, marjoram, thyme, and cayenne pepper. Porto is the site of Portugal's early industrialization and is known for its manufacturing, textiles, food canning, chemicals, and leather goods. The city has a strong liberal tradition and its inhabitants believe they are Portugal's hardest-working people.

CENTER

The midsection of Portugal, roughly between the Douro and the Tejo rivers, is called Beira. Meaning "border," the name was given to this region during the reconquest and resettlement, when it was a frontier between the Christian north and Moslem south. It is subdivided into three provinces: Beira Litoral (Coastal Beira), Beira Alta (Upper Beira), and Beira Baixa (Lower Beira).

Beira Litoral, which encompasses the districts of Aveiro, Coimbra, and the northern part of Leiria, in contrast to the mountainous Minho, is a coastal plain as much as 30 miles wide, containing salt marshes and long stretches of sand dunes. Around the *ria* (lagoon) near Aveiro, the district capital, there is a substantial section of land reclaimed from the sea. Aveiro is considered Portugal's Venice because of its picturesque canals, and the land around the town is likened to that of the Netherlands because it is extremely flat. During the late fifteenth and early sixteenth centuries, Aveiro was Portugal's most prosperous fishing port and center of the country's salt industry. Because of the growth of other ports, Aveiro is no longer as important as it once was, although it is still known for its fishing industry and salt pans.

Beira Litoral is bisected by the lower course of the Mondego River, Portugal's third most important waterway, which empties into the Atlantic at Figueira da Foz. The land to either side of the river is some of the most fertile in Portugal and produces rice, corn, grapes, and forest goods for domestic consumption. Small-scale agriculture under a mixture of owner cultivation and sharecropping is characteristic of the region. About 25 miles upstream from the mouth of the Mondego is the most important town of the Beiras, the district capital of Coimbra, Portugal's third largest city (74,616 inhabitants) and the site of one of Europe's oldest universities (founded in 1290). Coimbra University has faculties of arts and letters, medicine, science, pharmacy, and law. The faculty of law, probably the university's best, has produced a high proportion of the country's political leaders. Students come from all regions and social backgrounds, but those from the highest social classes are more in evidence.

In contrast to Beira Litoral, Beira Alta, which contains the districts of Viseu and Guarda, is generally bleak and desolate. Guarda, the farthest east of Beira Alta's two districts, contains a major portion of the Serra da Estrela, Portugal's highest mountain range. This makes the town of Guarda, the district's capital, Portugal's highest city (2,427 feet). The ruggedness of the mountains, cold, and aridity prohibit a large population (only 93 inhabitants/mi^2). Sheepraising is common in the district, and the area is known for its wool, milk, and cheeses, especially the *Queijo da Serra* (mountain cheese); similar to Brie, *Serra*, as it is commonly called, is made from the milk of longhorn sheep that graze the valleys of the Serra da Estrela. In the district of Viseu the inhabitants cluster along river valleys; in one of these, the valley of the Dão near the town of Viseu, the climate is similar to that of the Alto Douro. This allows the making of Dão, a full-bodied, fruity wine much like Burgundy and probably the best wine produced in Portugal.

Young and old villagers, central Portugal.

Beira Baixa, which is roughly coterminous with the district of Castelo Branco, is a dry and windswept extension of the Spanish meseta. The economy of the region is mixed stockraising and cereal crop cultivation with some mining and manufacturing. In Beira Baixa is Monsanto, chosen in 1938 as Portugal's most "Portuguese" village. One of the country's most authentically preserved villages, it is situated on the slopes of a granite hill, and its houses, made of the same material, perch on the rocks as if they were a natural part of the hillside.

The Estremadura province, which includes the southern part of Leiria and the districts of Lisboa and Setúbal, is the coastal region to the south of Beira Litoral between the Atlantic Ocean and the Tejo River. The good soils, moderate climate, and even rainfall support an intensive agriculture and make the Estremadura Portugal's most densely settled province (710 inhabitants/mi^2). It is known for its wines, which are second only to those of the Douro and Dão regions, the most notable being the reds of Colares and the whites of Bucelas. The area of the Estremadura just north of Lisbon is known collectively as the Saloio and its inhabitants as Saloios (which has come to be a derogatory term meaning "hicks"). The gardens of the Saloios produce the lemons, strawberries, pears, quinces, peaches, tomatoes, almonds, and olives

Villagers from Soutocico parading in traditional dress during Portugal Day celebrations, Leiria.

consumed in Lisbon. Ceramics, marble quarrying, and timber are also important industries in the region.

Tourism and local industries, such as fishing, mix in various locales in the Estremadura. The fishing village of Nazaré, which claims to have been founded by the Phoenicians; the Batalha Monastery, a masterpiece of Portuguese and Manueline architecture dedicated to Portugal's victory over the Castilians on the plain of Aljubarrota in 1385; Alcobaça, a Cistercian monastery founded in 1178; and the palace and monastery of Mafra, the Portuguese Escorial, attract huge numbers of tourists annually. The Serra de Sintra, a microenvironment of exceptional natural beauty less than 20 miles from Lisbon, also draws visitors. The summer residence of Portuguese kings for more than 600 years, the town of Sintra is clustered around the Palácio Nacional (National Palace) and the Palácio da Pena (Pena Palace), built in the nineteenth century in a variety of architectural styles (Arab, Gothic, baroque, and Manueline) and perched on the top of one of the Serra's highest peaks. Between Lisbon and Sintra is the national palace at Queluz (What Light) built in the eighteenth century and modeled on Versailles.

The Estremadura also contains Lisbon, Portugal's political, economic, and cultural capital and, with about 800,000 inhabitants, is the country's

A view of Lisbon from Edward VII Park, with the statue of the Marquês de Pombal in the center.

largest city. About one in five Portuguese lives in the greater Lisbon area, which makes Portugal macrocephalic, like many less-developed countries. Portuguese are drawn to Lisbon because living conditions and employment opportunities are better there than anywhere else in the country. The city has the highest proportion of doctors and medical personnel per capita, the country's biggest and best-equipped hospitals, the most extensive social services, several large universities, government ministries, major economic and industrial enterprises, and a rich cultural and intellectual life.

Lisbon is a typical Mediterranean city of broad avenues, wide squares, palm trees, and pastel-colored buildings. It has a noisy street life, and Lisboetas (Lisbonites, though more correctly it would be "Lisbonenses") exude a self-confident superiority toward the rest of the country that comes from living in the capital city. The city's largest square is the Praça do Comércio (Commerce Square), which is flanked on three sides by the imposing buildings of government ministries and, on the fourth, the Tejo River. Directly behind the square is the Baixa (Downtown) of three long avenues cut at regular intervals by parallel streets built by the Marquês de Pombal after much of Lisbon was destroyed by a massive earthquake in 1755. The buildings in the Baixa

A street scene in the Alfama, Lisbon.

are uniform in height and design, constructed according to a masterplan drawn up by Pombal's architect, Eugénio dos Santos, in order to rebuild the city as rapidly as possible. At the opposite end of the Baixa from the Praça do Comércio is the Rossio, the heart of the city during medieval times as it is today. Beyond the Rossio is the Praça de Restauradores, which is dedicated to and named for those who restored Portugal's independence from Spain in 1640. From this square begins Lisbon's principal thoroughfare, the Avenida da Liberdade, a broad, tree-lined avenue similar to the Champs-Elysées. At the top of the avenue, in the center of a vast traffic circle, is a statue of Pombal. Behind this statue is the Parque Eduardo VII (Edward VII Park), built to commemorate the visit of Edward VII to Portugal in 1902. To the east of the Baixa is the

The Torre de Belém.

city's oldest quarter, the Alfama, which, spared in the earthquake of 1755, dates to the time of the city's Moslem occupation. Dominated by the Castelo São Jorge (Saint George's Castle), the Alfama is a quarter of narrow, precipitous, winding streets and contains Lisbon's minster (*sé*), an imposing Romanesque cathedral built to resemble a fortress. On the hills to the west of the Baixa is the Bairro Alto (Upper Quarter), which is known for its elegant shopping streets, night clubs, and discos.

Greater Lisbon extends from the Praça do Comércio along the estuary of the Tejo to Cascais on the Atlantic Ocean. In Belém, one of these suburbs, are located the presidential palace, the Torre de Belém (Tower of Bethlehem), and the Mosteiro dos Jerónimos (Monastery of Jerome). The 1966 construction of Europe's longest suspension bridge, the Ponte 25 de Abril (25th of April Bridge) has permitted greater Lisbon to extend to the opposite bank of the Tejo estuary as well. This area, from the river to the city of Setúbal, some 20 miles to the south by *auto-estrada* (super highway), is heavily industrialized, with steelworks at Seixal, chemical industry at Barreiro, and shipbuilding at Almada. Interspersed among the various suburbs of greater Lisbon are numerous shantytowns (*bairros de lata*, literally, "tin quarters," in reference to the tin roofs of the shacks) without running water, sanitary systems, or paved streets. In these bairros de lata live the city's poorest residents

The Jerónimos Monastery, Belém.

who have been unable to find affordable housing in the established suburban neighborhoods.

The region upriver from Lisbon and south of Beira Baixa has been designated as the province of Ribatejo (meaning "banks of the Tejo"). More or less coterminous with the district of Santarém, this province is divided into two zones by the river itself. The northern bank resembles the Estremadura in topography and climate. This zone is intensively cultivated, with corn, grapes, other fruit, and olives the principal crops. From this region comes Portugal's *vinho da mesa* (table wine), reds from Cartaxo and whites from Chamusca. In the northern part of the Ribatejo, very nearly in the province of Estremadura, is the religious shrine of Fátima, where the Virgin Mary is said to have appeared to three peasant children on the thirteenth day of each month from May to October 1917. Fátima has since become one of the Catholic world's greatest shrines, attracting many thousands of pilgrims each year. The northern Ribatejo also contains the town of Tomar, which is the site of the great Convento de Cristo (Convent of Christ) built by the Portuguese order of the Knights Templar. The southern bank of the Ribatejo, with rolling hills and wide plains, resembles the land of Alentejo.

SOUTH

The Alentejo (meaning "beyond the Tejo") is subdivided into two provinces, the Alto Alentejo (Upper Alentejo), which contains the districts of Évora and Portalegre, and the Baixo Alentejo (Lower Alentejo), which is nearly coterminous with Beja, Portugal's largest district. In earlier times, most of the land of the Alentejo was in the hands of a few nobles and the military and ecclesiastical orders of the church who had received large grants of land from Portuguese kings as recompense for their services during the reconquest. Liberal reforms of the 1830s, designed to boost cereal production, transferred these lands through sale to private individuals, who—instead of working the land themselves as the reformers intended—became a class of absentee landlords.

The principal crops of the Alentejo are wheat and barley. It also produces the great bulk of one of Portugal's chief exports, cork, which is made from bark cut from cork oaks at nine-year intervals. There are vast olive groves around Elvas, Serpa, and Estremoz. Sparsely populated (54 inhabitants/mi^2), the region is made up of widely scattered towns, as in southern Spain. A staple of the Alentejano diet is *gaspacho*, a cold soup made from tomatoes, onions, cucumbers, and pimentos. The Alentejo is the least religious part of Portugal, and family ties are looser because of the seasonal migration to Lisbon of the region's landless work force.

The most southern region of Portugal, the Algarve, is simultaneously a province and district. The last part of Portugal reconquered from the Moslems, the Algarve forms a distinct geographical as well as cultural area, which is reflected in local speech patterns and architecture. Algarvian houses are single-storied, flat-roofed, and whitewashed, like those in Algeria. Although the low mountains (Caldeirão and Monchique) that separate the Algarve from the Alentejo are quite dry and thinly populated, the coastal area is fertile and densely settled (173 inhabitants/mi^2).

Because its warm climate is favorable for citrus trees, the Algarve is Portugal's main producer of oranges, pomegranates, figs, and carobs. Almonds are also cultivated in the region. Fishing is important in the Algarve; as in Estremadura, this local industry mixes with tourism. With numerous good beaches, the province has in recent years become a tourist mecca (principally for northern Europeans) that rivals the Costa del Sol in Spain. The Algarve is the site of the most southwesterly point of the land mass of Europe. It was there on a promontory between the Ponta de Sagres (Sagres Point) and the Cabo de São Vicente (Cape Saint Vincent) that Prince Henry the Navigator founded a school of navigation and planned the famous Portuguese voyages of discovery from 1437 to 1460.

ATLANTIC ISLANDS

The Azores archipelago, named after the great number of birds thought to be goshawks (*açores*) by Diogo de Silves, who discovered these uninhabited islands in 1427, is about 800 miles west of Lisbon and is composed of three clusters of nine islands: São Miguel and Santa Maria in the east; Terceira, Pico, Faial, São Jorge, and Graciosa in the center; and Flores and Corvo in the northwest. The archipelago totals about 5,821 square miles, has a population of about 250,000, and is subdivided into three administrative districts: Ponta Delgada on the island of São Miguel; Angra do Heroísmo on Terceira; and Horta on Faial. Volcanic in origin, the Azores have rich soil that, combined with the locally moderate climate, has produced an intensive agriculture. On small, family-owned holdings throughout the islands, Azorean farmers grow a wide variety of crops such as cereals, vegetables, pineapples, sugarcane, tobacco, and wine grapes. The island of São Jorge is a dairy and meat production center. After agriculture, fishing is the next important economic activity of the archipelago. Terceira Island is the site of a U.S. Air Force base, Lajes; because the base is jointly administered and provides employment, the Açorianas, as the archepelagoe's inhabitants are called, do not oppose it.

The islands of the archipelago of Madeira, about 700 miles southwest of Lisbon, were also uninhabited when discovered in 1418 by the Portuguese navigator João Gonçalves Zarco, who subsequently undertook their colonization. The archipelago consists of the island of Madeira (Timber Island), Porto Santo (Holy Port), the uninhabited Desertas (Deserted Islands), and the Selvagens (Rugged Islands). The archipelago is encompassed by the district of Funchal, and the capital city of the same name is located on Madeira, the largest of these islands. The two inhabited islands have a population of about 250,000. Madeira, like the Azores, is of volcanic origin and consequently has a rugged terrain. The island rises from sea level to a height of 6,106 feet at Pico Ruivo. The climate is generally subtropical at lower elevations and temperate at upper ones. Good soils and mild climate permit the cultivation of bananas, pineapples, sugarcane, avocados, mangos, vegetables, and grapes from which the famous Madeira wine is made. Most agriculture is concentrated on the coastal fringe in a semifeudal fashion that has forced many Madeirense to look to the sea for their livelihoods: Fishing is a major economic activity, especially on the island of Porto Santo. Madeira is known for its needlework and embroidery, a cottage industry employing about 70,000 women. Tourism is important for the economy of Madeira; as elsewhere in Portugal, it mixes with the local fishing industry, especially on Porto Santo, where the archipelago's best beach is found.

REFERENCES

Bradford, Sarah. *Portugal.* New York: Walker and Co., 1973.
Eppstein, John. *Portugal: The Country and People.* London: Queen Anne Press, 1967.
Robinson, Richard. *Contemporary Portugal.* London: George Allen & Unwin, 1979.
Stanislawski, Dan. *The Individuality of Portugal: A Study of Historical-Political Geography.* New York: Greenwood Press, 1959.
──────. *Portugal's Other Kingdom: The Algarve.* Austin: University of Texas Press, 1963.

3
Portuguese Society

PEOPLE

The first recorded inhabitants of Portugal were Paleolithic hunters. These were followed by Neolithic peoples from the eastern Mediterranean. Near the end of the second millennium B.C., a pre-Celtic Bronze Age people from central Europe appeared in the western Iberian peninsula. About the first millennium B.C., agro-pastoral Celts arrived, bringing their families, flocks, and wagons. The Celts were drawn to Galicia and northern Portugal, where the topography and climate were well suited to their herding-farming way of life. They settled in large numbers and blended with indigenous peoples, the descendants of the pre-Celtic settlement from central Europe a millennium earlier. The Celts, who dominated Iberia until the arrival of the Romans, built hilltop forts called *castros*, some of which gradually became fortified cities.

Phoenicians founded several fishing villages on the south coast of the Algarve and explored the western coast of Portugal as far north as Lisbon. Greeks from Asia Minor colonized along Portugal's south and west coast during the ninth and eighth centuries B.C. In the sixth century the Greeks were replaced by Carthaginians, who sought the silver, tin, and copper of Galicia. There were several Carthaginian settlements on the west coast, one as far north as the mouth of the Sado River.

Rome decided to enter Iberia when Carthaginian armies advanced as far as Barcelona. The Romans met the greatest resistance from the Celtic people of the interior, who were known for their physical exploits and pugilistic pursuits. Unlike the city dwellers of the coasts, Celtiberians resisted Rome's legions tooth and nail. The resistance was led by various chieftains, one of whom, Viriato, is reputed to have held up the Roman occupation for several decades. After his assassination, the Romans were able gradually to extend their control throughout the peninsula. The Portuguese have claimed Viriato as the country's first great national hero and in Viseu have erected a statue to his memory. The Celtiberians and Lusitanians (Celtic peoples from Portugal) withdrew to the northwest, where they continued to resist the Romans for several generations. It was not until the first century B.C., some 200 years after the initial Roman invasion of the peninsula, that the Lusitanians were finally conquered. Forced out of their hilltop fortifications, they were resettled on bottomlands. The Romans, who founded cities, built roads, imposed their language and legal code, and, after the conversion of the empire to Christianity, created bishoprics, left a lasting mark on Portugal and dominated the peninsula until the fifth century A.D.

In 408 and 409 Germanic peoples—Visigoths and Vandals from western Germany and Swabians from eastern Germany—entered the peninsula. Within two years they had spread to the west coast. The Swabians, like their Celtic forerunners, were primarily pastoralist and were drawn to Galicia and northern Portugal because these regions were similar in climate to what they had left behind. The Swabians settled among the Luso-Romans, who put up no resistance and assimilated them easily because many Swabians had served in Rome's legions and had adopted the Roman way of life. The collective life of the castros and Roman villas gave way to the Swabian custom of individual houses and small holdings, which is reflected today in the land tenure pattern of northern Portugal.

For almost two centuries Swabians maintained their dominance in the northwest while Visigoths controlled the remainder of the peninsula. By the eighth century, the Visigothic empire was rife with internecine fighting. A Moslem army from North Africa landed on the peninsula in 711 to support the hereditary rights of a certain Visigothic noble. Composed of Berbers and led by Tarik, this army swept through Iberia without meeting resistance, marching as far north as Asturias. In the wake of this success, other Moslem armies invaded the peninsula. The Alentejo fell under Moslem control in 713; Coimbra fell in 716. The Moslem conquest stopped short of complete control of Iberia most likely because the conquerors, who preferred the dry, sunny south of the peninsula, were insufficiently interested in the mountainous, rainy north to overcome the fierce opposition they met there.

Since the Moslem invasions, Portugal has not experienced major influxes of outside peoples. The Christian reconquest resulted in the expulsion of a great number of Moslems and the complete assimilation into Christian culture of those who chose to renounce Islam and convert. Thus, Portugal's present inhabitants are the descendants of a historical mélange of peoples—Celts, Phoenicians, Greeks, Romans, and North Africans—who have been greatly homogenized and amalgamated into a single people. The only exception would be Portugal's indigenous gypsy population of about 92,000 who live principally on the fringes of society in the Alentejo and support themselves by begging, fortune-telling, smuggling, and petty theft. They have successfully thwarted attempts by various Portuguese regimes to settle and integrate them into the mainstream of national life.

Throughout Portugal's recent history, the population of the country has steadily increased, from 4,287,000 in 1864, the year of the first census, to 9,833,014 in 1981, the date of the most recent enumeration. The only time that the population declined was during the 1960s, when many young men who wished to avoid compulsory military service in Africa illegally left the country, adding to the already substantial number who, having completed their service, were emigrating primarily to France, Canada, and the United States to find work. Portugal's population is not spread evenly throughout the national territory but is concentrated in a 50-mile-wide coastal zone stretching from Setúbal south of Lisbon to Viana do Castelo in the north. Accounting for only 25 percent of the national territory, this area contains 70 percent of the population and is a result of natural growth and internal migration of people from the interior to urban areas such as Lisbon and Porto, where Portugal's major economic and industrial activities are located. Owing to the rigors of fishing and labor-intensive agriculture as well as the emigration of young men, women have substantially outnumbered men in the Portuguese population since the first census. This imbalance will increase as the population ages.

SOCIAL CLEAVAGES

The most distinctive feature of Portuguese society is its homogeneity. Consolidated and unified politically, economically, and linguistically in the thirteenth century, Portugal does not contain any readily identifiable subnational ethnic groups like the Catalans and Basques in Spain. Moreover, Portuguese society has never been plagued by the religious and linguistic struggles that have marred the development of other nation-states in Western Europe. The social cleavages that do exist are principally those between classes, regions (especially between the north and the south and between the mainland and the islands), and urban and rural areas. These cleavages cut deep into Portugal's past and were encouraged by its geography and the way in which Portugal developed as a nation-state.

Late medieval Portugal was a three-tiered, hierarchically structured society. The uppermost tier was composed of a military aristocracy that won power and influence through the reliance placed on them by Portuguese kings during the Christian reconquest. Its wealth was drawn from huge tracts of land in southern Portugal given as recompense for military service against the Moslems. This top tier included the knights of the military-religious orders—the Knights Templar, Hospitalers, and Calatravans—who served as soldiers to the king and to whom large tracts of land were also granted. Below this top elite was a much smaller group of commoner knights who received smaller parcels. The base of the hierarchy was composed of the peasantry, separated from the military aristocracy by a wide gap of poverty and life-style. This huge peasantry was divided into two groups: those living in the north, who retained hereditary renting rights over their land, and those in the south, who were essentially landless and worked as laborers on the estates of the aristocracy and military-religious orders.

Portugal's military aristocracy was not inclined to work its vast holdings, preferring to participate in the lucrative trading opportunities beginning to be made available by the voyages of discovery. Consequently, huge tracts of land in southern Portugal remained uncultivated, used primarily as hunting preserves, which resulted in severe shortfalls in food production. In order to increase the productivity of these lands, efforts were made toward land reform during the eighteenth and nineteenth centuries. Unfortunately, these policies did not benefit the local peasantry, as land merely changed hands among individuals at the top of the hierarchy, nor did food production increase, as the new owners were no more inclined to work the land than were their aristocratic predecessors. This new landed elite preferred to live in Lisbon and ape the ways of the nobility.

The trade created by the discoveries did, however, by the eighteenth century, spawn a class of wealthy merchants of nonaristocratic origin. This group, along with individuals from the free professions, was the embryo of Portugal's middle class. By the end of the nineteenth century, this class had been joined by the owners of Portugal's nascent industries and made up about 15 percent of the population. At about the same time, owing to the beginnings of industrialization, an urban working class began to emerge. The great bulk of the population, however, continued to be poor, rural peasants.

Although Portugal began to industrialize and urbanize during the early twentieth century, the pace of change was slow and uneven and did not much affect the social order. By the end of World War II, Portugal was still composed of a very small upper class; a larger, but small by European standards, middle class; a small urban working class; and a large mass of poor, rural peasants. The upper class consisted of the owners and managers of Portugal's major industries; top-level military officers; the owners of the *latifúndios* in the Alentejo; the country's leading lawyers, physicians, and university professors; and high government officials. The middle class was composed of rural proprietors, company and field-grade military officers, the owners of small businesses, shopkeepers, schoolteachers, and low-level civil servants. Finally, the lower class was made up of the land-owning and landless peasants of the north and south, respectively, as well as the small urban proletariat, concentrated principally around Lisbon.

Traditionally there has been very little vertical social mobility within Portugal's three-tiered class system. The upper class was, for all intents and purposes, closed to recruitment of new members from the lower social orders. Its members had similar values and tended to intermarry. They saw themselves as an influential and wealthy elite in which individuals moved easily among the country's top occupations in business, industry, government, the university, and the military.

Except among the urban proletariat and the rural peasants of the south, the lower class did not manifest a similar degree of class consciousness, for in the great majority of Portuguese villages poverty was evenly spread among the inhabitants. Class differences were conspicuous only when villagers came into contact with upper-class individuals from outside, which happened infrequently. Thus, class contrasts were ephemeral, distant, and not very important to daily life. Class consciousness did, however, develop among the peasants in the Alentejo because their social life was much more hierarchically stratified and the vast wealth of the absentee landlord was juxtaposed with the relative poverty of the small landowners, sharecroppers, and especially the landless laborers who worked for the other groups on a daily or seasonal basis. As these groups were in frequent contact with one another, class contrasts were close and regular, which produced class resentment and hostility.

Portugal's social class system remained unchanged from the end of World War II until the 1960s and 1970s, when urbanization and industrialization began to create new career opportunities. Within the upper class a relatively small number of owners of large industrial concerns rose to a position of great social prominence and economic and political influence, while the social position of the *latifundistas* declined because they were unwilling to put their land to productive use. A class of medium-sized landowners, who lived on and worked their holdings, arose in the Alentejo. This new group of landowners, not socially or culturally distinct in dress and manner from the landless peasants who worked for them, began to form the backbone of a class of commercial farmers who were dependent upon their land for their livelihoods. In the urban areas the middle class began to change as new service careers such as those of skilled technicians, computer programmers, mid-level business executives, and financial advisers were created as a concomitant to industrialization. Since 1974 Portugal's social class system has continued to move in the direction of greater complexity and social mobility.

The north-south cleavage grows out of this difference in class consciousness among the peasantry, which itself is the result of the contrasting land tenure systems and different socioeconomic ecologies of northern and southern Portugal. As mentioned previously, in the north the dominant form of agriculture is the small parcel of owned or rented land (the minifúndio), worked by an independent class of peasants who eke out a living on the region's mountainous terrain. There is little mechanization because of the small size and ruggedness of the holdings; hence, agriculture is intensive, with entire families (including women) working the land as a unit. This has reinforced the extended family and other traditional institutions such as the church. Even in the urban and industrial zones of the north around Porto, traditional structures and values prevail. Factories and businesses tend to be family affairs, and many employees maintain a small farm on the side. In the south, in contrast, the latifúndio system generated a much more class-conscious peasantry. Class consciousness was encouraged by the tendency of Alentejanos to migrate to Lisbon in search of work, which fueled the growth of Portugal's urban proletariat and broke down traditional structures such as the family and church. These two contrasting socioeconomic ecologies have predisposed northerners to be conservative and protective of traditional institutions and southerners to be more radical and desirous of socioeconomic change.

The urban-rural split has manifested itself in Portugal primarily as conflict between the countryside and Lisbon. For much of the peasantry, Lisbon represented the centralized state that, through its administrative apparatus, bureaucratic regulations, tax collectors, and military conscription, sought to extract resources from the local communities. Thus, the state was feared and avoided. Consequently, parochial values and ways of life were and remain extremely important in Portugal and are contrasted with urban culture and life-styles. Localism is particularly strong in northern Portugal and on the archipelagoes of Madeira and the Azores. In these regions urbanization and industrialization have not broken down the tight-knit, self-reliant families, sense of individualism, and attachment to the land as elsewhere in Portugal, especially in the south. Hence, the north-south cleavage is complicated by an urban-rural dimension.

These socioeconomic and regional differences have affected Portuguese political attitudes and voting behavior since the nineteenth century. The urban bloc tends to be bourgeois, secular, rational, democratic, and egalitarian. The rural bloc, especially in the north and the Atlantic islands, tends to be traditional, religious, parochial, hierarchical, and authoritarian. The rise of liberalism in the nineteenth century and the establishment of the First Republic (1910–1926) can be said to represent the political ascendancy of the southern urban secular bloc, whereas Salazar's regime (1932–1974) represents the rise of the rural, Catholic northern bloc. Support for Salazar's regime was the strongest in the north and on the Atlantic islands, especially among small farmers, practicing Catholics, and the poorly educated, and weakest in the south, especially among the urban bourgeoisie, industrial workers around Lisbon, and nonpracticing Catholics.

Since 1974 the connection between Portugal's urban-rural and north-south cleavages and political behavior has been obvious in the vote for Portugal's major parties: In election after election support has arranged itself into northern and southern as well as urban and rural zones. Small farmers in the north and on the Atlantic islands strongly support the two right-of-center parties, the Social Democrat party (Partido Social-Democrata, or PSD) and the Christian Democratic party of the Social Democratic Center (Partido do Centro Democrático Social, or CDS); the landless agricultural workers of the Alentejo and urban industrial and service-sector workers support parties to the left of center, the Portuguese Communist party (Partido Comunista Português, or PCP) and the Portuguese Socialist party (Partido Socialista, or PS). Industrial workers in the north, like small farmers in that region, tend to vote for the PSD or the CDS, whereas in the south they vote for the PS—except in the industrial zones of greater Lisbon, where they support the PCP. In the south, support for the PSD and CDS comes from the urban areas, especially the middle-class suburbs of Lisbon, and from the shopkeepers in the villages of the Alentejo. In the north and on the Atlantic islands, support for the PS and PCP is highest in the urban areas, especially Porto. Practicing Catholics of the north overwhelmingly vote for the CDS and the PSD, especially in rural areas. Generally speaking, support for the PS is strongest in the center region, except in the vicinity of Fátima, where there is a large number of practicing Catholics who vote for the PSD and CDS.

Within Portuguese society, except among the top elite and the peasantry in the Alentejo in recent years, the main bonds of social solidarity were based not on class loyalty or attachments to large-scale institutions, but on family ties and patronage. The cement that held Portugal's three-tiered society together was a vast number of patron-client networks that transcended class divisions and regional differences. As the family was the key institution, its advancement was essential. In order to advance, connections were needed. Hence, when necessary, individuals turned to relatives or friends higher up the social ladder to apply leverage, or a wedge (*cunha*), where it would do the most good for the individual and his family. In return for favors, clients were expected to do service for their patrons (*caciques*). This system of social interaction put a high premium on the need for individuals to know who was related to whom, who knew whom, and who owed whom a favor. Such behavior, which emphasizes ascriptive and particular norms and values, has worked against the emergence of achievement and universal modes of social interaction as well as loyalties and attachments to national institutions beyond the family.

Traditionally, the position of women in Portuguese society was subordinate to that of men. Until the 1960s, women had no political, economic, or personal rights. A woman could not vote during Salazar's time unless she was literate and the head of a household. She was prohibited from selling family property or entering into any economic arrangement without her husband's consent. Such gender discrimination was a reflection of Portuguese attitudes about the ideal roles of men and women in society. A woman was expected to be the moral mainstay of the family, Portugal's most important social unit, by being a faithful and obedient wife and mother. Only in certain circumstances was the position of women less subordinate: In rural areas, for example, poor women gained some degree of autonomy and influence because they were often engaged as domestic servants or marketed the produce of their farms. Toward the end of the dictatorship there was a limited upgrading of the status of women. Since 1974 a women's liberation movement has formed, and gender discrimination was outlawed by the constitution of 1976. Divorce and abortion (under certain circumstances) are now legal in Portugal, and a number of women have become politically prominent in recent years.

RELIGION

Portugal is overwhelmingly Roman Catholic. In many ways the history of Portugal until recently has been the history of church-state relations, which at times were cordial and at others conflictual. The country's fledgling monarchy was launched with help from the Holy See; Catholic missionaries accompanied Portuguese explorers during the epoch of the discoveries. In exchange for its support in the creation of Portugal's seaborne empire, the crown shared with the church the riches from the colonies. This mutually beneficial relationship persisted, despite minor disruptions, until the end of the eighteenth century, when powerful anticlerical sentiments appeared in Portugal, the result of the spread of the political and social doctrines of the Enlightenment to the Iberian peninsula.

Individuals who adhered to these sentiments began to mount a powerful challenge to the authority of the church. The church responded by fulminating against what it believed to be the spread of anti-Christian doctrine. During the era of the republic (1910–1926), measures were taken to disestablish the church. As the church had come to symbolize the old order, Republicans took extreme action against it: Church property was confiscated, diplomatic relations with the Vatican broken, and religious holidays abolished. The Republicans forced church-state separation and secularized education. They even forbade the ringing of church bells during certain times of the day and banned priests from wearing cassocks in the streets.

During the New State dictatorshp (1932–1974) the anticlericism of the republic was reversed. Under the New State the church was revived and given special recognition and privilege. This revival was assisted by the supposed apparitions at Fátima in 1917, which had reinvigorated the spiritual life of the Portuguese church. The position of the church was also aided by Salazar, who led a contemplative religious life and kept in close contact with church leaders. Although Salazar did not legally reestablish the church, he did give it special constitutional recognition because of its historical and cultural position in Portugal.

Probably the most important decision taken during the New State epoch affecting church-state relations was the negotiation of a concordat with the Holy See. This agreement, signed in 1940, maintained the separation of church and state but reversed most of the anticlerical reforms of the republican period. The church was granted exclusive control of religious instruction in public schools, which all children were obliged to take, and of the moral instruction of those serving in the military, and it was permitted to operate its own educational institutions. The concordat also forbade divorce for Portuguese couples married in the church and granted the church the right to incorporate and own property. Those properties expropriated by the Republicans were returned and the church made exempt from taxes and given many state subsidies.

Throughout the New State period, the church was kept under strict political control. The concordat allowed the government to approve all appointments to the church hierarchy, and Salazar expected the church to support his policies and the New State regime. Under Salazar church and state maintained a cozy and mutually reinforcing relationship.

The church's response to the golpe d'estado that overturned the New State dictatorship and ushered in Portugal's present democratic regime was mixed and cautious. This ambivalence reflected a split that had divided the church hierarchy over Portugal's colonial wars in Africa. During the 1960s and 1970s, Catholic opposition had been building against the colonial policy of the government, and a number of Portuguese Catholic missionaries and priests in the African colonies came out against the government. Despite its early hesitation, the church is now favorably disposed to Portugal's new democratic regime, which for its part has not manifested the extreme anticlericism of the republic. Generally speaking, religious questions like abortion and divorce, both opposed by the church, have not been big issues in Portugal. Religion affects present-day politics primarily in voting behavior, practicing Catholics supporting conservative parties.

Although census figures indicate that 95 percent of the population is baptized Catholic, only a small proportion of Portuguese attend mass regularly, except in the north, where the people are most devout. In that region of Portugal weekly mass attendance reaches 90 percent, and vows (*promessas*) to various saints and penance for transgressions are frequently performed, penitents often making long climbs to religious shrines or hilltop chapels on their knees. In the south such piety is almost unknown.

Religious practice for the Portuguese is highly personal; much religious activity takes place outside of the church. Rural Portuguese frequently establish a network of relationships with various saints, and all communities have a patron saint to whom many residents form an intimate bond and who acts as a lifelong spiritual guardian and mediator. The most popular of these guardian-mediators is the Virgin Mary. At the same time many Portuguese, especially in the rural areas, believe in witchcraft, magic, and the existence of benevolent and malevolent spirits. As late as the 1930s there were cases of witch burnings, and as late as the 1960s there were women working as "healing mediators" who mixed Christian and pagan rituals and invocations. Belief in the evil eye is also widespread.

Because the Reformation did not extend to the Iberian peninsula, Portugal has a very small number of Protestants, perhaps 1 percent of the population, who came by their religion as a result of the activities of missionaries. The Anglicans, Methodists, Brethren, and Congregationalists are the oldest denominations and have had the largest followings. Fundamentalist groups such as the Pentecostals and Baptists have made inroads in recent years.

The number of Jews in Portugal is even smaller than the number of Protestants. The early Portuguese crown valued Jews for their skills in various walks of life, and the prevailing mood was one of tolerance. During this period, Jews, although forced to live in ghettoes, faced few restrictions on their activities. The mood changed in the sixteenth century when the Inquisition began in Portugal. Those Jews who refused to convert to Christianity either fled the country or were forcibly baptized. Called New Christians (Maranos), many such Jews continued to practice Judaism secretly. In the early twentieth century several small isolated communities of Maranos were discovered in Trás-os-Montes and Beira Baixa where, since the Inquisition, they had lived publicly as Christians and privately as Jews.

EDUCATION

Education during Portugal's formative years was provided in cathedrals and monasteries to a small number of individuals who became the country's intellectual and ecclesiastical leadership. In 1290 a university was founded in Lisbon and remained Portugal's only university until the sixteenth century. The university did not, however, attract the best and the brightest, many of whom went abroad to study, especially to Spain and France, where there were particularly large concentrations of Portuguese students at the universities in Salamanca and Paris. In 1537 in an attempt to curb corporate privileges, the university was moved from Lisbon to Coimbra, where it has remained ever since. André de Gouveira, a pedagogical innovator, tried to improve the university but died before he could accomplish his task. The Inquisition did much to stifle intellectual life in Portugal, and the Jesuits came to exercise virtualy complete control over Portuguese education until they were expelled in the middle of the eighteenth century.

New universities were founded in Lisbon and Porto in 1911, thus breaking the monopoly on higher education held by the University of Coimbra. In 1931 the Technical University of Lisbon, which offered degrees in engineering and science, was founded. Three regional universities were established at Aveiro, Évora, and Braga in 1973, and the following year the Catholic University of Lisbon was accredited by the Holy See. Unfortunately, these universities tended to overproduce graduates in disciplines such as law and literature, which are of little use to a less-developed country.

A system of public education was begun in 1821, although the church retained responsibility for primary education. By 1900 the state had taken over the responsibility for educating all children, even gradeschoolers. The literacy rate, however, remained at no better than 25 percent of the population. In 1964 compulsory education was increased from four to six years. Emphasis was placed on the three Rs, but schools also taught literature, music, civics, history, and some type of physical education. Although 90 percent of Portuguese began school at age seven, 20 percent never completed the six-year program because of the financial burden and labor loss secondary education represented for the typical Portuguese family. Only some students received state stipends; secondary schools were not free until 1974.

During the 1960s and 1970s the Portuguese education system expanded considerably. This quantitative growth was not matched, however, by qualitative improvement. Outmoded teaching methods are still used, and scientific and technological education are inadequate to meet the needs of a developing country. The greatest growth has been in secondary education. The course of study in secondary schools (*liceus*) was divided into two tiers, the first tier consisting of three years and the second of two years intended to prepare students for the university. The number of well-trained, highly qualified teachers has not kept pace with the expansion. Many secondary school teachers were actually engineers, lawyers, and others with university degrees—but without formal pedagogical training—who had not found employment in their chosen professions.

The golpe d'estado on April 25, 1974, did not do much to better education in Portugal. If anything, the educational system suffered. Schools became revolutionary strongholds as many teachers who were thought to be too closely identified with the New State were purged and replaced by politically acceptable ones, who, along with their students, were encouraged to participate in school administration. Curricula and texts were changed to reflect revolutionary precepts. The Ministry of Education became highly politicized. Although the school system has not yet emerged from this chaos, there have been improvements. Nonetheless, the minister of education's job is one of the most difficult in Portugal.

THE ARTS

The Portuguese language evolved from the vulgate Latin used on the western coast of the Iberian peninsula more than 1,000 years ago. Portuguese is the most archaic Romance language, having changed little since the thirteenth century. Spoken by about 200 million people, in Portugal and in Brazil, Angola, Mozambique, Guinea-Bissau, the Cape Verde Islands, São Tomé and Príncipe, and Macão, Portuguese is the fifth most widely spoken language in the world.

The earliest known examples of Portuguese poetic writing are a collection of songbooks (*cancioneiros*) that date from the twelfth century and contain songs (*cantigas*) written by court troubadours, aristocrats, and clerics with musical talent. The cantigas were gradually replaced by ballads (*romanceiros*) popular at court. One of these, written in the wake of Portugal's victory over the Castilians in 1385 at Aljubarrota, is considered to be the Portuguese version of the Arthurian legend.

Portuguese literary prose began in the fourteenth century with the compilation of chronicles written by court bureaucrats who were commissioned to make a record of the activities of a particular monarch. The first of the great court chroniclers was Fernão Lopes, who was commissioned by Duarte (1433–1438) to write a history of the house of Avis. In his chronicles, Lopes stressed the degree to which the Avis dynasty owed its successes to the ordinary townsfolk and artisans who had supported João I during the struggle for succession. Gomes Eanes de Zurara, who followed Lopes as court chronicler, highlighted the role of the aristocracy in building the nation, reflecting the changed political climate under Duarte's successor, Afonso V (1438–1481).

During the sixteenth century chroniclers directed their attention to the discoveries and Portugal's growing seaborne empire. Using the records of the Casa da Índia (India House), João de Barros wrote his *Décadas*, a history of the Portuguese in Goa. Fernão Lopes de Castenhada, who had served for many years in Asia, wrote a ten-volume chronicle of the Portuguese conquest of India. Gaspar Correia and Diogo do Couto, both of whom spent many years in the Orient, also wrote unofficial chronicles of Portuguese life in India. Both authors concluded that the colonial experience had had a detrimental effect on Portuguese character. Consequently, their chronicles were suppressed by the crown and were not published until some 250 years after they were written. The most famous chronicle from this period was the *Peregrinaçam* (Pilgrimage) written by Fernão Mendes Pinto, whose vivid imagination produced a work of great literary merit but dubious historical accuracy.

The Portuguese theater was founded by Gil Vicente (ca. 1470–1536), court poet to Manuel I. Vicente was a figure as important to Portuguese artistic expression as William Shakespeare was to the English; throughout his thirty-year career no court occasion was complete without a performance of one of his plays. These religious dramas or farces were written and performed for a bilingual audience in Portuguese and Castilian. Typical of the medieval genre, these plays had almost no plot and called down from heaven the power to right wrongs. Characters were generally stereotyped in order to draw the largest contrasts on stage, and Vicente used slapstick to poke fun at the clergy, women, and courtiers.

Perhaps the best-known Portuguese poet is Luís de Camões, who penned an epic poem modeled on the *Aeneid*. *Os Lusíadas* recounts the voyage of Vasco da Gama to India as well as Portugal's history up to that time. Camões was an adventurer who spent twenty years in the Orient and Africa. His poetry introduced new words into everyday usage and enriched the Portuguese language. Critics regard Camões as the greatest Iberian poet, the master of every type of verse. The Portuguese people consider him a national hero; his remains are buried alongside those of da Gama in the Jerónimos Monastery in Belém on the outskirts of Lisbon.

When Portugal was under the domination of Spain (1580–1640) the preferred language of literary expression was Castilian. The finest Portuguese writer of this era was Francisco Manuel de Melo, who was a poet, historian, essayist, and statesman. His best work was a history of the Catalan uprising of 1640 that allowed the Portuguese to regain their independence.

Little of note was written in Portuguese during the seventeenth century with the exception of the *Lettres Portugaises* (Portuguese Letters). An enormously popular work, it is believed to have been written by a nun, Sister Mariana Alcoforada, to her French lover, the Comte de Chailly, and describes their affair with great passion. The eighteenth century was also lacking in poetry and prose above the ordinary except that of Pedro António Correia Garção, who dedicated his life to ridding Portuguese literature of Castilian influence, and Manuel Maria Barbosa du Bocage, who, capitalizing on his image as a rascal, wrote somber, brooding poetry.

This paucity of extraordinary writers of prose and poetry was filled during the nineteenth century with the appearance of the poet-playwright Visconde de Almeida Garrett and the historian-novelist Alexandre Herculano. Representing the Romantic strain in Portuguese liberalism and the increasing power of the middle class, their writings, in addition to making literary statements, proposed the modernization of Portuguese society by overcoming its isolation through literature. This was an important task because, generally speaking, the Portuguese historical experience was too far from the mainstream of European development to be much understood and appreciated by those not part of its heritage. The second half of the nineteenth century was dominated by the poet Antero de Quental (1842–1892), an intellectual aristocrat from the Azores who was influenced by the French positivists and rejected the romanticism and individualism of Herculano and others. He became the guiding light for a group of like-minded writers called the "generation of 1870," which included the historians Teófilo Braga and Joaquim Martins, the novelists Eça de Queiros and José Ortigão, and the poet Abílio Junqueiro.

Of the generation of 1870, Queiros was the most forceful and original. A diplomat who lived abroad much of his life, Queiros's best-known novels were *O Crime do Padre Amaro* (The Sin of Father Amaro) and *O Primo Basílio* (Cousin Basílio), which exposed the vices of the middle class and the foibles of the clergy and women. Although Queiros deplored Portugal's backward state, he knew from his experience abroad that the situation could not be improved by imposing mainstream European values on Portuguese society. Queiros gradually lost faith in the reforms of the liberals and infused his last works with characters defeated by life (*vencido da vida*).

The most famous Portuguese writer of this century is without doubt Fernando Pessoa (1888–1935). Although he only published one small volume of poetry during his lifetime, Pessoa is considered Portugal's greatest poet since Camões. His impact on Portuguese literature is comparable to that of T. S. Eliot on English. Pessoa wrote under various pseudonyms, each work with a distinctive style and representing a different aspect of his personality. He became the model for a school of poet-scholars who wrote in the 1940s and 1950s, the best known of whom are Alexandre O'Neill and Jorge de Sena.

The most famous literary work from Portugal in recent times is the book *Novas Cartas Portuguesas* (New Portuguese Letters), written collectively by Maria Teresa Horta, Maria Isabel Barreno, and Maria Fátima Velho da Costa. This book, a collection of stories, letters, and personal pastiches, had the common theme of the oppression of women by men and male-dominated society. Suppressed in 1972 as obscene, the book appeared in the post–April 1974 period and has been hailed as a landmark in feminist literature.

The purpose of the media during the Salazarist dictatorship was to communicate official attitudes; the government therefore censored newspapers, magazines, books, radio, and television. Censorship gave rise to an underground language used by writers and broadcasters to circumvent the censor's pen. For example, the word *dawn* came to stand for socialism and *spring* for revolution. Juxtaposing photographs and hiding political meaning in crossword puzzles were also devices used to communicate points of view the regime disliked. Immediately after the coup, the media were nationalized and taken over by the Communists. This resulted in a backlash by the other parties, who were able to force the government to institute a policy that assigned to the nationalized press the political orientations of the various parties in order to ensure balanced reporting. Guidelines also instructed the media to make a clear distinction between hard news and editorial comment. The 1976 constitution now guarantees freedom of the press.

Portuguese newspapers cater to a comparatively small, largely urban reading public. Regular reading of newspapers in the countryside is much lower than in cities because of problems of distribution and higher illiteracy rates. The vast majority of Portuguese receive their news and entertainment from a number of public, private, and church-owned radio stations. Television, a government monopoly until the recent passage of a law that allows private stations, is broadcast on two channels, one for light entertainment, sports, films, and popular drama, and the other for serious entertainment similar to that aired by PBS in the United States. The lack of a well-developed film industry has forced Portuguese television to rely on Brazilian productions, especially sitcoms and serialized novels (*telenovelas*), which are extremely popular.

Portugal's musical tradition began in the fifteenth century when the cantigas were set to music. Early in the sixteenth century the cathedral in Coimbra became a center for the composition of polyphonic music and produced several composers of note. Portugal's musical tradition was carried throughout the seaborne empire. Gil Vicente used incidental music in his religious plays, some of which could be described as musicals. Until the seventeenth century, musical training was in the hands of the church, and clergy dominated the field of composition. During the eighteenth century Portuguese monarchs lavished money and attention on music teachers and composers, which gave Portugal the best and liveliest court music anywhere in Europe. During this era, the Italian Domenico Scarlatti was court choirmaster, infusing Portuguese church music and opera with the Neopolitan style. João de Sousa Carvalho was one of the most popular composers of opera and musical drama in Europe during the second half of the century.

Perhaps the best-known Portuguese composer is João Domingos Bomtempo (1775–1852). A prolific composer, Bomtempo, as head of the National Academy of Music, assured that the classical style would remain integral to Portuguese music until well into the Romantic era. Gradually, however, Romantic music from Europe was accepted, having been introduced by Alfredo Keil, a student of Franz Liszt. Portugal's only Romantic composer of note, Keil's patriotic hymn *A Portuguesa* became the national anthem.

The most widely known musical form of Portugal is the *fado*. The fado (literally, fate) is a song that expresses a melancholy longing intermingled with sadness and resignation and reflects Moorish, African, and indigenous influences. The fado is most often sung by a *fadista* dressed entirely in black and accompanied by two guitarists. There are two types of fado, the Coimbra fado, most often sung by a young man, usually a student at the university, and the Lisbon fado, most often sung by a woman of a certain age. Both kinds are mournful, soulful tunes, but the Lisbon fado tends to be more rhythmic and lively.

The art of oil painting began to develop in Portugal in the fifteenth century. The most famous Portuguese painter of this early period was Nuno Gonçalves, who was court painter to Afonso V. During the sixteenth century two schools of Flemish-style painting developed, one around the portrait painter Jorge Afonso and the other around Vasco Fernandes, who painted early themes in a vigorous style.

At the end of the sixteenth century, Portuguese painting adopted the Italian style of the late Renaissance. No Portuguese artist of note emerged, however. By the late seventeenth century Portuguese tastes in painting had shifted to the Dutch style, but, there were still no major artists, except perhaps Bento Coelho and Josefa de Óbidos.

It was not until the eighteenth century that Portugal produced an artist of sufficient ability to garner recognition outside of the country. This painter was Domingos António Segueira (1768–1837), who became well known for his allegorical religious and historical paintings in the neoclassical style, which matched in a technical and artistic sense similar work being done in Europe. He also painted portraits in the style of Goya.

For the first half of the nineteenth century Portuguese painting was very academic and unable to keep pace with developments in the rest of Europe. During this period, painters strove for a particularly Portuguese national style. Portugal's best painters lived in Paris. The most successful was Amadeus da Sousa Cardoso, a friend of Amadeo Modigliani and Georges Braque who studied under Paul Cézanne and produced both cubist and expressionist painting of considerable quality.

All styles of architecture common throughout Europe can be found in Portugal: The Temple of Diana in Évora built in the second century A.D. is one of the best-preserved Roman buildings in the Iberian peninsula; the country is dotted with castles built during the period of the reconquest; there are four great Romanesque cathedrals, one each in Lisbon, Porto, Évora, and Coimbra; the monastery at Alcobaça is one of the best examples of Cistercian architecture in Europe; the monastery at Batalha, built by English stonemasons, is a fine example of early Gothic architecture; the Renaissance style can be found in the monastery and palace of Mafra, Portugal's Escorial; the baroque, in Lisbon's Igreja de Santa Engrácia (Church of Saint Engrácia); the neoclassical, in Lisbon's Teatro Nacional de Dona Maria, II (National Theater of Dona Maria II); and the modern and postmodern style are evident in the new buildings of Lisbon and Porto.

Portugal did produce two unique styles of architecture. One has been dubbed "Pombaline" after Portugal's chancellor, the Marquês de Pombal, who rebuilt the downtown of Lisbon in a severe, neo-Palladian style after the earthquake and fire of 1755. The Pombaline style can also be found in Pombal's own palace in Oeiras. The other style is called "Manueline" after King Manuel I (1495–1521), during whose reign it developed. Portugal's most original contribution to European architectural expression, the Manueline style was used most frequently in the decoration of porches, windows, portals, and interiors. Sometimes called Atlantic Gothic, Manueline architecture was an expression of the spirit of the age of the discoveries and employed an iconography of nautical motifs such as ropes, sails, barnacles, and various sea creatures. Exuberant and opulent, Manueline architecture was meant to startle and astonish the viewer—and so it does, as all will attest who have seen the Manueline embellished window at the Convento de Cristo in Tomar.

Portugal has not produced significant sculpture. Most early sculpture was done by English and French stonecutters. Portuguese stonecutters accomplished little of note after their brilliant work during the Manueline

The Manueline window at the Convento de Cristo, Tomar.

period. Recently, the preference has been for neoclassical, Romantic, and monumental sculpture. The best-known monumental works are the Padrão dos Descobrimentos (Monument of the Discoveries), built in 1960 to commemorate the 500th anniversary of the death of Prince Henry the Navigator, and the giant statue of Christ across the Tejo from Lisbon and clearly visible from the city.

Of the crafts, Portugal is probably most famous for its ceramics, especially tiles (*azuleijos*). Introduced from Andalusia in the fifteenth century, Portuguese ceramics initially continued the polychromatic, Moorish, geometric style but later shifted to the Delft blue after the Dutch fashion. Azuleijos (literally, blues) began to be mass produced after the earthquake in 1755 in order to meet the demand of rebuilding Lisbon. Ever since they have remained a distinctive interior and exterior decorative feature of Portuguese architectural design.

REFERENCES

Keefe, Eugene K., et al. *Area Handbook for Portugal.* Washington, D.C.: U.S. Government Printing Office, 1977.

Makler, Harry M. "A Case Study of the Portuguese Business Elite, 1964–1966," in Raymond S. Sayers (ed.), *Portugal and Brazil in Transition.* Minneapolis: University of Minnesota Press, 1968, pp. 228–241.

Martins, Herminio. "Portugal," in Margaret S. Archer and Salvador Giner (eds.), *Contemporary Europe: Class, Status and Power.* New York: St. Martin's Press, 1971, pp. 60–89.

Pimlott, Ben, and Jean Seaton. "Political Power and the Portuguese Media," in Lawrence S. Graham and Douglas L. Wheeler (eds.), *In Search of Modern Portugal: The Revolution and Its Consequences.* Madison: University Press, 1983, pp. 43–57.

Reigelhaupt, Joyce Firstenberg. "Saloio Women: An Analysis of Informal and Formal Political and Economic Roles of Portuguese Women." *Anthropological Quarterly* 40 (July 1967):109–126.

Robinson, Richard. *Contemporary Portugal.* London: George Allen & Unwin, 1979.

4
From Castilian Province to Portuguese Republic

THE BIRTH OF PORTUGAL

The emergence of Portugal in the late Middle Ages as a distinct nation-state is intimately connected to the appearance of a separate Portuguese monarchy on the Iberian peninsula. As the Christian reconquest proceeded southward, lands taken from the Moslems were reorganized and resettled by counts appointed by the kings of Asturias (later León). In 1096 one of these kings, Alfonso VI bestowed upon Henri, a crusading knight from Burgundy, the province of Portucalense, which he was to govern as a fief. Count Henri, who subsequently married the king's favorite but illegitimate daughter, Teresa, built his manor at Guimarães. Bound by the usual ties of vassalage to his suzerain, Henri was expected to be faithful and loyal to the king and render him service whenever required. Until Alfonso's death in 1109, Henri dutifully carried out his feudal obligations by attending royal councils and giving the king military aid in his campaigns against the Moslems. Alfonso's death plunged the kingdom of León into a civil war among Aragonese, Galician, and Castilian barons who desired the crown. Count Henri stayed neutral throughout this struggle and gradually ceased to carry out his feudal obligations. When he died in 1112 his wife inherited the province and continued Henri's policy of nonalignment.

The victor in the struggle for the Leonese crown was Alfonso VII, who, when he ascended the throne, decided to assert his suzerainty over Teresa, his aunt, and her consort, a Galician nobleman named Fernando Peres. Teresa refused to do homage and was forced into submission after a six-week war in 1127. Her barons, who saw their fortunes and independence declining, took this opportunity to align themselves with her son and the heir to the province, Afonso Henriques. Only seven years old when his father died, Afonso Henriques had become a vigorous, visionary, and robust young man. Supported by the barons, he rebelled against his mother's rule. On July 24, 1128, Afonso Henriques defeated his mother's army at São Mamede near Guimarães, and Teresa was forced to flee to Galicia. Afonso Henriques thus gained control of Portucalense.

In 1135 Alfonso VII of León, having gained supremacy over Aragon and Castile, decided to designate himself emperor and convoke a great council in order that all the princes of northern Spain could pay him homage. Afonso Henriques, again encouraged by his barons to resist control by León, refused to attend the council and even marched on Galicia to regain territory lost to Alfonso during his mother's reign. The emperor met this challenge by ordering Galician barons to make war on Afonso. Open conflict was avoided, however, because negotiations between Alfonso and Afonso Henriques resulted in a treaty that established peace between Portugal and León in 1143. According to the treaty, Alfonso VII recognized Afonso Henriques as king of Portugal in exchange for which the new king gave the emperor military assistance and did him homage. Thus, the house of Burgundy and Portugal were born.

Afonso Henriques was a brilliant military commander and during his reign pushed the Moslems farther south than any other of the Christian kings on the peninsula. As early as 1135 he had built a castle at Leiria, and in 1139 he carried out a raid across the Tejo River deep into the heart of Moslem territory, where he decisively defeated a Moslem army at Ourique. In 1147 he took advantage of a series of religious rebellions among the Moslems and, with the help of Crusaders sailing for Palestine, captured Lisbon. Continued internecine fighting among the Moslems and Lisbon's strategic location eventually allowed Afonso to advance across the Tejo and capture and hold large sections of Al-Andulus, the heartland of Moslem Iberia. Beja fell in 1162. Three years later a local freebooter and adventurer named Geraldo Geraldes, considered by some the Portuguese Cid, attacked Évora and captured several towns in Spain's Estremadura province. In 1160 Geraldo attacked Serpa and in 1168 Badajoz, still Moslem but under Leonese protection. This attack, unauthorized by Afonso Henrique, provoked the intervention of Ferdinand II of León. In the ensuing struggle between Portuguese and Leonese forces, Afonso Henriques, who had subsequently arrived to take command, broke his leg and was taken captive. After two months in Leonese hands he was ransomed for his renunciation of all territorial claims in Galicia and Castile. This vigorous prosecution of the reconquest resulted in official papal recognition in 1179. Afonso Henriques and his successors were granted all conquered lands over which neighboring kings could not prove rights. At his death in 1185, Afonso Henriques had carved out an officially recognized Christian kingdom that extended well into Moslem Iberia.

Although Sancho I (1185–1211), Afonso Henriques's son and heir, continued the reconquest, he directed most of his energy and time to the consolidation of the new monarchy. During his reign ambitious programs of road building and resettlement of Christians on lands taken from the Moslems were carried out. Afonso II (1211–1223) continued his father's policy of strengthening the monarchy. Sancho II (1223–1246), Portugal's fourth king in the Burgundian line, was the least successful of early Portuguese monarchs. Dominated by powerful barons, his reign was characterized by considerable internecine fighting. He was eventually deposed and replaced by his younger brother, Afonso III (1246–1279).

With the collapse of the Almohad empire during the reigns of these last three kings, the Portuguese monarchy, again assisted by passing fleets of Crusaders, was able to reconquer the entire western peninsula. The reconquest was completed in 1249 during the reign of Afonso III, when an isolated enclave of Moslems in the extreme south of the Algarve was overrun. This last campaign carried the Portuguese to the sea and established the approximate territorial limits Portugal has had ever since. Large tracts of land were granted to nobles and the military-religious orders (Knights Templar, Hospitalers, and Calatravans) as recompense for their military services during the reconquest.

Thus, by the end of the thirteenth century Portugal was a compact, unified kingdom well before such unity appeared among the other monarchies of Europe. This was the result of Portugal's good fortune to be ruled early by long-lived, energetic, and able kings who reigned for an average of thirty years each. Afonso Henriques, the founder of the monarchy, ruled for fifty-seven years, a very long reign for medieval times. Unity was also fostered by policies designed to amalgamate Christian north and Moslem south. During this early period the exodus of Moslem peoples from the south to unconquered areas of Spain was balanced by large migrations of Christian settlers from the north to the south. Moslems who stayed behind were gradually assimilated into Christian society. During the reign of Dinis (1279–1325) the decision was taken to write all official documents in the vernacular, which stimulated the development of the Portuguese language as the national medium of communication. The founding of schools in monasteries and cathedrals as well as a university in 1290 fostered a unified national culture. This distinctively Portuguese culture of song, literature, and poetry was disseminated by learned tutors in manor houses, educated priests at court, and troubadours among the ordinary people. A sense of unity was also encouraged by the revival and restoration of the bishoprics of the church throughout Portugal as they were thought to have existed before the Moslem conquest. At the end of the reconquest, Portugal had its own church hierarchy organized into nine bishoprics united under the archbishop of Braga. Finally, national unity was heightened by the decision taken during the reign of Afonso III to move his court from Coimbra to Lisbon, where the climate was more to his liking. About midway between north and south, Lisbon gradually pulled these two regions together by becoming the center of this emergent nation-state's political, economic, and cultural life.

INVASION BY CASTILE

During the reign of Afonso IV (1325-1357) conflict broke out between Portugal and Castile, to which the Portuguese crown was still tied by vassalage. This conflict resurfaced after a peaceful interlude during the rein of Pedro (1357-1367), Afonso IV's son and heir. When in 1383 Pedro's son, Fernando, died, he left no heir to the throne. His only child, Beatriz, was married to Juan I of Castile on the provision that their offspring would inherit the Portuguese crown. At Fernando's death, the government fell to his queen, Eleanor Teles, a Spaniard who was seen as an interloper and was consequently unpopular. The queen's principal rival for control was Fernando's bastard son, João, who was the master of the Order of Avis, the Portuguese section of the Knights of Calatrava. Civil war and dynastic revolution ensued. João and his supporters, principally from southern Portugal, where the Knights of Calatrava were situated, drove Teles from Portugal. This action precipitated an invasion by Castilian forces who found support in the north, where there was much sentiment for the legitimist cause. From 1383 to 1384 fighting between Portuguese and Castilian forces waxed and waned, neither side able to deal a decisive blow to the other. Finally, in the summer of 1385, the war reached a climax when fewer than 7,000 Portuguese under the command of João's skillful military leader Nun'Alvares Pereira, aided by a contingent of English longbowmen, inflicted a crushing defeat on the imposing Castilian army of 10,000 infantry and 20,000 cavalry on the plain of Aljubarrota. This defeat ended the Burgundian line of kings and established a new ruling dynasty in Portugal, the house of Avis. Random hostilities between Portugal and Castile continued until permanent peace was established in 1411.

The Portuguese had been able to assert themselves over their more powerful neighbor because of English help. In order to ensure Portugal's future independence, João (1384-1433) decided to solidify the relationship with England. This he did by signing the Treaty of Windsor in 1386, and by taking as his queen in 1387 Philippa of Lancaster, the daughter of John of Gaunt. Philippa introduced an English style into the court and provided royal patronage to English commercial interests. She was also the mother of an extraordinary line of princes, the most well known of whom was Dom Henriques (Prince Henry the Navigator). These princes, called the "marvelous generation" by the poet Camões, led Portugal into its golden age, the age of the discoveries.

VOYAGES OF DISCOVERY

With the question of independence from Castile settled and a new ruling dynasty on the throne, Portugal embarked on new fields of conquest. In 1415 Portuguese troops captured the town of Ceuta in Morocco. Shortly thereafter Portuguese navigators began to explore the uncharted waters of the Atlantic. In 1419 João Gonçalves Zarco discovered the archipelago of Madeira and subsequently undertook its colonization. In 1427 Diogo de Silves found the archipelago of the Azores, which was also colonized. In 1434 Gil Eanes rounded Cape Bojador and explored the mouth of the Gambia River. These early efforts at exploration and colonization proved to be highly profitable and encouraged the organization of further voyages.

The voyages of discovery were made possible because Portugal possessed a sense of national unity and purpose well ahead of other, more powerful European proto-nation-states; was led by the strong visionary leadership of the early kings of the Avis line; and enjoyed a superiority in maritime and navigational technology embodied in the small, fast, lateen-rigged *caravela* (caravel). The voyages were driven by a mixture of economic, strategic, and religious motives. Economically, Portugal wanted to obtain the spices and luxury goods from the Orient that were in high demand among the European nobility at the time. Strategically and religiously, the Portuguese were fearful of the rise of Moslem power in the southeast of the Mediterranean and consequently sought to outflank it by sea. The principal strategic objective was to contact and make an alliance with the mythical Christian kingdom of Prester John, thought to be located somewhere in the vicinity of Ethiopia. To achieve these objectives, Prince Henry established a maritime school on a promontory at Sagres, where he trained Portuguese captains and planned voyages from 1437 until his death in 1460.

During the first decade of the reign of Afonso V (1438–1481), no voyages were launched because of a dispute among the military aristocracy over whether Portugal was to achieve its strategic objectives against the Moslems by conquering Morocco or by a seaborne flanking maneuver. After this interlude, interest revived in the latter tactic as profits were realized from the importation of slaves from Africa. During the reign of João II (1481–1495) the voyages were given the boost of royal patronage,

The Monument of the Discoveries, Belém.

and a plan for opening a sea-lane to India was devised. Possessing an accurate measurement of the circumference of the earth, the Portuguese rejected the westward route advocated by Christopher Columbus and knew that an eastward route around the southern tip of Africa was more practical. The crown, in exchange for its patronage, received a 22 percent share of the profits, the "royal fifth," of all voyages. In order to safeguard Portugal's edge in maritime and navigational technology, outside investors were discouraged and the voyages were conducted in secret.

The revival of the voyages under João II's patronage and direction led to discovery after discovery. Between 1482 and 1498 Diogo Cão explored the mouth of the Congo (now Zaire) River and the coast of Angola. Bartolomeu Dias rounded the Cape of Good Hope in 1487. Ten years later, Vasco da Gama sailed up the east coast of Africa to Mombasa and from there, with the aid of Arab pilots, to the Malabar coast of India. In 1500 Pedro Alvares Cabral's flotilla of thirteen caravels, following da Gama's route, was blown off course and discovered Brazil. On his third voyage to India in 1503, da Gama, escorted by fourteen men-of-war, constructed a string of fortresses at strategic points along the littoral of the Indian Ocean from Mozambique to India.

In 1509, one of the greatest strategic planners in the history of European imperial expansion, Afonso d'Albuquerque, was made viceroy of India. From his headquarters in Goa, captured in 1510, he succeeded in establishing Portuguese military and commercial supremacy throughout the Indian Ocean. He defeated the Turks, Arabs, Maylays, and the Moghul empire. He captured Ormuz and Muscat, thereby taking control of the mouth of the Persian Gulf. He established factories in Sumatra, Timor, the Molaccas, and Ceylon. Under his viceroyship the Portuguese expanded into the Mekong Delta and arrived in Canton in 1513, before making contact with Japan. The manpower for this vast imperial system was provided by the Portuguese policy of miscegenation, which produced a Eurasian population that, because they were assimilated into Portuguese culture, identified Portugal as their homeland.

During the reign of Manuel I (1495–1521), Portugal became the richest monarchy in Europe, a result of the wealth generated by the discoveries and the crown's monopoly of the spice and luxury goods trade from Asia. This newfound wealth did not, however, transform Portugal's social structure, nor did it lay the basis for further economic development. As the voyages of discovery were essentially a state-run enterprise, no middle-class or commercial sector of any consequence emerged as it had in other parts of Europe. Moreover, the persecution of the Jews, who possessed vital technical skills, robbed the country of an important force for modernity and reinforced feudal elements. Much of the profit from the Asian trade was used by the court, church, and nobility to purchase land and build cathedrals and palaces. Consequently, the wealth from Asia passed through Portugal and flowed toward northern Europe for the requisition of manufactures and played no small part in the industrialization of England. Lisbon grew by leaps and bounds during this period, becoming the third largest city in Europe. The growth was, however, at the expense of other coastal cities, such as Aveiro, which had been Portugal's chief fishing port, and gave rise to the present macrocephalic condition of the country.

As the wealth from the discoveries did not produce a middle class of competent, trained individuals to whom the affairs of state gradually fell, leadership in Portugal remained in the hands of the military aristocracy and the crown. This failure to transform the class system had a detrimental effect on Portugal's political and economic development and was exacerbated by the high degree of governmental centralization of the imperial system. Centralization meant that, more than would ordinarily be the case, the quality of national policy was intimately connected to the personal abilities of the top leadership, especially the king himself. Unfortunately, the house of Avis did not produce a king of great merit after João II.

When João III (1521-1557), the sixth in the Avis line of kings died, the heir to the throne was his three-year-old son, Sebastião. Sickly and poorly educated, Sebastião proved to be mentally unstable and, as he grew to young manhood, developed a fanatical obsession with launching a great Crusade against Moslems. In 1578, when he was twenty-four years old, he organized a military campaign in Morocco, where Moslem counterattacks had reduced Portuguese influence. His army, poorly equipped and incompetently led, was overwhelmed and destroyed at Alcazar Quivir. Sebastião, who was never seen again, was presumed killed. A large number of the nobility were captured and held for ransom. This event, the most disastrous military defeat in Portuguese history, eliminated much of the aristocratic leadership, drained the coffers of the treasury, and plunged Portugal into a period of confusion and intrigue.

IBERIAN UNION

Because Sebastião left no heir, Henrique, the last surviving son of Manuel I, was proclaimed king. This solved the problem of succession only temporarily, for Henrique was an infirm and aged cardinal who was unable to obtain dispensation from the pope to marry. Of the contenders, Philip II, the king of Spain and grandson of Manuel I, had the strongest claim to the throne. Consequently, he began to bribe the hispanophile members of the Portuguese nobility, who saw themselves as part of a broader Spanish community and identified strongly with Castilian language and culture. The Spanish monarchy sought to use the leadership vacuum created by the disaster at Alcazar Quivir to incorporate Portugal into Spain in order to realize the long-held desire to unite Iberia under one crown. In January 1580 the Portuguese Cortes (made up of the three estates of the realm) met to decide the succession. Unlike the hispanophile members of the nobility, however, the commoners rejected a Spanish king.

Active opposition to Philip II's intrigues to gain the crown came from António, the prior of Crato and the illegitimate son of Luís, one of Manuel's brothers. When Henrique died in 1580 António was proclaimed king by the commoners and marched on Lisbon with an improvised army. Eight days later, a well-organized Spanish force invaded Portugal and routed António's ragtag army at Alcântara on the outskirts of Lisbon. António fled northward and went into exile in France. Thus, Portugal was annexed by Spain.

In 1581 Philip II of Spain was declared Philip II of Portugal and proclaimed Spain and Portugal to be unified. He decreed that Portugal would be governed by a six-member Portuguese council; that the Portuguese Cortes would meet only in Portugal; that all civil, military, and ecclesiastical appointments would remain Portuguese; and that the language, judicial system, coinage, and military would remain autonomous. In 1582 Philip's navy subdued the island of Terceira in the Azores, which had remained loyal to António. In 1586 preparations were begun for the conquest of England. The combined Portuguese-Spanish armada assembled to carry out this mission was defeated in 1588. In retaliation, Elizabeth I attempted to capture Lisbon and install António on the throne. The Portuguese-English army, led by Sir Francis Drake, failed in this endeavor because of the strength of Spanish defenses and the inexperience of António's troops. After this loss, no further attempts were made to dislodge the Spanish from Portugal, and António died in Paris in 1595, thus ending the Avis dynasty.

During the reign of Philip II, the terms of the proclamation of the union of the two crowns were generally upheld. With Philip II's death in 1598 and the ascension to the Spanish throne of his son, Philip III, much less respect began to be paid to the provisions that preserved Portugal's autonomy. Philip did not visit Portugal until 1619, very near the end of his reign, and he began to appoint Spaniards to the six-man governing council as well as to lesser posts. His son and heir, Philip IV, had no interest in government and consequently turned over the administration of Portugal to the Duke of Olivares. The duke alienated Portuguese of all classes, including the hispanophile nobility when, in order to prop up the waning power of the Spanish monarchy, he levied excessive taxes and troop requisitions on Portugal to support Spanish military activities, especially against France.

The French, anxious to weaken Spain, offered to support with men and ships a pretender to the Portuguese throne. The best candidate was Duarte, Duke of Bragança, the son of João III's niece and an extremely powerful and wealthy landowner. In 1640 the Catalonians rebelled against Philip IV and, thus encouraged, a group of Portuguese nobles persuaded Duarte to take the crown of Portugal for himself. On December 1, 1640, Duarte and his supporters occupied the royal palace in Lisbon. Five days later he was crowned João IV, thus restoring the Portuguese monarchy and founding a new ruling dynasty, the house of

Bragança. Occupied with the rebellion in Catalonia, the Spanish were unable to send troops to prevent the restoration. Intermittent attempts to reincorporate Portugal into the Iberian union continued until 1666, when a permanent peace recognized Portugal's independence.

ABSOLUTISM

During the last forty years of the Iberian union, Portugal lost most of its colonial possessions in Asia to the Dutch but managed to retain Brazil and keep control over the West African slave trade. The wealth produced by slaving and Brazilian gold and sugar allowed the Braganças to reign in the opulent style of their Avis predecessors. As before, little was done to develop the Portuguese economy, and vast sums flowed through Portugal or were diverted for the construction of cathedrals, mansions, and palaces, built in the costly baroque style. Increasingly, the Portuguese economy came to be dominated by British commercial interests. In fact, a kind of colonial relationship emerged between Portugal and Britain that was solidified in the Methuen Treaty of 1703, by which the British agreed to import Portuguese wines instead of those of France in exchange for open access to Portugal for British textiles.

The first of the Bragança line of kings, João IV (1640–1656), was not a brilliant or charismatic ruler. He was cautious and stubborn, and, as he grew older, he contracted gout, which sapped his energy. When he died in 1656 his queen, Luisa, became regent because the royal couple's eldest son, Teodósio, had predeceased his father by three years and the youngest son, Afonso, was only ten years old. Although a disease in infancy had left Afonso partially paralyzed in his left arm and leg and had impaired his intelligence, his mother, who had a strong determination to continue her line, succeeded in having him proclaimed king against the wishes of some members of the Cortes. Afonso grew into a degenerate who was easily manipulated by his advisers. His marriage to Marie-Françoise Isabelle of Savoy was unconsummated, and in 1667, aware of the need for a successor, Afonso consented to his own abdication in favor of his brother, Pedro. Pedro ruled as prince-regent until Afonso's death in 1683 and then in his own right until 1706. Pedro introduced absolutist rule into Portugal, copying the style of the royal court of Louis XIV of France.

Absolutism went hand in hand with the nature of Portuguese government, which, by the seventeenth century, had achieved a high degree of centralization and bureaucratization. During previous centuries Portuguese kings had taken steps to establish control by the crown over the national territory. In the reigns of Afonso II, Afonso III, and Dinis, royal commissions called *inquirições* (inquiries) had been appointed to investigate land ownership, in order to protect the royal patrimony against the church and nobility, both of whom were not averse to changing boundaries in order to defraud the crown of royal income. At the same time the crown began to assert its control over the administration of justice. After the middle of the fourteenth century all local magistrates had to be confirmed by the king, who could order the election of new judges if necessary. Somewhat later, during the reign of Manuel I, the military and religious orders were nationalized and absorbed into the king's patrimony. At the same time Manuel turned the separate military aristocracy into a dependent court nobility, which had to rely upon royal appointments and annual allowances from the crown.

Centralized administration was encouraged in the fifteenth century as medieval town charters were revised in an attempt by the crown to standardize tax collection. It was during this period that the feudal division of Portugal into *terras* was replaced by provinces (*comarcas*) for administrative purposes. To facilitate the collection of taxes, the country was also divided into financial districts called alms-shires (*almoxarifados*), each under the jurisdiction of an alms-sheriff (*almoxarife*), empowered to collect the king's revenue. As central control was achieved, government became increasingly complex and bureaucratized. In 1736 the titles of the king's secretaries were changed to correspond to their functions: secretary of state for the interior, foreign affairs, war, navy, overseas, and the like. The secretary of state for the interior acted as the prime minister.

By the reign of João V (1706–1750), Portuguese government was a highly centralized, bureaucratic apparatus managed by ministers appointed by and responsible to the king, who exercised as much power as a particular monarch saw fit. João V's successor, José I (1750–1777), was indolent and consequently placed the reins of government into the hands of Sebastião José de Carvalho e Melo, later the Marquês de Pombal. A petty noble who managed to surmount Portugal's rigid class system by a combination of energy, intelligence, good looks, and a shrewd marriage, Pombal became the veritable dictator of Portugal. Using the absolute authority of the crown to achieve his objectives, he undertook the reorganization of the state administration in order to solve Portugal's recurring economic problems. Once Portugal's ambassador to Great Britain and Austria, Pombal had been influenced by the ideas of the Enlightenment. Realizing how backward his country was, he sought through a ruthless despotism to reform the country's economy and society by encouraging the development of a middle class. Those nobles who opposed him were arrested, brutally tortured, and executed. His greatest challenge came on November 1, 1755, All Saints' Day, when Lisbon was leveled by an earthquake followed by a tidal wave and fire that killed 60,000 of the city's inhabitants. Despite the hysteria about him, Pombal kept his presence of mind and devised a scheme to reconstruct Lisbon. Rebuilt in record time because of the architectural genius of Eugénio dos Santos, Lisbon emerged as the first planned city of Europe.

When José died in 1777, his queen, Maria I (1777–1816), banished Pombal to his estate in Oeiras and dismantled the dictatorship. Although Pombal's policies had succeeded in restoring some degree of economic prosperity, the strong middle class that he hoped to create did not materialize, and the old social order quickly restored itself. Portugal was unaffected by the French Revolution and initially resisted entreaties by Napoleon to participate in the continental blockade against the importation of British goods. Claiming that he had sent his army under General Junot to liberate Portugal from British economic domination, Napoleon invaded and quickly occupied Portugal in 1807. Maria I and her son, the future João VI (1816–1834), fled to Brazil in 1808, where a government in exile was established. A British army under the command of the Duke of Wellington forced the French out of Portugal and held off two subsequent invasions. The Portuguese army was reorganized and put under the command of William Carr Beresford, one of Wellington's officers, who acted as regent while the royal family was in Brazil.

CONSTITUTIONAL MONARCHY

Although the ideology of liberalism was known in Portugal in the late 1700s by way of the American and French revolutions, it was not until the turn of the eighteenth century that it became a force with which absolutists had to contend. Freemasonry introduced by foreign merchants played an important role in spreading liberalism in Portugal. In 1801 there were five Masonic lodges in Lisbon, and the first Portuguese grand master was elected in 1804. The invasion by the French encouraged the spread of liberal ideas; by 1812 the number of Masonic lodges had increased to thirteen. In 1818 Freemasons founded the Sinédrio, a secret society that was a major motive force in the liberal revolution of 1820. Radical ideas were also spread by Portuguese who lived in London and Paris, where they had observed and been influenced by the functioning of the British and French systems. Newspapers and pamphlets published by these exiles were smuggled into Portugal and widely read by the small, but increasingly important, middle class. After the Napoleonic wars, the exiles themselves returned to Portugal and began to agitate for the establishment of a liberal, constitutional monarchy. They were eventually to be successful because of a crisis in royal leadership.

The king, João VI, had been absent from the country since 1808 when the court fled to Brazil to escape Napoleon's army. The regency headed by Beresford was almost bankrupt because of the drain on the treasury necessitated by the crown's location in Brazil. The Portuguese were exhausted and war-weary from three French invasions. Liberalism was thus an attractive ideology, at least to the middle class in the coastal towns. They held out hope for a new system of political organization that would afford them some opportunity to participate in the government as well as to reform the country's economy. Liberalism was especially appealing to this group because its proponents posed not as revolutionaries who wanted a clean break with the past but as restorers of traditional, individual rights they claimed had been suppressed by absolutism. Portuguese liberals and their supporters, therefore, were content with a constitutional monarchy and established church.

The struggle to create a constitutional monarchy began in the early days of 1820 when a liberal insurrection broke out in Spain, forcing Ferdinand II to accept the Spanish constitution of 1812. These events, as well as the departure for Brazil of Beresford, who had earlier executed the head of Portuguese Freemasonry, General Gomes Freire de Andrade, encouraged Portuguese liberals and helped spread their influence within the army. In August 1820 military units in Porto revolted. The liberal revolution quickly spread. A provisional government was organized and elections held for a constituent Cortes.

The constitution, which emerged in 1822, established a hereditary limited monarchy with a strong central government responsible to a unicameral parliament elected by literate males. João VI accepted the limits on his powers outlined in the constitution and returned to Portugal, leaving behind his son, Pedro, to govern Brazil. The first Cortes elected under the new constitution attempted to reassert Lisbon's control over Brazil, which, because of its growing sense of nationhood, was beginning to agitate for independence. In 1822, with British support, Pedro declared Brazil independent and took the title of emperor, although he remained the heir to the Portuguese throne.

The unicameral Cortes had a precarious existence and did not long endure. From the outset the liberals had antagonized the nobility and clergy by failing to give them representation as they had been accustomed in the traditional Cortes. The aristocracy thought that the king had been humiliated when the constitution stripped the monarchy of many royal prerogatives. Moreover, the radicals even succeeded in antagonizing some of their own supporters, particularly merchants, because they were unable to improve Portugal's economy, devastated by the Napoleonic wars.

Portugal's first constitution also appeared at an inauspicious time in European history. Throughout Europe in the decade following the

Congress of Vienna (1815), numerous attempts were made to reestablish absolutism. In 1823 the Holy Alliance intervened in Spain, whose turbulence was considered a threat to European peace. Thus isolated, Portuguese liberals faced great odds. Their base of support, the middle class, was small, not more than 9 percent of the population, and concentrated principally in Lisbon and Porto. Absolutists were still strong and had established headquarters in Vila Real in the province of Trás-os-Montes. France's restoration of Ferdinand to the throne in Spain gave impetus to an absolutist uprising in Portugal (known as the Vila Francada), which occurred at the end of May 1823 in Vila Franca de Xira, near Lisbon. The rebels were joined by João VI's youngest son, Miguel, who had fallen under the influence of young nobles who saw their power and privilege threatened by liberalism. The constitution was suspended and absolute monarchy restored with the promise that a new constitution would be drafted more in keeping with Portuguese traditional institutions. The promised document never materialized, however, and many liberals fled to France and Great Britain. Portugal was governed by João's moderate absolutism until his death in 1826.

João's death created a problem of royal succession. The rightful heir to the throne was his eldest son, Pedro, emperor of Brazil. Neither the Portuguese nor the Brazilians wanted a unified monarchy; consequently, Pedro abdicated the Portuguese crown in favor of his daughter, Maria da Glória, a child of seven, on the condition that when of age she marry his brother Miguel. In April 1826, as part of the succession settlement, Pedro granted a new constitution to Portugal, known as the Constitutional Charter (Carta Constitucional). Pedro returned to Brazil, leaving the throne to Maria, later Maria II (1834–1854), with Miguel as regent.

The Constitutional Charter attempted to reconcile absolutists and liberals by allowing them both a role in government. The Cortes was divided into two chambers: The upper chamber, the Chamber of Peers (Câmara de Pares), was composed of life and hereditary peers and clergy appointed by the king without numerical limit. The lower chamber, the Chamber of Deputies (Câmara de Deputados), was composed of 111 deputies elected to four-year terms by indirect suffrage from local assemblies, which were themselves selected by a franchise restricted by tax-paying and property-owning requirements.

The compromise between the historical Cortes of appointed delegates and the unicameral Parliament of 1822, however, did not satisfy the absolutists. In February 1828 Miguel, who had been exiled for his role in a failed absolutist uprising of 1824 (the Abrilada), returned to Portugal to take the oath of allegiance to the charter. Immediately upon his arrival, he was proclaimed king by his supporters. Although it initially appeared that Miguel would abide by the charter, pressure mounted for a return to absolutism. A month after his return, Miguel dissolved the Chamber of Deputies and, in May, summoned the traditional Cortes of the three estates of the realm to proclaim his accession to absolute power. At the same time the charter was nullified.

Miguel's accession sparked a military uprising by the liberals in Porto and other regions of Portugal. This led to six years of repression of Portuguese Jacobins. Many thousands fled, and, among those who remained, many thousands were detained by Miguel's police. This oppression eventually plunged Portugal into a violent civil war.

The war was essentially a struggle for power among three main factions, each with its own ideology and notions about representative institutions and popular participation. The absolutists, who derived their power from the aristocracy and the peasantry, especially in the north, wanted no written constitution and the traditional, appointed Cortes of the three estates of the realm. The moderates, backed by the upper bourgeoisie in the cities and towns, wanted the charter and a parliament of two houses, one indirectly elected and the other appointed by the crown. The radicals, supported by the urban middle class and merchants in the major cities, wanted a return to the constitution of 1822 and a directly elected unicameral parliament.

In July 1833 allied moderate and radical liberal troops under the command of Pedro IV, who had a romantic belief in liberal principles and who had in the meantime abdicated the Brazilian throne, established a beachhead in Porto. Later that month, Pedro's naval commander succeeded in defeating Miguel's fleet, and a second landing was made at Faro in the Algarve. The liberal army marched northward and captured Lisbon on July 24. A stalemate of nine months ensued, during which time the absolutists controlled the rural areas, where they were supported by the aristocracy and the peasantry, and the liberals occupied Portugal's two major cities, Lisbon and Porto, where they commanded a sizable following among the middle classes. The War of the Brothers, as it was known, was finally ended when liberal forces supported by the Quadruple Alliance defeated the absolutists in May 1834. Miguel was banished from Portugal, never to return, and Pedro restored the charter.

A new Cortes met in August 1834. Although there were no political parties as such, the delegates were deeply divided between moderates, who supported Pedro and the charter, and radicals known as vintistas (Twentiests), who wanted a return to the constitution of 1822. In September 1836 the radicals rebelled and reestablished the constitution of 1822. At the same time, the Septemberists, as the radicals were now called, convoked a constituent assembly that was given the task of revising the 1822 document to make it more compatible with changed social and economic circumstances. This resulted in a violent reaction from the moderates, who saw their power threatened and considered the charter the symbol of the liberal victory in the civil war. As a compromise, the constituent assembly was remanded to make alterations in both the constitution of 1822 and the Constitutional Charter, with the aim of establishing a constitutional monarchy similar to those elsewhere in Europe. In April 1838 Portugal's third constitution was promulgated.

The constitution of 1838 attempted a compromise between the charter and the constitution of 1822. It abolished the moderative authority and returned to liberalism's classical tripartite division of power into legislative, executive, and judicial branches of government. The 1838 document reaffirmed, as in 1822, that sovereignty rested with the nation. It abolished the Chamber of Peers and substituted a Chamber of Senators (Câmara de Senadores), and it established the direct election of the Chamber of Deputies, although under a restrictive franchise. The king's role was enhanced, and the Chamber of Senators was restricted to notables.

After four years of inept radical government and a marked decline in liberal sentiment, the charter was restored in 1842, with a bloodless golpe by the moderates. This second restoration did not, however, immediately bring stability to Portugal's political life. There were still two distinct concepts of who ought to govern. The moderates still advocated a Chamber of Peers nominated for life and a Chamber of Deputies elected indirectly. The radicals, on the other hand, wanted direct election of both houses. The moderates finally recognized that the charter had to be modified to allow more participation by the population. Therefore, starting in 1852, amendments called Additional Acts (Actos Adicionais) gradually introduced a number of democratic reforms. The first of these acts called for the direct election of the Chamber of Deputies but maintained income qualifications for voting and office holding. The second, passed in 1885, eliminated hereditary parity, limited the number of life peers to 100, created fifty elected peerages, and restricted the crown's moderative power. The third, passed in 1896, lessened the reforms of the 1885 amendment somewhat by restoring life peerages.

Despite continued differences between the moderate liberals, who came to be called Regenerators (Regeneradores) and radicals, who were known first as Historicals (Históricos) and later as Progressives (Progressistas), these amendments as well as the tacit agreement between them that each faction would govern as long as they were able and then turn power over to the other, lent some measure of stability to Portuguese government. This system of government, known as rotativism (rotativismo), operated from 1871 until it collapsed in the first decade of the twentieth century. The Regenerators and Historicals were not politial parties in today's sense of the term. The electorate was not more than 1 percent of the population; therefore, the Regenerators and Historicals were essentially loose coalitions of notables based on personal loyalties and local interests. Elections were held after a change in governing faction in order to provide the new faction with a majority in Parliament.

Although rotativism produced stable government, it failed to solve Portugal's underlying social and economic problems. Portugal did not have sufficient reserves of indigenous capital required for industrialization. Exports were largely wine, olive oil, salt, nuts, and cork, domestically produced or reexported from the colonies. Liberal legislation designed to boost cereal production in the Alentejo by converting the latifúndios into commercial farms failed to have the desired effect because the new owners became a class of absentee landlords. The government was in perpetual deficit, and periodic financial panics disrupted the economy. Foreign investment was scarce; the government was forced to borrow from abroad for the building of public works projects, which aggravated the country's considerable debt. Despite these difficulties, during much of the liberal period Portugal was free from radical social movements. Socialism and republicanism, though known among the political elite, had little following among the ordinary people. This was to change, however, in the decades after 1890.

THE FIRST REPUBLIC

The year 1890 was a watershed in the history of Portugal. It marked the emergence of a political awareness that eventually brought down the constitutional monarchy and the establishment of a republic twenty years later. The event that sparked the awakening was the confrontation with Portugal's old ally, Great Britain, over the publication by Lisbon of a map (the so-called mapa côr de rosa, or rose-colored map) on which Portugal's territorial claims in Africa were shown (in red) to extend across Africa's midsection from Mozambique to Angola. These claims, based on earlier cross-continental expeditions by Portuguese explorers such as Serpa Pinto, clashed with Cecil Rhodes's plan to build a railroad from Capetown to Cairo through central Africa. In 1890 the British issued an ultimatum to the Portuguese to withdraw their claims. The Portuguese, aware they did not have the means to resist, acquiesced to British demands.

This foreign policy humiliation was denounced by Portugal's growing band of Republicans, who had organized themselves into a formal party in 1878. The Republicans based their appeals on crude nationalism and played on the fears of many that a continuance of the inept government of the liberals would make Portugal either a British colony or a province of Spain. Teachers, journalists, small-business people, clerks, and artisans were drawn to republicanism, with its appeals to nationalism, universal suffrage, separation of church and state, and the abolition of the monarchy and nobility, which were seen as irrational institutions that sapped the strength of the country. The consolidation of the French Third Republic and the overthrow of the Brazilian monarchy in 1889 also encouraged the spread of republican sentiments. As a result, three Republicans were elected to Parliament in 1899 from Porto and, in 1906, four from Lisbon.

The appeal of republicanism was also enhanced by the collapse of rotativism. Between 1896 and 1906 the system ceased to function smoothly. Conflicts between the Regenerators and Historicals, formerly settled in secret, were brought into the open in an effort to generate public support for the system. This was new and unsettling in a society as depoliticized as was Portugal's and did not fulfill its intended purpose. By 1906 it was impossible for either faction to arrange a parliamentary majority. In May 1907 the situation came to a standstill. King Carlos (1889–1908) dissolved Parliament and gave to Prime Minister João Franco the power to govern by decree. In January 1908 an attempted military golpe supported by the Republicans resulted in the cancellation of fresh elections and a crackdown on the Republican party. In February the king and his youngest son, Luís Philipe, were assassinated by two disgruntled Republicans, Manuel Buiça, a teacher, and Alfredo Costa, a clerk. The crown was left to Manuel II (1908–1910), eighteen years old at the time.

In an effort to salvage the monarchy, Franco stepped down as prime minister and called new elections. Factionalism among Regenerators and Historicals again prevented the formation of a stable government even after six attempts. On October 3, 1910, the army refused to put down a mutiny of the crews of two Portuguese warships anchored in the estuary of the Tejo. Manuel II fled with the royal family to Great Britain and, on October 5, a provisional Republican government was established with the historian Teófilo Braga as president and Afonso Costa, a radical Republican, as prime minister.

In May 1911 the provisional government held elections for a constituent assembly, which set about the work of writing a new constitution. This document, which appeared on August 21, abolished the monarchy and inaugurated Portugal's first Republican government. The constitution secularized the state by disestablishing the church, forbidding religious instruction in the public schools, and prohibiting the military from taking part in religious observances. It granted workers

King Manuel II (1908–1910), Portugal's last reigning monarch. Photo courtesy of General Directorate of Social Communication, Lisbon.

the right to strike and opened the civil service to merit appointment. The constitution vested legislative power in the bicameral Congress of the Republic (Congresso da República). The upper house, called the Senate (Senado), was indirectly elected from local authorities for six-year terms; the lower house, or Chamber of Deputies (Câmara de Deputados), was directly elected for three-year terms. Executive power was vested in a cabinet and prime minister responsible to the Congress, which also chose the president of the republic, the nominal head of state.

The Portuguese Republican party (Partido Repúblicano Português, or PRP) was, perhaps, Portugal's first political party in the modern sense of the term. Although its base of support was primarily urban, the PRP had a nationwide organization that extended into the rural areas. In 1904 the party was reorganized to provide a coherent structure by linking Republican centers (centros republicanos), which recruited new members, and Republican revolutionary boards (juntas revolucionários) in almost every parish, municipality, and district throughout the country. After the revolution was proclaimed in Lisbon, the previously organized boards assumed power in local government.

The PRP did not, however, remain unified. In 1911 moderate and radical Republican deputies divided over the election by the constituent assembly of the president of the republic. The candidate of the radical Republicans, led by Afonso Costa, was defeated by the candidate of the moderates, led by Brito Camacho and António José de Almeida, who opposed Costa's radical and intransigent republicanism and feared that he would gain control of the new government. The split widened at the PRP congress in October 1911, when the moderates were hooted down and left in disgust. The moderates then formed the Republican National Union (União Nacional Repúblicana, or UNR), the directorate consisting of Camacho, Almeida, and Aresta Branco. The UNR was essentially a personal clique of several moderate leaders whose purpose was to get through Parliament a program that would mitigate the impact of the more radical Republican government. After this breakup the PRP became known as the Democratic party (Partido Democrático).

In February 1912, the UNR leadership itself split into two Republican splinter parties. The immediate cause of the rift was disagreement over the UNR program, drawn up by Camacho, but it also involved personal rivalry between Camacho and Almeida. The rump, led by Camacho, was renamed the Republican Union (União Repúblicana, or UR), and its members became known as Unionists. The other group, led by Almeida, was called the Republican Evolutionist party (Partido Repúblicano Evolucionista, or PRE). The program of the PRE was quite similar to that of the UR but urged a policy of moderation and conciliation and advocated proportional representation and revision of intolerant laws.

The fragmentation of PRP, personalism, and petty squabbles produced acute governmental instability during the First Republic. In its fifteen years and eight months of existence, there were seven elections for Parliament and eight for president and forty-five governments. Instability was also encouraged by the government's total dependency upon Parliament, where no stable majority could be organized. This political turmoil led to several hiatuses of military rule during the First Republic and eventually to its overthrow.

In January 1915 senior military officers, who were becoming increasingly alienated from the republic, imposed a period of military rule at President Manuel de Arriaga's request. In May of the same year, however, pro-Republican junior officers and sergeants returned the government to civilians.

In 1916 Prime Minister Afonso Costa, who feared that a German victory in World War I would mean the loss of Portugal's African colonies of Mozambique and Angola, sent an expeditionary force of 40,000 men to fight on the side of the Allies. Poorly trained and equipped, this force suffered horrendous casualties in Flanders. This debacle, as well as severe food shortages caused by the war mobilization, paved the way for a second military intervention in December 1917, led by Major Bernardino Sidónio Pais. Pais, who had held a diplomatic post in Prussia some years before, was sympathetic to Germany and antiliberal. He was an energetic, charismatic individual who sought to build a broadly based popular following. Gradually, however, he came to rely increasingly on upper-class youths, young army officers, students, and sons of big landowners who were antiliberal and traditionalists. In December 1918, while boarding a train in Lisbon, Pais was assassinated by José Júlio da Costa, a radical Republican corporal recently returned from the front. Portugal's government was returned to civilians.

Political instability continued under civilian government. A small-scale civil war erupted in northern Portugal as monarchists led by Henrique Paiva Couciero attempted to restore the monarchy. A wave of violence swept the country, and leading Republican figures, including António Machado Santos and Prime Minister António Granjo, were murdered. Political instability and violence brought economic life to a standstill. The middle class, which had initially supported the republic, began to turn toward traditional values as liberal and republican ideals were increasingly discredited.

By 1925 the republic had become the butt of ridicule and cynicism. Those dissatisfied with the republic viewed the authoritarian governments established in Italy (1922) and Spain (1923) as attractive alternatives. Many military officers, despite their previous negative experiences in government, thought that only they could save Portugal from disintegration. Their inclination once again to intervene was heightened by grievances over low pay and poor equipment. During the last thirteen months of the republic, there were three attempts to overturn the regime. The last of these was successful. On May 25, 1926, General Manuel Gomes da Costa, who had been selected to lead the golpe d'estado by the young officers who had organized it, announced from Braga his intention to march on Lisbon and take power. This was followed by a massive military uprising that met little resistance. On May 28, General Gomes da Costa symbolically entered Lisbon, a dramatic gesture emulating Benito Mussolini's march on Rome in 1922. Prime Minister António

Maria da Silva resigned on May 29 and the First Republic came to an end.

REFERENCES

Livermore, H. V. *A New History of Portugal.* Cambridge: Cambridge University Press, 1969.

Marques, A. H. de Oliveira. *History of Portugal.* 2 vols. New York: Columbia University Press, 1972.

Payne, Stanley G. *A History of Spain and Portugal.* 2 vols. Madison: University of Wisconsin Press, 1973.

Wheeler, Douglas L. *Republican Portugal: A Political History, 1910–1926.* Madison: University of Wisconsin Press, 1978.

5
Corporatists and Monarchists Versus Republicans

MILITARY DICTATORSHIP

The officers who carried out the golpe d'estado of May 28 and the civilians who supported it did so for a mixture of motives. Republicans in and out of the military simply wanted to change the unpopular government of Prime Minister António Maria da Silva, which they believed could only be accomplished through military intervention. Monarchists hoped that the golpe would bring about the restoration of the crown. For others, the military represented the will of the nation and salvation from the chaos and turmoil of the First Republic.

The golpe itself was relatively bloodless because no military units came to the aid of the government. On May 30 the president of the republic, Bernardino Machado, turned the government over to Commander José Mendes Cabeçadas, a naval officer and staunch Republican, not to General Gomes da Costa, the titular leader of the military uprising. This resulted in two months of extreme instability and behind-the-scenes infighting among the various factions of the military. The promonarchist tendency within the May 28 Movement, as the golpe was called, was led by General João Sinel de Cordes. This tendency had allied itself with right-wing but not necessarily monarchist junior officers who wanted some form of authoritarian state. In the hope of preventing the rise of a monarchist or authoritarian regime, Mendes Cabeçadas formed a duumvirate with Gomes da Costa on June 1. On June 17, Gomes da Costa ousted Mendes Cabeçadas and his followers from the provisional government. General da Costa's supremacy was temporary; he, too, was ousted on July 9. On the same day General Óscar Fragoso Carmona was named head of the military government and Sinel de Cordes, minister of finance.

The military government was now in the hands of monarchist and authoritarian officers, and it seemed as if a restoration of the monarchy would follow. This was not to be, however, because of the reaction that such an outcome would have provoked among the substantial number of Republicans among the officer corps and the rank and file of the military as well as from the populace at large, among whom republican sentiments were quite widespread. Carmona, who was both a Republican and devout Catholic, was acceptable to a broad range of views. Having spent most of his career as a staff officer, he was skilled at smoothing over differences and forging compromises between pro- and antimonarchist and pro- and anticlerical officers. He carefully preserved a balance between each side in order to ensure that the military regime would survive.

Despite Carmona's ability to balance one side against the other, thus preventing either victory, some Republican military officers still feared a restoration. On February 3, 1927, the army garrison at Porto, commanded by General Adalberto Sousa Dias, who had opposed the golpe of May 28, revolted against the government. The government responded with heavy artillery and air strikes. Although the rebels deployed a sizable force, General Dias and his followers had to surrender after a six-day siege in order to save the city of Porto, which was being reduced to rubble by government forces. This battle, the bloodiest in Portugal since the War of the Brothers a century earlier, resulted in 120 dead and 650 wounded. The outcome might have been different, however, if an uprising of Republican naval personnel and police in Lisbon a week later had been better coordinated with the rebellion in Porto.

Despite this uprising, the government remained Republican, and monarchists pinned their hopes on Sinel de Cordes, the finance minister. These were to be dashed by his incompetent management of the government's finances. During his term of office, government spending rose by 40 percent and the budget deficit increased to 38 percent beyond revenues. Because of the influence of exiled Republicans in Paris, de Cordes was unsuccessful in raising money independently from private banks in Europe. In order to balance Portugal's accounts, de Cordes sought a foreign loan, which he finally procured from the League of Nations.The league's supervision of Portugal's finances raised the specter of international interference in Portugal's internal affairs, which generated negative feelings against de Cordes, even among his monarchist supporters. Carmona removed him from office in April 1928. The ousting of de Cordes, the election of Carmona to the presidency of the republic on March 25, 1928, and the appointment of Colonel José Vicente de Freitas, a staunch Republican, as prime minister virtually assured, at least for the time being, that the monarchy was not to be restored.

Sinel de Cordes was replaced as finance minister by António de Oliveira Salazar, a professor of political economy at Coimbra University.

Salazar accepted the post on April 27, 1928, only after he had demanded and had been granted complete control over the expenditures of all government ministries. In his first year at the ministry he not only balanced the budget but achieved a surplus, the first since 1913. This was accomplished by centralizing financial control, improving revenue collection, and cutting public expenditures. Salazar remained finance minister as military prime ministers came and went. In January 1930 the most prominent Republican survivor within the military government, Francisco Cunha Leal, president of the Bank of Portugal, was forced to resign after a dispute with Salazar over the banking system in Angola.

From his first successful year as finance minister, Salazar gradually came to embody the financial and political solution to the turmoil of the military dictatorship, which had not produced a clear leader. Salazar easily overshadowed military prime ministers and gradually gained the allegiance of Portugal's young intellectuals and military officers, who identified with his authoritarian, hierarchical, antiliberal, anticommunist view of the world. Moreover, Salazar's ascendancy was welcomed by the church which saw in him a savior from the anticlericism of the Republicans. It was also welcomed by the upper classes of landowners, businesspeople, and bankers, who were grateful for his success in stabilizing the economy after the financial chaos of the First Republic.

SALAZAR

Salazar was born on April 28, 1889, in the village of Vimieiro, near the town of Santa Comba Dão, a few miles north of Coimbra. His father, who was fifty when Salazar was born, divided his workdays between his own small plot of land and that of a local landowner for whom he was a bailiff. His mother, Maria de Resgate Salazar, who was forty-three, ran a cafe at the local railway station. Salazar had four older sisters. Although Salazar's mother and father were poor, they were not destitute. Both parents were deeply religious.

Salazar began his education in earnest at a small private school in Vimieiro operated by José Ribeiro, who gave lessons to the children of the village whose parents could afford a few escudos per month. Later, Salazar attended the public school in Viseu and at the age of eleven won a place in the local seminary, where he studied for eight years. Salazar was a good student and, being deeply religious, took minor orders but eventually decided against the priesthood. In 1910 he entered the University of Coimbra, where he studied law and economics. Although he was not an ardent monarchist, he did not, like his fellow undergraduates, celebrate the collapse of the monarchy. His years spent in the seminary had deepened his Catholicism and impelled him to

Prof. Dr. António de Oliveira Salazar, prime minister from 1932 to 1968. Photo courtesy of General Directorate of Social Communication, Lisbon.

oppose the anticlericism of the First Republic. Known as a bookish student, Salazar refused to involve himself in politics, preferring to make his views known by writing articles in various journals. He received his bachelor's degree in 1914.

Between 1915 and 1918 Salazar shared rooms in Coimbra with Manuel Gonçalves Cerejeira, who later became the cardinal patriarch of the Portuguese Catholic Church, and Mário de Figueiredo, a future minister of justice and education. During these years he wrote his doctoral dissertation and continued to contribute articles to journals, especially that of the Academic Center of Christian Democracy (Centro Académico da Democracia Cristã, or CADC), a Catholic study group of which he was a member. As a lecturer at the university, Salazar began to establish his reputation by writing and speaking about the problems of wheat production and the commodity crisis in Portugal. His known antirepublican, mildly monarchist sympathies resulted at one point in his suspension from teaching duties, the university accusing Salazar of using the lectern to propagate monarchist ideas. Salazar was exonerated of these charges by an official inquiry, and he returned to teaching. He received his doctoral degree in 1918 and accepted a professorship at the university.

After receiving his doctorate, Salazar became more active in politics. In 1919 he stood for Parliament on the Catholic party list for the constituency of Viana do Castelo, but he was defeated. Two years later he stood for the constituency of Guimarães and was elected. On September 2, 1921, he took his seat in Parliament; finding the activities of Parliament distasteful, he resigned his mandate the same evening. He was again a candidate on the Catholic party list in 1925 but failed to be elected.

Salazar never married. The person closest to him throughout his life was Maria de Jesus Caetano, his housekeeper, whom he had first employed during his student days in Coimbra. Dona Maria, as she was universally known, raised the two children Salazar adopted, Micas and Maria António. Throughout his life Salazar lived a solitary, ascetic existence. He was self-effacing, preferring to operate behind the scenes and to avoid the limelight. Although outwardly modest, he was inwardly convinced that he and he alone was right and knew what was best for Portugal.

Without a doubt, the dominant influence on Salazar's world view was the Thomist philosophy in which he had been steeped while a seminarian in Viseu. From the writings of Saint Thomas Salazar derived his basic views about social and political organization. Saint Thomas saw society as a harmonious, organic whole in which each individual was subordinated to the various functional groups composing the social order. State and society were organized hierarchically according to natural law and God's just ordering of the universe. The social order was fixed and immutable. Inequalities among men were part of the natural order, and it was one's duty to accept one's station in life. The state was authoritarian and hierarchical. The king's authority was paternalistic and absolute; his power derived from God but was to be exercised for the common good and to promote the general well-being.

Salazar's Thomism was reinforced by the teachings of the church, especially by Pope Leo XIII in the encyclical *Rerum Novarum* (1891) and Pope Pius XI in *Quadragesimo Anno* (1931). Usually referred to as the church's labor charter, *Rerum Novarum* argued that the family and labor organizations were part of the natural social order and that workers were justified in striking so as to obtain a just family wage. Leo's encyclical taught that it was the duty of the state to see to it that distributive justice was achieved not by abolishing private property, which was essential for human fulfillment, but by controlling its use. Pope Leo was opposed to unchecked industrial capitalism, which he believed was dehumanizing and destructive of the individual personality. *Quadragesimo Anno* reaffirmed the church's insistence on class collaboration as a barrier against socialism and its denunciation of the economic imperialism of monopolistic capitalism.

Salazar was also influenced by the writings of the Lusitanian integralists who in turn had been inspired by the works of Georges

Sorel and Charles Maurras and the Action Française. Integralismo Lusitano fulminated against liberalism, republicanism, democracy, communism, indiscipline, and secularism. The group supported traditional, authoritarian monarchical rule based on corporatist principles. Although Salazar accepted much of what Integralismo hoped to obtain, he rejected its sometimes violent tactics.

As Salazar came to be seen as the civilian mainstay of the military dictatorship, he increasingly took it upon himself to lay out the country's political future. He set forth his plans in two key speeches, one on May 28, 1930, and the other on July 30 of the same year. In the first speech, Salazar went beyond the financial subject of his talk and spoke of the need for a new constitution that would create a strong, authoritarian, political order, which he dubbed the New State (Estado Novo). In the second speech he declared his intentions to establish such a state, a state in which individuals would be able to procure their "liberty" and "rights" within its natural organizations: families, parishes, municipalities, and corporations.

The military approved of Salazar's speeches and on May 28, 1932, awarded him the Order of the Tower and Sword, Portugal's highest decoration. On July 5, 1932, after the collective resignation of the government of General Júlio Domingos de Oliveira (which had come to power two years earlier), Salazar was appointed prime minister by President Carmona, a post he held until 1968.

THE CONSTITUTION OF 1933

Before being appointed prime minister, Salazar and other like-minded individuals, civilian and military, organized the National Political Council, which was created to give advice on a constitution for the New State. The council's first draft of a new basic law appeared on May 28, 1932, and was approved in a national plebescite on March 19, 1933. Of the 1,214,159 eligible voters (heads of households), the constitution received 719,364 votes in favor, 5,955 against. Nearly a half million (488,840) voters abstained. Counting abstentions as favorable votes, backers claimed the constitution had overwhelming support, and it was duly promulgated.

The drafters of the 1933 constitution drew on sources as different as the Constitutional Charter, the 1911 constitution, the 1919 constitution of the Weimar Republic, and the corporatism of Salazar. The 1933 constitution essentially represented a compromise between republican and corporative principles. Articles 5 and 6 proclaim Portugal to be a corporative and unitary republic in which the state is to function as a promoter of moral unity and coordinator and stimulator of social activity with the aim of harmonizing all social interests.

The 1933 document consciously reversed the balance of power between the legislative and executive established by the constitution of the First Republic (1911). Giving supreme authority to the executive rather than the Parliament, the constitution divided the executive between a president of the republic and a prime minister (officially called the president of the Council of Ministers). The president of the republic was to be directly elected for a seven-year term. Although the constitution appeared to give the president more weight than the prime minister by granting the president the power to appoint the prime minister and to dissolve the legislature, the chief functions of the president, as head of state, were ceremonial. The power to dismiss the prime minister was a mere fiction never exercised during Salazar's long tenure in office. In fact, it was Salazar who chose the president and not the other way around.

Real power was thus in the hands of Salazar, who was in complete charge of running the government on a day-to-day basis. The constitution gave to the prime minister extensive appointment powers as well as the authority to issue decree-laws without parliamentary approval. The constitution eschewed the notion of collective responsibility and permitted the prime minister to conduct the government's business either individually with each minister or with the cabinet as a whole. Salazar used this provision to the maximum. During his years as prime minister, Salazar never consulted the cabinet collectively, preferring to deal with ministers on a one-to-one basis. This meant that individual ministers were responsible to Salazar and Salazar alone, who hired and fired ministers as he saw fit. The cabinet as a unit was thus unable to exercise any power, even the limited power it had been granted by the constitution.

The legislature, the National Assembly (Assembleia Nacional) was clearly placed in a subordinate position by the 1933 constitution. Its function was consultative, not initiative. Meetings were brief and its sessions short (three months per year). The prime minister could suspend its sittings, and ministers were not required to be deputies, nor were they, or the prime minister, accountable to it. The only concession to popular democracy made in the constitution was the election of one-half of the National Assembly's membership of 90 deputies (raised to 120 in 1945, 130 in 1959, and 150 in 1971) every four years from a limited electorate. The other half was appointed by the Corporative Chamber. Elections to the National Assembly were not competitive, there being only one list of candidates permitted, although some limited opposition was allowed after World War II. As Salazar controlled Portugal's single party, he essentially handpicked deputies. For most, membership in the National Assembly was primarily honorific, a form of patronage given in return for demonstrating loyalty to Salazar. A high percentage of deputies were actually New State civil servants.

In keeping with Salazar's corporatist philosophy, the 1933 constitution also created a Corporative Chamber (Câmara Corporativa). The chamber consisted of 150 proctors (*procuradores*) chosen from the several interest sectors of Portuguese society, such as agriculture, commerce, industry, the military, the church, the bureaucracy, and local government. Like the National Assembly, the chamber's function was principally advisory and consultative. It divided its sessions among each of its twenty-four corporate sections, the chamber never meeting as a whole. These sections were organized around the nation's major economic and social activities as well as its principal moral and spiritual concerns. Each of these sections would conduct hearings, after which an advisory opinion (*parecer*) would be issued and sent to the National Assembly and the government. Theoretically, the system was supposed to permit appropriate opinion to be heard before decisions were made. Salazar, however, paid little, if any, attention to the opinions expressed by the Corporative Chamber or the National Assembly.

The constitution identified the family as the primary organizational unit of society, followed by local government. Each of the country's administrative districts was subdivided into *concelhos*, roughly equivalent to counties. These were further divided into *frequesias*, or parishes. Major urban areas, such as Lisbon and Porto, were divided into wards (*bairros*) and these in turn into parishes. Each parish was administered by a *junta* composed of a variable number of members (depending on the size of the parish population) who were theoretically elected from heads of households but in practice chosen by the mayor. The county was administered by a municipal chamber (*câmara municipal*) headed by a mayor (*presidente*) and composed of councilmen (*vereadores*), one from each board within the county. The civil governor of each district, who was appointed by the minister of internal administration, saw to it that local government carried out its administrative tasks and could dismiss local officials who failed in their responsibilities.

Although the constitution created a nominally strong president, executive power actually rested with Salazar. This, and because the legislature was filled with Salazar's handpicked supporters, meant that the constitution of the New State was little more than window dressing for his personal authority. The republican features of the constitution were suppressed and the New State became a civilian version of the military dictatorship.

THE NEW STATE

The 1933 constitution set up the governmental framework of Salazar's new political order, but the organizational aspects of the New State were defined by several statutes decreed in conjunction with the constitution's promulgation. The first of these was the 1933 Labor Statute, which outlined the state's obligation in social and economic life. The statute reflected Salazar's Thomist-corporatist philosophy, placing the good of the individual worker below that of the group and the good of the group below that of the society. It was the first attempt in Portuguese history to create some institutionalized way to satisfy labor's claim to representation in the decisionmaking process. The statute held that the relationships among labor, capital, and property were to be regulated according to corporatist principles by the state, which had the right and duty to control economic and social life. The statute outlawed strikes but also forbade lockouts by owners and decreed that disputes between labor and owners were to be resolved by collective bargaining under state auspices. In order to give concrete meaning to his corporatist principles and to implement the labor statute, Salazar established a secretariat of state for corporations and social welfare. It was the job of this secretariat to oversee the collective bargaining process, support the establishment and development of corporative organizations, and create a nationwide network of social assistance, or *caixas de providências*. Salazar named Pedro Teotónio Pereira, who had been one of the principal leaders of the integralist youth movement, to head this secretariat.

In addition to the labor statute, five additional decree-laws were promulgated that established a network of grassroots corporative organizations. One of these laws set up a system of guilds (*grêmios*), which were associations of employers and owners in various areas of business, commercial, and industrial activity. These associations were monopolistic, and, as with labor, they were subordinate to society. They were to eschew class conflict and were obligated to cooperate with labor organizations.

A second decree-law created a national network of unions (*sindicatos*) that paralleled the system of grêmios. Like grêmios, sindicatos were subordinate to the society and the public good. They were monopolistic, and their charters had to be approved by the state. Sindicatos were required to represent the interest of labor and provide for the social, moral, and educational betterment of their members. Although this law seemingly formed the infrastructure of a strong labor movement, the reality was quite different: Sindicatos were organized by districts, which prevented labor from unifying at the national level. Labor's strength was also inhibited by the law's requirement that a factory have at least 100 workers to qualify for a sindicato. This meant that the great majority of Portugal's workers remained unorganized because much of the country's industrial sector at that time was composed of small, family-owned firms. Organization actually occurred in large concerns, of which there were only a few. This decree-law also created separate organizations called orders (*ordens*) for the liberal professions: lawyers, physicians, engineers, agronomists, and the like. These, too, were monopolistic and subordinate to the general good.

The third decree-law of 1933 set up a system of community centers (*casas do povo*), one in each of the country's freguesias. These community centers had two types of members: effective members, who were the parish's heads of families and males over the age of eighteen, and protective members, who were local landowners. This membership system allowed the casas do povo to be dominated by local bigwigs and not the small farmers and peasants, their putative beneficiaries. The casas do povo, then, did little to promote rural, social progress through cooperation.

The fourth decree-law created a network of fishermen's centers called *casas dos pescadores*. These centers, like the casas do povo, were designed to provide for the social welfare and betterment of fishing communities. Like the casas do povo, they did not fulfill this objective because they were dominated by the owners of the large fishing companies, owners of big boats, and harbormasters who were also required to join.

The fifth decree-law designed the capstone of the system, the corporations, which were conceived as the supreme agencies through which lower-level corporative organizations were to work out conflicts and harmonize differences. The corporations were to encourage the corporative ideal, promote national solidarity, and integrate grassroots and intermediate-level corporative units. They also provided technical and advisory opinions to the government. Despite having been decreed, the corporations did not, in fact, begin to be organized until 1956, some two decades later, when the directives for their establishment were finally issued.

Because Salazar was aware that the creation of the corporations was going to take considerable time, he issued several decree-laws in 1936 to establish a series of organizations for economic coordination that would act as intermediaries between the state and lower-level corporate groups. These provisional agencies were to be disbanded once full corporatism had arrived. Three basic types of agencies were decreed: regulatory commissions, which were to control the production of various agricultural products such as wheat; juntas, which were established to encourage and regulate exports of various products such as wine and olive oil; and institutes, which were supposed to monitor the quality of Portuguese products such as bread, canned fish, and wine. It was through these agencies that the state controlled virtually all of Portugal's economy throughout the duration of the New State. The economy was, in effect, guided, directed, and regulated from above.

In addition to grassroots corporative units, Salazar created a number of collaborative agencies designed to harmonize class differences, unify the nation, and spread his corporative ideology. The most important of these agencies was the National Union (União Nacional, or UN), which was proclaimed to be a nonpartisan association, rather than a political party. The UN was not a mass-based movement as were the Nazi party in Germany or the Fascists in Italy during the same period. It was essentially a skeletal organization made up of caciques or local notables loyal to Salazar and civil servants, who were obliged to join as a condition of state employment. It functioned as a vast patron-client network that dispensed favors in exchange for fidelity to Salazar. In addition to its patronage function, the UN was responsible for screening and nominating candidates for political office. This was done by the president of the UN and the minister of internal affairs in consultation with civil governors and local caciques. Lists of nominees were presented to Salazar, who carefully scrutinized them and struck off those he found unacceptable.

Two other collaborative agencies were the Portuguese Legion (Legião Portuguesa) and Portuguese Youth (Mocidade Portuguesa). Created on May 19, 1936, the Mocidade represented Salazar's effort, following the fashion of the time, to create a militant youth organization. This organization, subdivided into age groups—Lusitos (7–10), Infantes (10–14), Vanguardistas (14–17), and Cadetes (17–21)—had its own uniforms, insignias, and symbols and functioned as a paramilitary organization. Few Portuguese youth took the Mocidade seriously, however, and it became Portugal's version of the Boy Scouts. The Legião was the adult complement to the Mocidade. Organized into land, air, and naval brigades, it was a disciplined armed force that stressed military virtues and acted as a military reserve that could be mobilized in an emergency. Its job was to defend the nation and uphold domestic order.

In addition to these organizations of state control, Salazar had at his disposal the instruments of law and order: the armed forces and police. Salazar was quite deft at keeping the military happy through flattery and sizable budgets. As most of the military saw in him the best solution to Portugal's problem of governability, they were content to let him run the country. At this stage there was also a patriotic closing of the ranks around Salazar and, by 1945, civilian control of the military was clear. The police consisted of the Public Security Police (Polícia de Segurança Pública, or PSP), which had responsibility for policing urban areas, and the Republican National Guard (Guarda Nacional Repúblicana, or GNR), which functioned as a rural gendarmerie. Both were commanded by army officers. The most infamous of the New State's instruments of control was the secret police, the International Police for the Defense of the State (Polícia Internacional e do Defesa do Estado, or PIDE). Set up and trained by the Germans and Italians, the PIDE was under the jurisdiction of the minister of internal administration and was empowered to detain without charge for three months anyone considered a threat to state security. The PIDE itself was small and relied on a vast network of informers. Its victims were the regime's opponents, who were arrested and deported to camps in the Azores and Timor and to the infamous Tarrafal penal colony in the Cape Verde Islands, where prisoners suffered unspeakable living conditions and harsh physical punishment. The PIDE also used the regular prisons on the mainland at Peniche, Aljube, and Caxias.

The New State also sought to control Portuguese social and political life through censorship. An April 1933 decree established committees that had the power to censor published matter that "perverted" public opinion and to "defend" society from attacks on truth, justice, morality, and the public good. Moreover, Salazar demanded from the civil service formal pledges of loyalty and oaths that they were not members of secret societies or clandestine opposition organizations.

With the arrival of the New State, school curricula changed and textbooks were rewritten to reflect the official shift toward Salazar's Thomist Catholicism and nationalistic and authoritarian views. Relations with the church were patched up, and decree-laws signed in April and October 1936 ordered crucifixes to be returned to the classrooms in primary schools and established the post of teacher of moral education, with instructors being selected from lists prepared by the church.

In May 1940, a concordat was signed with the Holy See primarily to safeguard Portuguese missionary rights overseas. The concordat also gave the church autonomy it had not had in Portugal since the rise of Jacobinism. The church was permitted to buy and sell property like any other property owner. Churches and seminaries were given the right to operate tax-free. The Holy See was empowered to name bishops, priests were made liable for military service (but only as chaplains), and the church was allowed to run its own schools, which the state was authorized to inspect and subsidize if it so desired. Religious instruction was to be given in schools by ecclesiastically approved persons, canonical marriages were again recognized as legal, divorce was forbidden, and Portugal was to have representation in the Vatican at the ambassadorial level. The concordat intertwined Catholic and Portuguese national tradition.

OPPOSITION TO THE NEW STATE

Opposition to the New State came from monarchists, who wanted the restoration of the crown, and Republicans, socialists, anarchists, and Communists, who wanted a popular democracy. Although monarchists saw Salazar as the instrument for an eventual restoration, he made it clear that this was not going to happen soon. In a speech after the death of King Manuel in July 1932, who left no heir, Salazar indicated that restoring the crown to Duarte Nuno of the Miguelist branch of the royal family would upset Republicans too much. Later, in November 1933, Salazar nationalized the properties of the house of Bragança. This action forced the monarchists to come to terms with the New State, at least for the time being. Salazar, however, either because of his private monarchist sympathies or because he wanted to play the monarchists along, was careful never to completely dash their hopes for a restoration. During the New State, the Monarchist Cause (Causa Monarquia) was, apart from the UN, the only political association Salazar tolerated. Moreover, Duarte Nuno was discreetly given an allowance paid from the foundation set up to administer the nationalized Bragança properties.

Having co-opted the monarchists, Salazar faced opposition principally from Republicans, socialists, anarchists, and Communists. The first phase of this democratic and left-wing opposition began almost immediately and was designed to prevent the establishment of the New State. In 1931 old politicians from the First Republic organized themselves into the Republican and Socialist Alliance in an attempt to overturn Salazar's regime. In 1933, in the wake of the promulgation of the Labor Statute, an aviator named Sacramento Beires attempted a coup, which was supported by a general strike organized by a broad front of socialists, anarchists, and Communists. Earlier, in 1929, Communists had taken up arms and declared a soviet in the glass-manufacturing town of Marinha Grande. The uprising was quickly put down; 350 party militants were arrested and shipped off to prison camps in southern Angola. On September 9, 1936, the crews of three Portuguese men-of-war anchored in the estuary of the Tejo mutinied and attempted to join the Spanish Republican navy. The mutineers were deported to Portugal's penal colony of Terrafal in the Cape Verde Islands. On July 4, 1937, anarchists threw a bomb at Salazar but missed. From 1937 to 1945 there was a lull in overt attempts to topple Salazar, but the opposition made its feelings known in a series of strikes in 1942, 1943, and 1944.

The second phase of opposition activity began after World War II. The victory of the Allies raised the hope of the opposition that following the war the New State would soon collapse. In keeping with the change in the international situation, Salazar sought to spruce up Portugal's image in the eyes of the victors by permitting a certain amount of partisan political activity during, but only during, the official monthlong campaign period immediately preceding elections. Before this, elections (of Carmona for president in 1935 and 1942 and the National Assembly in 1934, 1938, and 1942) had been plebiscites, as it were, with only officially UN-approved candidates permitted to stand. Salazar's concession to popular democracy consisted principally of a partial lifting of the restrictions on the press and the freedom to assemble. These concessions were, however, counterbalanced by increased harassment by the PIDE and the systematic disqualification on minor technicalities of opposition candidates. Consequently, the opposition tended to expend much energy in discrete but ineffective episodic activity and failed to sustain its organizational activities beyond the electoral period.

Continuity from election to election was provided not by any organized entity but by a loose aggregation of individuals representing diverse ideological orientations. The basic goal of this opposition was to Europeanize Portugal's politics by replacing the New State with some type of democracy. The first manifestation of opposition to the regime in the postwar years came in October before the 1945 elections. The Movement of Democratic Unity (Movimento de Unidade Democrática, or MUD) was organized by a former minister of the First Republic, Mário de Azevedo Gomes. Joined by oppositionists associated with Cunha Leal, the MUD criticized the New State for its lack of political freedoms. Faced with an intransigent Salazar, the MUD in the end abstained from the elections. In 1948 the movement was officially suppressed.

During the postwar period Portugal also experienced sporadic armed oppositional activity. In early 1945 an army captain, Fernando Queiroga attempted a military golpe that involved Admiral Mendes Cabeçades of 1926 fame, General José Norton de Matos, and several civilian ministers from the First Republic. Queiroga's golpe planned for simultaneous uprisings at various barracks throughout Portugal, but the conspirators' only support came on October 10, 1946, from Queiroga's own Sixth Cavalry Regiment in Porto. The uprising was easily smashed, and Queiroga surrendered north of Coimbra.

Conspiracy against the New State inside the military, however, continued under the auspices of the Military Junta of National Liberation (Junta Militar de Libertação Nacional, or JMLN). The JMLN planned to channel the discontent within the ranks of the military that had built up against Salazar's minister of war, General Fernando dos Santos Costa, into a movement led by Mendes Cabeçades against the New State itself. It was believed by some that Carmona was, at that time, willing to exercise his constitutional powers and dismiss Salazar. This plan came to naught on April 10, 1947, and the government proceeded to dismiss those implicated.

The government continued to contain the opposition, but this did not prevent those opposed to the New State from supporting the candidacy of General Norton de Matos in the presidential election of 1949. In his campaign speeches, Norton de Matos made it clear that if he were elected he would dismiss Salazar. Although he was backed by a broad spectrum of oppositionists, de Matos eventually withdrew from the race for lack of sufficient freedom to campaign. President Carmona, who was then eighty years old, ran unopposed and won his fourth term. He died two years later on April 18, 1951.

Carmona's death once again raised the question of a restoration. Salazar lifted the ban that had kept the claimant, Duarte Nuno, from returning to Portugal; in 1952 the pretender to the throne took up residence at the Casa São Marco north of Coimbra. Duarte Nuno had expressed his belief in a Christian monarchy founded on the family and corporative institutions. Salazar, for his part, had hinted that a restoration might be a permanent solution to Portugal's governance problem. When Carmona died, however, Salazar decided that a restoration would be more trouble than it was worth because of the rift it would generate between Republicans and monarchists. Although some believed that the best solution would be for Salazar himself to become president, he thought differently and chose an air force general, Marchal Higino Craveiro Lopes, to be the regime's candidate.

There were two candidates from the ranks of the opposition. One was Admiral Manuel Quintão Meireles, who had served in the Vicente de Freitas government of 1928–1929 with Salazar, and who thought that Salazar had betrayed the May 28 Movement. The other was a professor of mathematics from Porto, Rico Luís Gomes, who carried the banner of a new electoral coalition of the left, the National Democratic Movement (Movimento Nacional Democrático, or MND). As before, oppositionist candidates were harassed by the PIDE. Shortly before the election, Gomes was disqualified because he was a Communist, and Meireles discontinued his campaign. Consequently, General Lopes was duly elected and Salazar retained his post as prime minister.

After this defeat, opposition to the New State died down and a period of lassitude ensued. The cold war and Khrushchev's revelations about Stalin gave those on the left good reason to rethink their positions. Nevertheless, during this time a few of the regime's former supporters came out in opposition to Salazar. One was Captain Henrique Galvão, who had been involved in an attempt to restore the monarchy in 1927. In conjunction with several important figures from the First Republic, Galvão clandestinely organized the National Civic Association (Associação Cívica Nacional, or ACN) and began to plot the regime's overthrow. He was arrested and sent to prison in 1952.

Just as the opposition was beginning to despair, hope was rekindled by the 1958 presidential election in the form of the candidacy of an air force general, Humberto Delgado. Like Galvão, Delgado had earlier been a supporter of the May 28 Movement. He had served as the military adviser to the Portuguese Legion and even authored a radio play dedicated to Salazar. All factions of the opposition rallied to Delgado, who initiated his campaign by announcing that, if elected, his first act as president would be to dismiss Salazar. This would be followed by a general dismantling of the New State. Although Delgado, who had a genius for campaign rhetoric, generated an extensive following among ordinary Portuguese, the regime's candidate, the lackluster Admiral Américo Tomás, was elected. Many suspected that if the regime had not rigged the election, Delgado would have won.

Despite his defeat at the polls, Delgado did not abandon his efforts to oust Salazar and dismantle the New State. He continued to oppose it by organizing the Independent National Movement (Movimento Nacional Independente, or MNI), which Salazar banned. For these activities, Delgado was dismissed from the air force. Faced with additional charges, he fled to the Brazilian embassy on January 12, 1959, seeking political asylum. By May, he and Galvão surfaced in Latin America, where they continued their oppositionist activities.

In 1961 the *Santa Maria,* a Portuguese cruise ship, was hijacked by a group of Portuguese and Spanish exiles, including Galvão, whom Delgado had made secretary general of the MNI. The hijackers planned to sail the *Santa Maria* to the island of Fernando Pó and establish governments to rival those on the Iberian peninsula. After thirteen days at sea, the *Santa Liberdade,* as the ship had been rechristened, short of food and water, surrendered at Recife, Brazil. It is not clear if Delgado was directly involved in this operation. A short time afterward he expelled Galvão from the MNI, accusing him of treason and exhibitionism.

In the summer of 1961 Delgado conceived a plan to overturn the New State by organizing a small group of people who would take over a military unit in a specific region of the country. In order to implement the plan and coordinate the general uprising he thought would follow, Delgado relocated to Morocco. While in Morocco he made several clandestine visits to Portugal. The uprising, which was scheduled to begin on January 3, 1962, actually began on January 1 without Delgado's knowledge. Thirty men led by Captain Varela Gomes and Manuel Serra, a former merchant marine officer and radical Catholic socialist, climbed the walls of the headquarters of the Third Infantry Regiment in Beja. Confusion reigned, and the mutiny was quickly put down by troops rushed from Lisbon. Sixty-five people were subsequently arrested; Delgado escaped to Spain.

Delgado then moved his activities to Algeria, where he organized the Patriotic National Liberation Front (Frente Patriótico de Libertação Nacional, or FPLN). Whatever effectiveness the FPLN might have had was never realized because of internal disputes over tactics and infiltration by the PIDE. Delgado was adamant about the need to spark an immediate armed rebellion followed by urban guerrilla struggle. Other entities within the FPLN, principally the Communists, advocated a more methodical, disciplined, and cautious approach. Delgado gradually came to live in a world of fantasy. The PIDE took advantage of his diminished mental state as well as the divisions within the FPLN and lured Delgado and his secretary to a supposed secret conference with Portuguese supporters at the Spanish border town of Badajoz. Both were murdered and buried in shallow graves.

Meanwhile, within Portugal, the opposition continued to attempt to organize itself. In 1963 all factions, except the Communists, monarchists, and Catholics united in the Democratic Social Action (Acção Democrática Social, or ADS). Led by old republicans like Cunhal Leal and Azevedo Gomes, the ADS also included a new generation of oppositionists, such as Mário Soares, Portugal's current president. The ADS advocated full electoral freedom and independence for Portugal's colonies in Africa, where, by this time, national liberation movements had been organized and were fighting against Portuguese colonialism. With the death of Azevedo Gomes in 1965, the ADS began to fragment. Young socialists like Mário Soares wanted to form a left-wing democratic movement in alliance with the Communists, whereas moderates wanted a less radical approach.

During the official campaign periods preceding the 1969 and 1973 National Assembly elections, three opposition electoral coalitions were organized. One was the Democratic Electoral Committee (Comissão Democrática Eleitoral, or CDE), which represented left-wing Catholics and Communists. The second was the Electoral Committee for Democratic Unity (Comissão Eleitoral para a Unidade Democrática, or CEUD), which brought together socialists and social democrats. The third was the Monarchy Electoral Committee (Comissão Eleitoral Monarquica, or CEM), an amalgamation of radical monarchists that had evolved from within the officially recognized Monarchist Cause. Thus, even as late as the 1960s there were still a substantial number of monarchists in Portugal, and many expected a restoration when Salazar died.

After 1970 opposition to the New State came from several underground urban guerrilla groups. These groups harassed the regime with random violence in the hope of crippling Portugal's capacity to wage war against the liberation movements in the African colonies. The most active of these, the Revolutionary Brigades (Brigadas Revolucionárias, or BR) was led by Isabel do Carmo, an endocrinologist who believed that violent revolution was the only way to bring down the regime.

Toward the end of the New State a certain amount of dissent began to develop even within the regime itself. The key organizational framework for these dissidents was the semilegal Society for Economic and Social Development (Sociadade para o Desenvolvimento Económico e Social, or SEDES). The SEDES brought together a new elite of younger men who had been youth leaders during the 1950s and who had been profoundly influenced by Pope John's encyclical *Pacem in Terris*. The SEDES sought to democratize the New State by focusing public attention on Portugal's economic and social problems and by sponsoring seminars and panel discussions on such issues. This organization still exists as a nonpartisan civic group that seeks to stimulate public debate about significant social and economic issues in Portugal.

In 1966, when the New State celebrated the fortieth anniversary of the May 28 golpe, that brought down the First Republic, Salazar seemed to be as firmly entrenched as ever, despite the activities of the opposition and the outbreak of fighting in the African colonies. Although the New State was to survive for another eight years, Salazar did not. On September 6, 1968, he suffered a cerebral hemorrhage, and over the next few weeks it became evident that he would not recover his faculties. President Tomás replaced him with Marcello Caetano. Salazar died on July 27, 1970, at the age of seventy-nine, still believing he was prime minister, apparently never having been told that he had been removed from office.

REFERENCES

Figueiredo, António de. *Portugal: Fifty Years of Dictatorship*. New York: Holmes and Meier, 1975.

Gallagher, Tom. *Portugal: A Twentieth-Century Interpretation*. Manchester: Manchester University Press, 1983.

Kay, Hugh. *Salazar and Modern Portugal*. New York: Hawthorn Books, 1970.

Raby, Dawn L. *Fascism and Resistance in Portugal*. Manchester: Manchester University Press, 1989.

Soares, Mário. *Portugal's Struggle for Liberty*. London: George Allen & Unwin, 1975.

Wiarda, Howard J. *Corporatism and Development: The Portuguese Experience*. Amherst: University of Massachusetts Press, 1977.

6
Downfall of the New State

CAETANO

Marcello José das Neves Alves Caetano was born on August 17, 1906, to a primary school teacher. When he graduated from secondary school, he entered the University of Lisbon, where he studied law. Like Salazar, with whom he began a long association when he was appointed as a legal adviser in the finance ministry in 1929, Caetano spent his young manhood during the turmoil of the First Republic. Like Salazar, he had been a militant, right-wing student leader and had contributed prolifically to various right-wing journals and newspapers. He emerged as Portugal's leading constitutional lawyer and was intimately involved in drafting the 1933 Constitution. In 1933, when only twenty-seven years old, he was chosen to head the faculty of constitutional and administrative law at the University of Lisbon and, seven years later, was named to head the Mocidade Portuguesa, the New State's youth organization. From 1944 to 1947 he was minister of the colonies and from 1949 to 1955 president of the Corporative Chamber. In 1955 he was made minister to the presidency of the Council of Ministers, a post something like that of deputy prime minister. He was appointed prime minister on September 26, 1968.

Unlike Salazar, Caetano came to realize that the New State could not survive in the post–World War II world unless it adapted to changing times. In 1962 he fell out with Salazar over an unauthorized occupation by police of the University of Lisbon campus, which had been entered in order to quell a student demonstration. Despite his resignation as rector of the university in the wake of this event, Caetano continued to serve as a member of the Council of State.

Also unlike Salazar, Caetano was a family man and had an engaging personality. He was more cosmopolitan, having been born in Lisbon and traveled widely before becoming prime minister. He was reform-minded, and his objective was to revitalize and update the New State. These qualities and goals were reflected in his leadership style, which

Prof. Dr. Marcello José das Neves Alves Caetano, prime minister from 1968 to 1974. Photo courtesy of General Directorate of Social Communication, Lisbon.

was outgoing and friendly. He made numerous tours to "meet the people" of Portugal and the African colonies and held televised "fireside chats" (*conversas en família*) with the people concerning his programs. The slogans of his prime ministership were "evolution without revolution" and "renewal in continuity."

In order to achieve his aims, Caetano sought to build a base of support among the moderates in the regime and to avoid a direct confrontation with the *ultras*, the die-hard Salazarists still in many positions of power throughout the government. He also attempted to gain the credibility of the opposition and international respect by demonstrating a commitment to social, economic, and political change. In the social sphere, Caetano extended Portugal's family allowances as well as old age, sickness, and accident insurance to rural workers. Additional casas do povo were built so that by 1973, 70 percent of Portugal's freguesias had such a facility. In 1970 fishermen, newspaper vendors, and domestic servants were included in the social insurance scheme. In order to boost wages, Caetano introduced the thirteen-month year for paying civil servants. More hospitals were constructed, and rents were frozen in order to deal with the country's critical housing shortage.

In the political sphere Caetano relaxed press censorship and allowed some political exiles to return home. He appointed Guilherme de Melo e Castro, a progressive Catholic, to head the UN, which had been renamed the National Popular Action (Acção Nacional Popular, or ANP). Melo e Castro's assignment was to revitalize Salazar's nonpartisan association and through it engage the opposition in a political dialogue. The electoral law was modified in order to expand the franchise to include all literate adults. Younger, dynamic, politically neutral technocrats were brought into government. The PIDE was reformed, reigned in, and renamed the General Directorate of Security (Direcção-Geral de Segurança, or DGS). The requirement that the government had to approve all individuals elected to lead the sindicatos was relaxed, allowing many important sindicatos to fall into the hands of the opposition.

In all sectors of Portuguese society, especially the opposition, these changes raised expectations that far-reaching and fundamental changes were on the horizon. These expectations were dashed, however, after 1970: Despite having created a more open political climate and improved living conditions, Caetano's liberalization had come up against the resistance of the ultras, and fundamental change in the New State would not be forthcoming. The final brake was applied in 1972 when President Tomás decided, against Caetano's wishes, to stand for a third seven-year term. The seventy-eight-year-old Tomás received 616 of 669 votes in the electoral college. (The electoral college had been instituted after the Norton de Matos scare to ensure that the dictatorship would never lose a presidential election.) The overwhelming margin of victory given to Tomás was a clear signal from the ultras that Caetano's liberalization was over. This led to the resignation of several reform-minded deputies in the National Assembly—Francisco Sá Carneiro, Francisco Pinto Balsemão, Joaquim Magalhães Mota and Correia Cunha—who attempted to form an opposition force given voice by Balsemão's weekly newspaper, *Expresso*. Although the 1969 elections to the National Assembly had been the freest since the First Republic, the elections of 1973 were a throwback to those held when Salazar was alive: The ANP's candidates were elected for want of challengers, their opponents having all been previously disqualified on technicalities.

Disillusionment with Caetano soon became widespread, and after 1972 a malaise settled over Portugal that was to last until the regime collapsed two years later. Furthermore, the negative feelings about Caetano's stewardship were exacerbated by a steady worsening of the country's economic situation. Although Portugal's industrial sector had been growing at an annual rate of 9 percent and direct foreign investment was steady during the 1960s, increased government spending on social services and wars in the colonies began to cause budget and balance of payments deficits. Even though these were offset by Portugal's vast gold reserve, amassed by Salazar through tightfisted economic policies over the course of the New State, commodity prices (especially that of oil) began to inflate between 10 and 20 percent per annum, which cut deeply into living standards. Many small firms went bankrupt. The disparities of wealth, always wide in Portugal, gaped even wider. Emigration accelerated as young men sought to escape unemployment and military service. The New State, unable to be changed from within and unable to bring the colonial wars to a close either by defeating the independence movements on the battlefield or negotiating a settlement, was moving rapidly toward a crisis.

THE COLONIAL WARS

Of all the problems Caetano faced, the colonial wars in Angola, Mozambique, and Portuguese Guinea loomed the largest. The independence movements that had sprung up in each of Portugal's African colonies during the early 1960s were generated by the same underlying socioeconomic conditions. Since the latter part of the nineteenth century, the African colonies were important for Portugal's image of itself in the world. Although Portugal was a small country in Europe, its colonies made it into a world-class nation, the center of an extensive and racially diverse pan-Lusitanian community scattered across the globe and held together by the mutual bonds of Portuguese language and culture. The Portuguese, like the French with respect to Algeria, propounded the notion that Angola, Mozambique, and Portuguese Guinea were simply extensions of Portugal overseas, indissolubly linked to the metropole. The Portuguese claimed to be carrying out in Africa a nonracial, Christian, civilizing mission as they had successfully done in Brazil. Theoretically, an African inhabitant of the colonies could become the legal equal of any metropolitan citizen, if willing to abandon traditional African ways of living and adopt Portuguese language and culture.

Although the Portuguese were less racist than the British, the effect of their policy of cultural superiority created within each colony marked socioeconomic and racial disparities. The standards for being officially recognized as an *assimilado* (one assimilated into Portuguese culture) were so high that only an extremely small percentage of Africans ever achieved this status. Hence, the great majority of Africans remained classified as *indígenas* (natives), which permitted the colonial authorities to subject them to numerous indignities and certain forms of forced labor.

By the late 1950s, the New State began to face serious challenges to its African policies from the opposition in Portugal and African nationalist movements in each one of the colonies. While decolonization was proceeding apace in other parts of Africa, however, Portuguese ultras remained committed to the idea of one nation from the Minho to Mozambique. Gradually, the nationalist challenge grew into a generalized guerrilla war for independence in each colony.

During the 1960s the military situation did not give cause for concern. The guerrilla armies of the national liberation movements were at that time relatively small and ineffective. Caetano and the ultras believed that surrender to small and unrepresentative groups would betray the general population. At first the military problem was principally a matter of maintaining internal security. But in the 1970s the liberation movements began to step up military operations, and the Portuguese armed forces began to lose the initiative. This happened initially in Portuguese Guinea where Portuguese efforts to weaken the African Independence party of Guinea and the Cape Verde Islands (Partido Africano de Independência para a Guiné e Cabo Verde, or PAIGC) by manipulating its internal ethnic divisions had failed. Even the assassination of the PAIGC's president, Amílcar Cabral, by internal rivals with Portuguese help, did not break the unity of the party.

In order to salvage the situation, the military commander and governor-general of Portuguese Guinea, General António de Spínola, sought to use the good offices of President Léopold Senghor of Senegal to negotiate a settlement with the PAIGC. Spínola offered the PAIGC the opportunity to participate as a partner in governing an independent Guinea within a broad Luso-African-Brazilian community. Both the PAIGC and the government in Lisbon rejected Spínola's plan. Caetano and the ultras saw such an arrangement as tantamount to total capitulation and believed that it would be preferable to be defeated militarily rather than agree to such a negotiated settlement. Among the officer corps in Guinea, Caetano's attitude created fear that Caetano would imitate Salazar (who in 1961 blamed the army for the loss of the Portuguese State of India) and blame them for the loss of Africa. Consequently, resentment against the government in Lisbon began to spread among the Portuguese armed forces in Guinea.

On September 24, 1973, Luís Cabral, Amílcar's brother, who had become president of the PAIGC, declared Guinea-Bissau an independent country. Within three weeks about sixty countries had recognized this declaration of independence, even though one-third of the country and its major towns were still occupied and controlled by the Portuguese armed forces. In early 1974 the military balance shifted decisively against the Portuguese when the PAIGC introduced SAM-7s onto the battlefield. The appearance of these weapons attested to the PAIGC's growing sophistication as a military force and destroyed Portugal's hitherto uncontested air superiority. The Portuguese air force began to suffer heavy losses, as did the infantry, deprived of adequate air cover.

During the 1960s the liberation movement in Mozambique, the Front for the Liberation of Mozambique (Frente de Libertação de Moçambique, or FRELIMO) had been confined to the Cabo Delgado and Niassa provinces in the extreme north of the colony. Experiencing serious internal ethnic and racial conflict at that time, FRELIMO was unable to carry the war to the south, where most Portuguese settlers lived. The movement was also weakened by the assassination, possibly with Portuguese help, of its founder and leader, Eduardo Mondlane. The Portuguese armed forces, under the command of General Kaúlza de Arriaga, had also successfully denied FRELIMO access to the indigenous population by resettling large numbers of Africans into *aldeamentos*, or strategic hamlets. During the 1970s, with the help of the neighboring independent states of Malawi and Zambia, FRELIMO was able to outflank Portuguese defenses in Cabo Delgado and Niassa and commence military operations in Tete Province. Their objective was to interdict the construction of the massive hydroelectric project at Cabora Bassa on the Zambizi River.

Although FRELIMO was not able to stop construction of the dam, their presence in Tete forced the Portuguese to divert considerable military resources and manpower to its defense. This stretched the Portuguese army too thinly across Mozambique, despite the recruitment of a sizable number of African troops, and permitted FRELIMO to penetrate the province of Manica e Sofala. The activities of FRELIMO in the "waist" of Mozambique threatened to cut the colony in two and spread panic among Portuguese settlers, who began to experience the war firsthand. In Vila Pery, Vila Manica, and Beira, settlers stoned army soldiers for failing to stop FRELIMO and protect their farms, which were increasingly coming under attack.

From 1973 to 1974, Angola was the one colony where there was no deterioration of the military situation. Angola was experiencing only sporadic guerrilla activity at that time. The Portuguese army had been successful in its containment strategy, however, principally because of the weakness of the independence movement, which was split along racial and ethnic lines into three rival parties. The Popular Movement for the Liberation of Angola (Movimento Popular de Libertação de Angola, or MPLA) was led by discontented assimilados and mulattoes from the Mbundu ethnic group. Because of this group's close proximity to Luanda, the capital of the colony, the movement was strongly influenced by Portuguese values and culture. The National Union for the Total Independence of Angola (União Nacional para a Independência Total de Angola, or UNITA), led by Jonas Savimbi, was less Europeanized and drew its support from the Ovimbundu people in southern Angola. The National Front for the Liberation of Angola (Frente Nacional de Libertação de Angola, or FNLA) was led by Holden Roberto and drew support from the Bakango people in northern Angola. These movements were as hostile to one another as they were toward the Portuguese.

The deterioration of the military situation in Guinea-Bissau and Mozambique and the refusal of the civilian leadership to countenance a negotiated settlement had disastrous consequences for the fighting effectiveness of the Portuguese armed forces. Morale plunged, discipline became lax, frontline officers frequently avoided contact with the enemy, and leadership was lethargic. Discontent within the officer corps over the government's decision to continue fighting was aggravated by hostility toward a permanent army staff corps that never rotated between their desks and combat duty. Combat officers, who faced almost continuous duty in the *mato* (bush) of Africa, came to resent their deskbound colleagues, who were never in danger and who frequently held lucrative civilian jobs on the side. Moreover, during the New State, as during previous regimes in Portuguese history, promotion of officers was based more on political loyalty than on professional competence. This meant that many talented officers were not promoted up to their abilities and many less skilled were promoted well beyond their abilities. The African wars gradually transformed the armed forces from a reliable instrument of the New State to a dissatisfied and discontented force that increasingly began to contemplate saving itself from disgrace and dishonor by overturning the government in Lisbon.

THE ARMED FORCES MOVEMENT

Although rumors of a golpe were rife during the early 1970s, it was not until the first months of 1974 that evidence that the armed forces were going to move against the New State actually became clear. The general belief was that the golpe was being prepared by high-ranking ultra officers who thought that Caetano's reforms would lead to independence for Mozambique, Angola, and Portuguese Guinea. In fact, the golpe was being planned by junior officers, captains and majors, who had become deeply angered and exhausted by years of combat duty and were determined not to be made the scapegoats for military defeat.

The first attempt to organize took place on September 9, when 140 junior officers met near Évora at a farmhouse owned by a cousin of one of the conspirators, Captain Dinis de Almeida. The specific purpose of the meeting was to protest a decree-law recently promulgated by the Caetano government designed to deal with the problem of officer recruitment and retention. In 1973 only 137 career lieutenants had been inducted into the army, which forced the government to make up the shortfall through conscription. This meant that a way had to be found to replenish the lower ranks of the officer corps by encouraging drafted officers to make careers in the armed forces. Decree-law 353/73 of July 13, 1973, permitted conscripted officers with combat experience to reenlist and attend a one-year crash course at the military academy. They could then reenter the ranks with their seniority dating from their initial appointment as conscripts. This policy particularly angered regular officers who, after attending the academy's four-year course, had slowly worked their way up to the ranks of captain and major and had served years in frontline units in Africa. They were afraid that *milicianos* (conscripted officers) would soon outrank them by being rapidly promoted to lieutenant colonel and colonel. The junior officers who gathered at the farmhouse drew up a document protesting the policy. It was eventually signed by 400 of their colleagues.

A second meeting, held at Oeiras on the outskirts of Lisbon on November 24, 1973, organized a coordinating committee. On December 1 a third meeting in Óbidos, north of Lisbon, brought together 186 officers, representing all army units, who decided to continue their protest against the government until more support could be organized. At a fourth meeting held on December 8 on the Costa da Caprica, across the Tejo from Lisbon, an inner steering committee composed of Captain Vasco Lourenço, Major Otelo Saraiva de Carvalho, and Major Vitor Alves was chosen.

For its part, the government responded to these meetings by transferring officers suspected of attending them and by revoking Decree-law 353/73. This did not, however, end the conspiracy. In January, junior officers met at the house of Colonel Marcelino Marques to consider how to proceed. Most of the conspirators were politically naive. Some argued for an immediate golpe; others counseled patience. Some were in contact with certain senior officers known to be dissatisfied with the government's African policy, such as General Francisco de Costa Gomes and General António de Spínola, the chief and deputy chief, respectively, of the general staff.

On February 22, 1974, Spínola published a book called *Portugal e o Futuro* (Portugal and the Future) in which he advocated a political rather than military solution to the African wars. The book was an elaboration of his idea of progressive autonomy for the colonies within a vast, worldwide Lusitanian community, first put forward while he was the commander of Portuguese forces in Guinea. Caetano, however, saw "progressive autonomy" as ultimately meaning "self-determination" because the history of the postcolonial French Union and the British Commonwealth showed that such federations do not last and complete independence results. Although Spínola's book embarrassed some officers because of its quasi-neocolonialist slant, it provided a catalyst for further organizing against the regime.

On March 5 the conspiracy to overturn the regime developed a formal structure. The conspirators began to call themselves the Armed Forces Movement (Movimento das Forças Armadas, or MFA) and to discuss a plan of action. Some adhered to the ideas Spínola had propounded in his book and wanted him to lead the golpe. Others wanted a more radical solution. There was no agreement among them on what type of political framework would replace the New State once it was overthrown. They were bound together principally by the common objectives of regime change, decolonization, democratization, and redemption of military honor.

At this point the government finally realized that a serious challenge to its authority was afoot and something had to be done to stave it off. Caetano, who was proving to be weak and vacillating, suggested to President Tomás that a new prime minister be chosen and a new government formed. Tomás thought it would be better if Caetano stayed on as prime minister. After arranging a vote of confidence in the National Assembly, Caetano then asked Spínola and Costa Gomes to publicly pledge support for the government and its African policies. They refused, and Caetano dismissed them on March 14, 1974. Twenty-nine of the MFA conspirators were arrested and transferred to different units. Costa Gomes was replaced by the ultra general, Joaquim da Luz Cunha, Arriaga's brother-in-law. These actions, of course, only aroused the young officers more strongly against the government.

On March 15, Major Otelo Saraiva de Carvalho, or Otelo, as he became universally known after the golpe, gave the order to the military to move against the regime. Based on faulty information from one of the MFA's officers at Lamego, the order was premature, and the only unit that actually responded was the Fifth Infantry stationed at Caldas da Rainha, 50 miles north of Lisbon. A column of 200 men led by Major Casanova Ferreira marched on Lisbon only to be stopped by loyalist troops and GNR units on the city's outskirts. They were turned back to Caldas, where they surrendered. The government mistakenly thought that the danger of a golpe had passed.

This misfire only strengthened the resolve of the conspirators. Otelo drew up a new plan, and on March 18 the MFA issued a formal document protesting the arrest of those officers involved in the Caldas da Rainha incident. On April 23 military preparations were completed. April 25 was selected as the day for the move against the state. At twenty-five minutes past midnight of April 24, the Catholic radio station Rádio Renascença broadcast "Grandola, Vila Morena," a protest song about popular resistance by José Afonso. This song was the signal to march,

April 25, 1974, Carmo Square, Lisbon. Photo courtesy of General Directorate of Social Communication, Lisbon.

and military units throughout Portugal began to move on the country's key points. Government ministries in the Praça do Comércio in Lisbon were quickly occupied; Caetano took refuge in the GNR headquarters in Carmo. Having previously refused to give himself up to MFA Captain Salqueiro Maia, whose troops had surrounded the GNR building, Caetano surrendered at 5:45 p.m. to Spínola, the MFA's titular leader. Tomás was arrested at the presidential palace in Belém and, with Caetano and other government ministers, flown to Madeira the next day. A month later they were exiled to Brazil.

The New State had collapsed like a house of cards without a shot being fired in its defense. The golpe was greeted by the Portuguese people with great happiness and euphoria. Jubilant Lisboetas presented the soldiers with red and white carnations, which soon became the symbol of the revolution. From April 25, 1974, until July 1976, when

DOWNFALL OF THE NEW STATE 87

April 25, 1974, Trinity Square, Lisbon. Photo courtesy of General Directorate of Social Communication, Lisbon.

a new democratic regime was finally put in place, Portugal experienced an intense period of anarchy and disorder as various factions jockeyed with one another for power.

SPÍNOLA

Immediately after the golpe, the MFA met at Pontinha barracks, where Spínola announced the formation of a Board of National Salvation (Junta de Salvação Nacional, or JSN) composed of himself and the following officers: General Costa Gomes, Brigadier Jaime Silveiro Marques of the army; Admiral Rosa Coutinho and Admiral José Baptista Pinheiro de Azevedo of the navy; and Brigadier Diogo Neto and Colonel Carlos Galvão de Melo of the air force. Spínola was chosen as interim president of the republic and laid before the Portuguese people a political program based on that of the MFA. This program included the election of a constituent assembly; the abolition of the DGS, the Portuguese Legion, Portuguese Youth, and the ANP; amnesty for political prisoners; a general purge (*saneamento*) of high-level New State officials; the end of censorship; and the right to freely form political associations.

The first photograph of all the members of the Board of National Salvation meeting at the Cova da Moura Palace, April 28, 1974. *Standing, left to right:* General Diogo Neto, Admiral Rosa Coutinho, Colonel Galvão de Melo. *Seated, left to right:* General Costa Gomes, General Spínola, Admiral Pinheiro de Azevedo, and Brigadier Silveiro Marques. Photo courtesy of General Directorate of Social Communication, Lisbon.

The relationship between the JSN and the MFA, which had assumed a watchdog role in order to assure that its program would be carried out, was a difficult one from the start. The JSN was composed of high-ranking conservative officers who wanted to move cautiously, whereas the MFA was composed of low-ranking liberal and radical officers who wanted to move more rapidly and in a new direction. This was especially true of the officers of the MFA's coordinating committee: Vasco Gonçalves, Ernesto Augusto de Melo Antunes, Vitor Alves, Vitor Crespo, Almada Contreiras, José Inacio da Costa Martins, and Pereira Pinto.

This tension was aggravated by the political activity of exiled political leaders who were permitted to return under the MFA's amnesty. Álvaro Cunhal, the secretary general of the Portuguese Communist party arrived from Prague and took charge of the party. Capitalizing on its reputation for resistance to the repression of the New State, the PCP quickly expanded its membership and established several hundred cells throughout Portugal. Cunhal's strategy was to catapult the PCP into power not by winning elections but by occupying key positions in the media, state bureaucracy, local government, and the labor unions, a strategy made possible by the vacancies left by the saneamentos and the general chaos of the moment. Mário Soares, the secretary general of the Portuguese Socialist party, returned from Paris and began organizing the PS, which had been created the year before in Bad

Munstereifel, Germany. Although the founders of this party were avowed socialists, they did not envision an Eastern European-style regime for Portugal. Instead, they were strongly committed to Western European social democracy.

At the same time, the disillusioned ANP liberals who had resigned from the National Assembly in 1972 set about organizing their own political party, the People's Democratic party (Partido Popular Democrático, or PPD), which chose Francisco Sá Carneiro as its first secretary general. As the party solidified around the concept of social democracy, it changed its name to the Social Democratic party and billed itself as a non-Marxist party of the left. Also, at the same time, Diogo Freitas do Amaral, Adelino Amaro da Costa, Valentim Xavier Pintado, and Leite de Faria, all former members of the conservative wing of the SEDES and the ANP, founded the party of the Social Democratic Center, which was inspired by Christian humanism and traditional conservatism and favored a Western European-style democracy.

Spínola appointed an old-style republican, the sixty-nine-year-old Adelino da Palma Carlos, as prime minister and asked him to form a provisional government. The government included fourteen ministers: Álvaro Cunhal and Pacheco Gonçalves (without portfolios) of the PCP; Mário Soares (foreign affairs), Francisco Salgado Zenha (justice), and Raúl Rego (social communication and information) of the PS; and Sá Carneiro (deputy prime minister) and Magalhães Mota (internal administration) of the PPD. The rest of the government was left of center, and the only military man was Lieutenant Colonel Firmino Miguel, who held the portfolio of defense.

Palma Carlos, who was a constitutional lawyer and dean of the University of Lisbon faculty of law, saw his duty as prime minister to establish the legal basis for his provisional government and to normalize public life. In effect this meant creating a constitutional basis for Spínola's presidency. This proved impossible. The government was a shambles; unpopular New State civil servants were hounded from their jobs. A huge wave of strikes washed over the country, and workers occupied factories and firms abandoned by their owners. The walls of Lisbon were covered with revolutionary graffiti and murals. Palma Carlos, unable to develop a coherent, consistent policy concerning labor demands and broader economic issues, resigned on July 10 after fifty-six days in office.

Spínola then nominated his minister of defense, Firmino Miguel, to the vacant post of prime minister. But the MFA rejected Miguel, proposing two alternatives: Major Melo Antunes or Colonel Vasco Gonçalves. Spínola incorrectly perceived Antunes to be a dangerous radical and Gonçalves, who owned his own engineering consulting firm, as someone who could be trusted. What he did not know was that

Gonçalves had been a member of the PCP in his youth and was still very sympathetic to the party. That the MFA was able to reject Spínola's choice for prime minister and substitute its own showed clearly that the MFA, not the JSN, held power in Portugal. The MFA perceived that, with Spínola at the helm, the haughty, paternalistic style of leadership associated with the New State would continue. In order to give itself the power to control events, the MFA organized a special military strike force called the Continental Operations Command (Comando Operacional do Continente, or COPCON). An elite force of 5,000 handpicked men, this new military arm of the MFA was placed under the command of Otelo, the architect of the April 25 golpe and newly promoted to brigadier.

Spínola thus found that he had power over neither the MFA nor his own government. His foreign minister, Mário Soares, had begun on his own initiative to negotiate with the liberation movements for the independence of the colonies. In late July Spínola was forced to concede the right of the people of Angola, Mozambique, and Guinea-Bissau to self-determination, even though Spínola and other conservative members of the JSN saw rapid decolonization as a mistake. Spínola viewed the loss of Guinea-Bissau as unfortunate, but he believed that the loss of Mozambique and Angola would be tragic. At the same time the economic situation was worsening, anarchy continued, and latifúndios were beginning to be occupied in the Alentejo.

In order to strengthen his hand against the MFA, Spínola tried to assert his personal control over the situation by adopting a Gaullist-style leadership in the hope of rallying broad popular support for his person. On September 10 in a nationally televised speech he argued for "authentic" decolonization, not hasty abandonment. He called for a rally of the "silent majority," which he thought would give him the popular mandate he needed to reorganize the government and disband the MFA. Spínola hoped to capitalize on the violent reaction to the anarchy in the Alentejo by the conservative Portuguese of the north, who had begun to drive radicals and Communists from their villages and towns with pitchforks and shotguns.

The showdown between Spínola and the MFA and its radical civilian allies came the day before his rally of the silent majority, which had been arranged to take place in Campo Pequeno, Lisbon's main bullring, on September 28, 1974. On the eve of September 27, in order to interdict Spínola's supporters from entering the city, radicals and other leftists barricaded the roads that connected Lisbon to the north. The prime minister, Vasco Gonçalves, and Otelo, the commander of COPCON, were summoned to the presidential palace in Belém, where Spínola placed them under house arrest and told Otelo to issue orders to COPCON to remove the barricades. When Otelo gave such orders by telephone, the subordinate who received the call sensed that the command was given under duress and decided not to carry it out. Instead, COPCON announced that it would march on Belém if Otelo were not freed. Spínola conceded defeat by cancelling the rally and resigning the presidency on September 30.

The MFA and the Left saw themselves as defending the social, economic, and political gains of April 25 against the efforts of Spínola and other conservatives on the JSN to marginalize them and take control of the government. The basic degree of trust that was necessary for the maintenance of consensus between the MFA and the JSN broke down as each perceived the other in the most sinister of lights. The result was confrontation, and ultimately, Spínola's defeat.

THE SHIFT TO THE LEFT

Spínola was replaced by General Costa Gomes, the chief of the general staff. Costa Gomes, who was mildly leftist, saw himself as a mediator and conciliator, which won him the nickname "the Cork" for his ability to float with each new ripple of the political waters. He pledged himself to carrying out the program of the MFA. Gonçalves was retained as prime minister and a third provisional government, heavily weighted with MFA members, was installed.

Unlike Spínola, Costa Gomes was committed to rapid decolonization. On November 24, 1974, agreements were signed to grant independence to the islands of São Tomé e Príncipe on July 12, 1975. In December 1974 agreement was reached with the already recognized PAIGC for the independence of the Cape Verde Islands on July 5, 1975. Also in December Portugal arranged for the return of Goa, Damão, Diu, and Dadra to India. Independence for Mozambique, negotiated with FRELIMO, was also slated for July 1975.

An agreement on Angolan independence, however, was slower in coming because the nationalist movement was divided into three rival organizations. The MFA wanted to hand over the government to the MPLA, but the presence of UNITA and the FNLA made a compromise necessary. Each liberation movement was negotiating independently with the Gonçalves government in the hope of being named the legitimate government of independent Angola. Independence was finally negotiated for November 11, 1975, with the colony to be ruled until then by an interim government composed of Portuguese, FNLA, MPLA, and UNITA representatives. Elections were to be held in order to determine the legitimate government upon full independence. These elections never came about because civil war broke out among the liberation movements.

When the Portuguese departed on November 11, each movement proclaimed itself to be the legitimate government of independent Angola. One legacy of decolonization was the coming home of about 800,000 destitute and embittered Portuguese colonial settlers called *retornados*.

The general tendency after Spínola's resignation was a rapid shift to the left. Within the government and the MFA, talk began to move away from "democratization" to "building socialism." The MFA came to see itself as the vanguard of a popular revolution. The Fifth Division, the old psychological warfare unit under the New State, was reorganized by Colonel Varela Gomes, a Marxist, and began to communicate MFA ideas to the people, especially in the rural north. The avowed purpose of this "cultural dynamization" program was to overcome the lack of "revolutionary consciousness" among the people of that area. At the same time Prime Minister Gonçalves aligned the policies of his government with those of the PCP. In particular, he supported the Communists' attempt to maintain their monopoly over the labor movement, which was opposed by the socialists and moderates as well as elements from the extreme Left. Political disorder mounted. Rural workers in the Alentejo occupied more and more of the region's latifúndios; in Lisbon and Porto, squatters moved into unoccupied houses, and neighborhood committees sprang up and began to take over local government.

The shift to the left and increased levels of anarchy encouraged Spínola to make another bid for power, this time by golpe. His attempt was a fiasco: The golpe was poorly planned and the MFA and COPCON knew about it in advance. On March 8, 1975, Miguel Champalimaud, owner of the United Fiber Company (Companhia União Fabril, or CUF), a giant conglomerate with vast holdings in the former colonies, and Lieutenant Nuno Barbieri, the son of a former PIDE official, announced that they had seen secret plans drawn up by the MFA and certain leftist groups to arrest 1,500 moderates and conservatives and to liquidate them. Whether such a plan actually existed is not known. In any case, Spínola, who was one of those slated for elimination, took the announcement at face value and put his takeover plan into effect. On March 11, Spínola arrived at the Tancos air force base about 80 miles north of Lisbon, where he was to coordinate an air and ground attack on the First Light Infantry barracks near Lisbon, the seizure of radio stations, and the capture of the GNR headquarters in Carmo and other strategic points. Spínola calculated that only a small force would be necessary because the majority of military units would remain neutral. The attack on the First Light Infantry went off half-cocked, the barracks strafed in desultory fashion by only two aircraft. Only 160 troops arrived to take the Lisbon airport. The Fifth Division and COPCON quickly rounded up Spínola's supporters and Costa Gomes announced over national radio that the government was still in control. Spínola and his immediate coterie boarded helicopters and flew to Spain. In the aftermath, Prime Minister Gonçalves declared that the people and MFA had triumphed and their alliance was "irreversible."

THE GROUP OF NINE

The March 11 fiasco strengthened the hand of Gonçalves and MFA radicals. Spínola's followers were purged and the leftist tendency reasserted itself with renewed vigor. On March 14 the MFA met and decided to institutionalize itself. The JSN was abolished and all governing power was vested in a new organ called the Council of the Revolution (Conselho da Revolução, or CR), which included the president of the republic, the prime minister, the chiefs of the three branches of the armed forces, and a number of officers appointed by the MFA. The CR was made responsible to a newly organized Assembly of the Armed Forces (Assembleia das Forças Armadas), whose 240 members were elected from the ranks of the three service branches. The CR was given the power to oversee what was now being called a revolution.

The first official act of the CR was to nationalize Portugal's private banks and insurance companies. The second was to install the fourth provisional government, with Vasco Gonçalves again as prime minister. Nearly half of his twenty-one ministers were military men, and the civilian contingent was heavily weighted toward the left. At the same time, large private conglomerates, such as CUF, were taken over by their employees in moves coordinated by the PCP-dominated labor organization. In the Alentejo, farm workers who had occupied latifúndios were influenced by the PCP to transform them into collective farms. At this juncture it appeared as if Portugal was rapidly becoming an Eastern European–style Communist regime.

An atmosphere of fear and apprehension prevailed. Civilian political leaders, such as Mário Soares, Sá Carneiro, and others, were extremely concerned that the elections for a constituent assembly, which had been announced by Costa Gomes in February, would not take place in April as scheduled. This concern was dissolved when the MFA agreed to constituent assembly elections. If once elected, the parties would produce a constitution that institutionalized the MFA and made it the permanent guarantor of the transition to socialism. This accord also stipulated that the president of the republic would have to be a military officer chosen by an electoral college. Elections for the constituent assembly were held on April 25, 1975, the first anniversary of the golpe, using the d'Hondt system of proportional representation. Turnout was extremely high, with 91.7 percent of the eligible electorate going to the polls. Blank ballots, called for by the MFA as a sign of solidarity with the revolutionary process, were only 6.9 percent of the vote.

The PS polled 37.9 percent of the ballots, the PSD 26.4 percent, the PCP 12.5 percent, and the CDS 7.7 percent. The remaining 15.5 percent was divided among various parties of the extreme Left and the Popular Monarchist party (Partido Popular Monarquico, or PPM). Only one of these smaller parties, the Maoist Popular Democratic Union (União Democrática Popular, or UDP) managed to win a seat. These results revealed the relative and regional strengths of the four main parties. The PCP showed that, despite its superior organization, it was in reality a party of the Alentejo and the industrial belt surrounding Lisbon. The vote for the PSD and the CDS showed these parties to be strong in the conservative north, especially in rural areas. The PSD showed the greatest support in the archipelagoes of Madeira and the Azores. Support for the PS appeared to be spread over the whole of Portugal, and it emerged from the election as the major national party. The UDP won its single seat from the Lisbon constituency.

The PCP and parties of the extreme Left as well as the MFA, however, claimed that these election results signified nothing whatsoever. The MFA, now pulling closer to the extreme Left, was not going to allow a mere election stand in the way of the revolution. The PCP refused to align with the democratic parties and reaffirmed its support for the leftward-leaning MFA, which they saw as an ally in their attempt to gain power. This convinced some radical officers that the PCP was the only political party truly committed to liberating Portugal. On July 9 the assembly of the MFA approved a document that declared that the MFA itself was a liberation movement and called for the election of assemblies within all units of the armed forces and police, which would be unified at the national level in a People's Assembly.

This action by the MFA sparked a reaction by the political parties. On July 11 the PS, PSD, and CDS withdrew from the fourth provisional government in protest over the MFA's decision to link itself directly with "popular power." They announced that they were launching an international campaign against encroaching communism in Portugal. It also sparked a reaction in the north. On July 13 Catholics marched in Aveiro against the MFA, and on the same day a group of farmers sacked and burned a PCP headquarters in Rio Maior. By the end of the season, the "Hot Summer of 1975" as it is now generally known, the offices of a large number of leftist parties were attacked and destroyed by the deeply conservative farmers of northern Portugal, who saw the events taking place in Lisbon as a dire threat to their way of life. The situation in northern Portugal was paralleled in the archipelagoes of Madeira and the Azores, where the offices of the PCP and other leftist organizations were also sacked and burned.

At the same time, two right-wing underground organizations appeared: the Democratic Liberation Movement of Portugal (Movimento Democrático de Libertação de Portugal, or MDLP) and the Portuguese Liberation Army (Exército Português de Libertação, or EPL). These organizations smuggled small arms into northern Portugal from Spain and were composed of former servicemen and retornados from the colonies. General Spínola led the EPL from Switzerland, where he had been living in exile since the March 29 fiasco. The EPL was pledged to carry out the original MFA program and to create a pluralist democracy in Portugal. The EPL and MDLP were also supported by significant numbers of former members of PIDE and the Portuguese Legion, who had organized themselves into cells and were preparing for guerrilla warfare and a campaign of terror against the MFA-supported regime. By July 1975 Portugal was on the verge of civil war.

In order to solidify the victory of the Left, the Assembly of the MFA voted to establish a triumvirate composed of Costa Gomes, Vasco Gonçalves, and the COPCON commander, Otelo. These three leaders, however, were not in agreement on what kind of leftist regime should be created. Gonçalves's aim was to try to establish a regime in concert with the PCP's wishes. Otelo hoped to bring about a regime dominated by "people's assemblies." Costa Gomes preferred a moderate socialism. On August 7 Gonçalves formed a new cabinet, the most lackluster of the five provisional governments since April 25, 1974. It was at this time that Major Melo Antunes and eight other officers, generally known as the Group of Nine (Grupo dos Nove), published a document calling for a nonaligned democratic socialism in Portugal. Extolling traditional military values, it asked for an end to anarchy and respect for the results of the constituent assembly elections of April 25. This document was followed on August 13 by another, prepared by COPCON. Called the "Left Alternative," it criticized both the Antunes document for its democratic, Western European orientation and the Gonçalves-PCP alliance for its state socialism. The COPCON document advocated a direct link between the people and the MFA.

Although he tried, Gonçalves was not able to prevent open debate on the document of the Group of Nine. As it became evident to the PCP that the days of Gonçalves's cabinet were numbered, they began to seek an alternative strategy for gaining power. On August 20, Cunhal announced that a new direction was in the offing. On August 25, the United Revolutionary Front (Frente Unido Revolucionário, or FUR) was organized, which aligned the PCP with the extreme Left. The plan was to co-opt COPCON commander Otelo into this alliance.

On August 29, Costa Gomes prevailed upon Gonçalves to resign, having promised to nominate him chief of the general staff. He was replaced by Admiral José Baptista Pinheiro de Azevedo, who pledged his government to support the original program of the MFA. The Azevedo government had fourteen ministers: four from the MFA (Melo Antunes, Almeida e Costa, Tomás Rosa, and Vitor Alves); four from the PS (Jorge Campinos, Lopes Cardoso, Salgado Zenha, and Walter Rosa); three independents (Marques do Carmo, Almeida Santos, and Pinheiro Farinha); two from PPD (Magalhães Mota and Sá Borges) and one from PCP (Álvaro Augusto Viega de Oliveira). Former prime minister Vasco Gonçalves's nomination to be chief of the general staff was rejected by the MFA.

Under the sixth provisional government, anarchy continued unabated. Incidents of revolutionary outbursts in Lisbon provoked violent reactions in the north. The military itself became paralyzed as the chain of command broke down completely. Enlisted soldiers under the influence of the FUR organized Soldiers United Will Win (Soldados Unidos Vencerão, or SUV) and stopped obeying the orders of their officers. Military units in the north removed themselves from the command of Brigadier Eurico Corvacho, a staunch Gonçalves supporter, and placed themselves under Brigadier António Pires Veloso, who was linked to the Nine. Otelo vacillated, having opportunistically come out in favor of the Nine in order to oust Gonçalves, and was reluctant to throw in his lot with FUR and SUV. The Fifth Division under Major Dinis de Almeida moved further left.

The Group of Nine made plans to resist any attempt by the Communists and the extreme Left to exploit the anarchy that prevailed. On November 18 the MFA voted to replace Otelo with Major Vasco Lourenço as commander of COPCON and the Lisbon military region. Otelo defied this order and refused to step down. On November 24, the MFA reiterated its order. Revolutionary paratroopers occupied bases at Tancos, Montijo, Monte Real, and Monsanto. In response, Colonel Ramalho Eanes declared a state of emergency, seconded by Major Lourenço, and took charge of military operations. Commandos under the leadership of Colonel Jaime Neves surrounded one revolutionary base after another. By November 26 all mutinous units had surrendered and COPCON was abolished. Otelo, Almeida and 200 extreme leftists were arrested. A new sober and realistic mood settled over Portugal. Under the direction of the Group of Nine, the armed forces returned to its original role as guarantors of democracy, not the vanguard of the popular revolution.

REFERENCES

Abshire, David M., and Michael Samuels (eds.). *Portuguese Africa: A Handbook.* New York: Praeger Publishers, 1969.

Bruce, Neil. *Portugal: The Last Empire.* New York: John Wiley, 1975.

Bruneau, Thomas C. *Politics and Nationhood: Post Revolutionary Portugal.* New York: Praeger Publishers, 1984.

Chilcote, Ronald H. *Portuguese Africa.* Englewood Cliffs, N.J.: Prentice-Hall, 1967.

Duffy, James. *Portuguese Africa.* Cambridge: Harvard University Press, 1968.

Gallagher, Tom. *Portugal: A Twentieth-Century Interpretation.* Manchester: Manchester University Press, 1983.

Harsgor, Michael. *Portugal in Revolution.* Beverly Hills, Calif.: Sage Publications, 1976.

Harvey, Robert. *Portugal: Birth of a Democracy.* New York: St. Martin's Press, 1978.

Porch, Douglas. *The Portuguese Armed Forces and the Revolution.* London: Croom Helm, 1977.

7
Consolidation of Democracy

The victory of the Group of Nine was a major turning point in the evolution of Portugal's political system. The government of Pinheiro de Azevedo, backed by the Group of Nine, steered a middle course toward a Western European–style democracy. This was acceptable to the major political parties except the PCP, which disapproved of what it considered a move to the right. After November 25, individuals such as Vasco Gonçalves, Varela Gomes, Ramiro Correia, and José da Costa found themselves in disgrace and gradually faded from the political scene. The leaders of several left-wing terrorist organizations, such as Isabel do Carmo of the Revolutionary Brigades, were rounded up and sent to jail for their activities. Spínola was allowed to return to Portugal.

The MFA, now under the control of the Group of Nine, negotiated a second, reformulated pact with the political parties. In this agreement, signed on February 14, 1976, the MFA eschewed the idea of a permanent involvement in politics. This new arrangement made the military the guarantors of democracy for a fixed period of time, four years. The agreement allowed the constituent assembly to finish its work and elections to be held for a national legislative body and a president.

THE CONSTITUTION OF 1976

Portugal's new constitution was passed by the constituent assembly on April 2, 1976. It was not ratified by the citizenry in a national plebiscite but was simply signed by the president and promulgated. In the constituent assembly it received the approval of all parties except the CDS, which voted no on the grounds that the document was too "socialistic." Despite the party's opposition, the CDS did declare that it would abide by the constitution. Even as the constitution was being promulgated, however, certain political figures were declaring their intention to modify it as soon as the five-year prohibition on amendments had lapsed. Sá Carneiro of the PSD, for example, had drafted an entirely new document that he hoped eventually to substitute for the original.

Like the constitution of 1933, Portugal's new constitution drew on many sources. The influence of the Basic Law of the Federal Republic of Germany and the constitution of the French Fifth Republic was clearly evident. At the same time, the document was an amalgamation of the various partisan wants and desires of the parties in the constituent assembly and enshrined the role of the military in Portugal's transition to democracy as well as the economic "conquests" of the revolution. In the constitution's preamble of principles, Article 2 proclaimed:

> The Portuguese Republic is a democratic state based on popular sovereignty, on the respect for and the guarantee of fundamental rights and freedoms, and on the democratic pluralism of expression and political organization, which have as their objective the assurance of the transition toward socialism through the creation of conditions for the democratic exercise of power by the working classes.

Articles 3 and 10 acknowledged the role of the MFA in this transition, and Article 9 advocated the nationalization of the means of production.

Like those of other Western European democracies, the Portuguese document conceived of human rights not as natural but as social, economic, and cultural. In this conception, the state was to *achieve* such rights, not simply protect the individual for whom such rights are inalienable. Thus, in addition to rights to life, freedom, privacy, religion, expression, travel, and the like, Portuguese citizens were guaranteed such social and economic rights as a job, health care, housing, and a clean environment. A citizen's rights also included the right to private property, but this was limited by the proscription that it could be exercised only if it contributed to social progress. It was, however, forbidden in the basic economic sectors. In addition, the right to create trade unions, cooperatives, and worker self-management committees was recognized. In the section dealing with economic rights, the constitution enshrined agrarian reform, regional development, and economic planning. Article 82 declared that the nationalizations carried out after April 25, 1974, were irreversible.

Section II dealt with the organization of executive, legislative, and judicial powers. In effect, the constitution established a semipresidential system modeled on that of the French Fifth Republic, that is, one in which an independently elected president shares governing power with a prime minister responsible to a parliament. In the Portuguese system, the president is elected directly from the entire country for a five-year term. There is no limitation on the number of terms, but the constitution forbade an individual from succeeding himself after two consecutive terms. Individuals seeking the presidency must be at least thirty-five years old and, in order to be elected, must have received 50 percent of the vote. If no candidate reaches this minimum threshold, a runoff election is held two weeks after the first ballot between the two candidates with the highest number of votes. The president is the commander in chief of the armed forces and is empowered to appoint the prime minister, giving due consideration to the results of parliamentary elections; send messages to Parliament; and dissolve Parliament and call for fresh elections when necessary.

The constitution created a unicameral parliament, called the Assembly of the Republic (Assembleia da República, or AR), having 250 seats. Deputies sitting in the AR had to be twenty-one years old and were to be elected from a list of candidates put forward by each of the parties in electoral constituencies that correspond to the country's administrative districts. The apportionment of seats was made by the d'Hondt highest-average method, with no minimum threshold. The party with the most votes in each district was awarded a seat. Its total vote was then divided by two, and the vote received by the parties compared. The party with the highest vote after this division was given the next seat. Each time a party was awarded a seat, its original vote was divided by the number of seats it had already been awarded plus one. Distribution of seats continued until all the seats in the districts are allocated. Seats were allotted to the various districts in proportion to the number of registered voters in each. Registration was compulsory. There were twenty-two constituencies, eighteen for mainland Portugal, one each for the archipelagoes of Madeira and the Azores, one for Portuguese immigrants living in Western Europe, and one for Portuguese expatriates in the rest of the world.

Deputies were enjoined by the constitution to represent the entire country and not the constituency from which they were elected. Like members of parliaments everywhere, Portuguese deputies were given certain rights, privileges, and perquisites. The basic unit of organization among deputies was the parliamentary group (*grupo parlamentar*), composed of the members of each party represented in the AR and bearing that party's name. Membership in a parliamentary group carried certain responsibilities. Deputies were expected to vote in the manner prescribed by their parliamentary group and to submit to it for approval the bills they intended to introduce. The presidents of the parliamentary groups were important and powerful individuals who determined group strategy and led the debate on the floor. The presiding officer of the AR, the president, was chosen from among the parliamentary groups. The president represented the AR, presided over meetings, and supervised its technical staff.

The constitution designated the Council of Ministers (Conselho de Ministros) or cabinet as the chief policymaking body of the government. The cabinet was composed of a prime minister (presidente do Conselho de Ministros), ministers of the various government departments, and secretaries of state. The prime minister was appointed by the president of the republic after consultation with the parties represented in the AR. Ministers and secretaries of state were appointed by the president upon the recommendation of the prime minister. Thus, the constitution made the prime minister simultaneously responsible to president and Parliament.

The cabinet was empowered by the constitution to negotiate treaties; prepare the plan and budget of the state; make regulations for the execution of laws passed by the AR; issue decree-laws on matters not reserved to the AR, subject to legislative authorization; and direct the activities of the state bureaucracy. The prime minister was empowered to formulate the general policy of the cabinet and coordinate the administrative activities of the ministers and secretaries of state. Within ten days of being appointed, each new cabinet was required to submit to the AR its program for governing. If the AR rejected the program, the cabinet was dismissed by the president and a new one appointed. The cabinet was also dismissed if the AR passed a vote of no confidence. If no cabinet drawn from the AR was able to get its plan approved, the president could dissolve the AR and hold fresh elections.

The role of the military as the watchdog of the revolution and the transition to democracy was enshrined in the Council of the Revolution. Specifically, the CR, which was composed of the president of the republic, the chief of the general staff, the chiefs of the three service branches, and fourteen officers appointed by each branch of the armed forces, was constitutionally empowered to advise the president on the proper functioning of Portugal's new democratic institutions, guarantee faithfulness of government policy to the spirit of the revolution, pass decree-laws having the same weight as laws made by the AR, and make judgments on the constitutionality of all laws.

Below the national level, the constitution created two basic political administrative subunits subordinate to the AR, cabinet, and prime minister: the autonomous regions of the Azores and Madeira and the territorial administrative subdivisions of the mainland called local authorities (*autarquias locais*). Taking account of the special geographic, economic, and social conditions of the Atlantic archipelagoes, as well as their historic aspirations for autonomy, the constitution granted each island group special political status. Article 229 gave each archipelago the power to legislate on all matters of local concern and to exercise its own executive authority. The Azores and Madeira were thus authorized to elect regional parliaments for four years by direct suffrage. The executives of the autonomous regions are appointed by the minister of the republic, who is designated by the president and who coordinates and supervises the work of the national government's field offices.

On the mainland (as well as below the regional governments) the constitution retained the structure of local government laid down in the constitution of 1933 but democratized it by grafting on elected assemblies and subjecting the choosing of executives to election. Thus, in each parish the constitution created an assembly (*assembleia de freguesia*), elected for a three-year term and empowered to chose the executive (junta) of the parish. In each concelho an assembly (*assembleia municipal*) was elected for a three-year term and empowered to approve the plan and budget of the executive body of the concelho, the municipal chamber (*câmara municipal*). The constitution determined that the mayor and the councilmen be directly elected by the registered voters residing in the concelho.

A FREELY ELECTED GOVERNMENT

With the promulgation of the constitution, the way was cleared for elections to fill the offices it created. The first elections for the AR were held on April 25, 1976, the second anniversary of the Revolution of the Carnations. Turnout was 83.8 percent of the registered electorate, down from the 91.7 percent for the constituent assembly election the year before. Fourteen parties ran candidates. The PS campaigned under the slogans "Socialism, yes; dictatorship, no," a reference to the alternative posed by voting either CDS or PCP, and "Europe is with us," which aggravated the PSD. Soares declared that if the PS were victorious, he would not enter into a coalition with any other party and would govern alone. The PCP, for its part, campaigned against the PSD and CDS, calling them reactionaries who sought to resuscitate monopoly capitalism in Portugal and roll back the "gains of April 25." The Communists also favored a coalitional government of the Left. The PSD campaigned as a non-Marxist, left-of-center alternative to the PS, and CDS presented itself as the party of traditional conservatism and Christian humanism. The campaign was generally peaceful, marred only by the murder of a candidate of the Popular Democratic Union in Vila Real.

The 1976 elections produced the following results: The PS won 34.9 percent of the vote and 107 seats in the AR, down 3 percent from their constituent assembly showing; the PSD, 24.4 percent and 73 seats, also down about 2 percent; the CDS, 16.0 percent and 42 seats, up about 8 percent; PCP, 14.4 percent and 40 seats, also up about 2 percent; and the UDP, 1.7 percent and 1 seat. The nine other parties, all of the extreme Left, failed to win seats. The results again revealed the regional bases of support of the four main parties. The PCP continued to draw the bulk of its support from the Alentejo and the industrial belt around Lisbon. The PSD and CDS were strongly supported in the north, with the PSD especially strong in the Azores and Madeira, and the PS received support throughout Portugal, running strongest in urban areas and in the center. The UDP again won its single seat from the Lisbon constituency.

The elections for the AR were followed on June 27 by an election for president of the republic. The PS, PSD, and CDS threw their support behind Ramalho Eanes, the colonel who had been in charge of the military operations on November 25 that put the Group of Nine in power and since then promoted to general and made army chief of staff. Eanes had personal characteristics valued by many Portuguese, which made him a formidable candidate. He was ramrod straight—honest, stern, serious, and a competent military leader. During his tenure as chief of staff he demonstrated that he could get the job done by reducing the army to a small, disciplined, professional fighting force. He was backed by the PS, PSD, and CDS.

There were three other candidates in the race: the prime minister, Admiral Pinheiro de Azevedo, who unfortunately suffered a heart attack during the campaign; Octávio Pato, the candidate of the PCP who was ridiculed with shouts of "quack, quack" (a reference to his name, which means "duck" in Portuguese); and Otelo Saraiva de Carvalho, the ex-COPCON commander and darling of the far Left, who had recently been released from prison.

The campaign was lively but, compared to the constituent assembly and Assembly of the Republic elections, turnout was low, 75.4 percent of the registered electorate. This was probably a result of the almost foregone conclusion that Eanes would win, which he did handily, taking 61.5 percent of the vote. Otelo was a distant second with 16.5 percent, followed by Azevedo with 14.4 percent. Pato brought up the rear with 7.6 percent. Eanes ran well in all districts of the country except Setúbal, where he was outpaced by Otelo, who attracted a good share of the Communist vote in that PCP stronghold. On July 14 Eanes replaced Costa Gomes and pledged his presidency to the development of Portuguese democracy.

With parliamentary and presidential elections completed, a constitutional government could be organized. Eanes called upon Mário Soares to form Portugal's first freely elected government in nearly fifty years. Honoring his campaign promise to govern alone, Soares formed a cabinet made up almost entirely of PS members with a few independents and military men. He presented his program to the AR for approval on July 16, 1976. Soares faced an extremely grave economic situation because

General António dos Santos Ramalho Eanes, president from 1976 to 1986. Photo courtesy of General Directorate of Social Communication, Lisbon.

of Portugal's withdrawal from the African colonies; the drop-off of remittances by Portuguese immigrants, always a main source of government revenue; and the excesses of the post-1974 period, which had nearly depleted Portugal's foreign reserves. He sought to deal with these problems by holding down wages and public spending and by changing some of the legislation passed during the Gonçalves governments. With the help of the PSD and CDS, Soares was able to get through parliament a bill that returned certain smaller enterprises nationalized after 1974 to their previous owners and defined the limits of the public sector.

This first PS government also tried to bring order to the reform of agriculture. Between March 11 and November 25, 1975, about 2.5 million acres of land in the Alentejo and Ribatejo had been occupied by landless workers, frequently led by the PCP. These occupied estates were converted into collective farms (unidades da produção colectiva, or UPC) and financed by the Institute for Agrarian Reorganization. The Soares government, in order to prevent more land from being occupied, decided that land not already scheduled for expropriation would be returned to its owners. At the end of September 1976, Lopes Cardoso, the minister of agriculture, ordered the eviction of occupiers on about 100 farms. Violence broke out between the occupiers and police. Cardoso, who was a radical socialist, lost heart and was replaced by another member of the PS, António Barreto, who intended to carry the policy through. A new law of agrarian reform was pushed through the AR that enlarged the area of agricultural land exempt from expropriation, compensated owners for their losses, established cooperatives for small farmers, and restricted the size of UPCs.

Soares's policies and his growing partnership with the PSD gave rise to strong opposition by the PCP. Álvaro Cunhal condemned the PS for implementing policies that, in the view of PCP, not only favored the recovery of monopoly capitalism in Portugal but rolled back some of the "gains" of April 25, 1974, as well. The government's policies also eroded the internal cohesion of the PS, which had successfully reunified itself after a leadership quarrel in January 1975. That quarrel involved Manuel Serra, the radical Catholic socialist and one of the principals in the Beja uprising of January 1962, who had joined the PS in June 1974 bringing with him a group of socialist intellectuals called the Popular Socialist Movement (Movimento Socialista Popular, or MSP). Professing to be a new generation of radical socialists, Serra's group soon found itself in Soares's disfavor, bolted from the party, and subsequently organized the Popular Socialist Front (Frente Socialista Popular, or FSP).

The cohesion of the PS was again disturbed when two of the party's deputies in the AR, Carmalinda Pereira and Aires Rodrigues, voted against Soares's plan and budget. They were expelled from the party and later organized the unsuccessful Unified Socialist Workers' Party (Partido Operário Unificado Socialista, or POUS). After Lopes Cardoso was fired as the minister of agriculture, he accused the PS leadership generally and Soares particularly of abandoning the working class and following what amounted to little more than social democratic policies. Cardoso and a radical faction within PS called the Association of Socialist Culture–Workers' Brotherhood (Associação de Cultura Socialista–Fraternidade Operária) departed from the PS and organized a group called the Democratic and Socialist Left (Esquerda Socialista e Democrática), which in August 1979 transformed itself into an official party called the Leftist Union for Social Democracy (União de Esquerda para a Democracia Social, or UEDS).

It was, however, the economic difficulties faced by the PS government and not internal party quarrels or PCP opposition that proved to be Soares's undoing. Although government expenditures had been cut, unemployment continued at about 25 percent of the work force, and the balance of payments remained in deficit. Soares was therefore forced to negotiate a $7.5 million loan from the International Monetary Fund (IMF) in order to forestall bankruptcy. The IMF's terms were stringent: devaluation of the escudo, deflation, and austerity. Angered by these terms, the floating coalition in the AR that Soares had skillfully arranged on various issues collapsed; his government fell in December 1977, after sixteen months in office.

This led to the formation of a second PS government, with the participation of some members of the CDS in exchange for their support in the AR. This unlikely arrangement was purely a marriage of convenience. The PS wanted to stay in power, and the CDS wanted an opportunity to gain political legitimacy, something it had been denied during the heady days of the revolution when the party was deemed by the Left to be little more than an extension of Caetano's ANP. The involvement of the CDS with the PS, however, was not well received by the party's conservative supporters. Under pressure from this quarter and finding it difficult to agree on policy with the PS, the CDS withdrew from the coalition and the second socialist government collapsed. Eanes dismissed Soares as prime minister in August 1978.

THE DEMOCRATIC ALLIANCE

In the wake of the collapse of the PS-CDS government, hopes rose that a coalition between PS and PSD would follow. This was not to be because of the intense personal rivalry between Soares and Sá Carneiro. A coalition between PS and PCP was also not possible because of the long-standing hostility and distrust that existed between the socialists and Communists. Eanes did not want to call for fresh elections, because yet another election for the AR would have to be held within a year in order to begin the next legislative term. Without viable options, he decided to take the initiative in organizing a nonparty government. In August 1978 he appointed Alfredo Nobre da Costa, the manager of Portugal's steelworks, as his prime minister. Nobre da Costa recruited a cabinet of independent technocrats and submitted his plan and budget to the AR for approval as required by the constitution. The parties in the AR, resenting Eanes's attempt to govern without them, failed to give Nobre da Costa's government a vote of confidence. This defeat did not, however, deter Eanes from seeking an independent government. In October 1978 he turned to Carlos Mota Pinto, a professor of law at Coimbra University who had been a PSD deputy in the constituent assembly but had broken with Sá Carneiro and was considered an independent. Mota Pinto's government of technocrats was able to win a vote of confidence by the AR. But Mota Pinto's stringent austerity measures very soon made the government extremely unpopular. The PSD withdrew its support, and the second nonparty government of presidential initiative fell in July 1979. Faced with a second defeat, Eanes reluctantly decided to hold an interim election for the AR and appointed a caretaker government headed by Maria de Loudres Pintasilgo, a radical

Catholic engineer who was then Portugal's delegate to UNESCO and the first woman to hold the office of prime minister.

The opposition to Eanes's nonparty governments from within the AR had been orchestrated by Sá Carneiro, the leader of the PSD. His decision to withdraw the party from the Mota Pinto government provoked a leadership quarrel within the party. Sá Carneiro was challenged by a group of thirty-seven PSD deputies sympathetic to the Mota Pinto government, led by António Sousa Franco, António Rebelo de Sousa, and Magalhães Mota, who resigned from the party and remained in the AR as the Social Democrat Action (Acção Social Democrata, or ASD). In September 1979 the ASD transformed itself into a political party called the Independent Social Democrat Association (Associação Social Democrata Independente, or ASDI). With the departure of this group, Sá Carneiro, who represented the aspirations of and was strongly supported by the traditional conservative rural dwellers of the north against Lisbon, gained absolute control of the PSD.

In July 1979 Sá Carneiro announced the formation of an electoral coalition called the Democratic Alliance (Aliança Democrática, or AD). The AD was composed of the PSD, the CDS, the Reformers (a small group of socialists led by António Barreto and Madeiros Ferreira, who had split with Soares in the autumn of 1979), and the small Popular Monarchist party, which wanted not only to restore the monarchy but also to protect Portugal's environment. The AD produced a unified list of candidates for the interim elections set for December 2. It promised decisive action to solve Portugal's economic problems, continued membership in NATO, reapplication for membership in the EEC, reprivatization of certain sectors of the economy, replacement of collective farms by individually owned small- and medium-sized farms in the Alentejo, and revision of the constitution.

The formation of the AD sparked the PCP to organize its own electoral coalition called the United Peoples' Action (Acção Povo Unido, or APU). This coalition brought the PCP together with the Portuguese Democratic Movement (Movimento Democrático Português, or MDP). The MDP was the direct descendant of the CDE, the pre-1974 electoral coalition of radical Catholics and Communists, which appeared after the revolution as a broad movement of socialists, Communists, and social democrats. When it became evident that the coalition was controlled by the PCP and when the party decided that the MDP should become more than an electoral coalition, the socialists and social democrats departed. Although the MDP and PCP are considered one and the same by the PS, PSD, and CDS, they are in fact distinct parties with separate memberships, policy preferences, and bases of support.

On December 2 the AD won 45.2 percent of the vote and 128 seats (PSD 73, Reformers 5, CDS 45, and the PPM 5), an absolute majority of 3 seats; the PS received 27.3 percent and 74 seats; the APU, 18.8 percent and 47 seats (PCP 44, MDP 3); and the UDP, 2.2 percent and 1 seat. The AD's victory came primarily at the expense of the PS, whose vote dipped dramatically by 7.5 percent from 1976 as a consequence of the party's poor performance in government. The PCP's increase resulted from its coalition with the MDP, which was better organized in the north, as well as defections from the PS in the south, where dissatisfaction with the government's policy on agrarian reform was increasingly evident.

Although Eanes was not sympathetic to the AD and disliked Sá Carneiro for attacking his governments of presidential initiative, he was constitutionally bound to appoint him as prime minister. Sá Carneiro's long-term objectives were to send the military back to the barracks, revise the constitution, and open up the economy to private initiative. In order to begin the task of putting the military squarely under civilian control, he gave Adelino Amaro da Costa the defense portfolio, the first time since before Salazar's New State that the post of minister of defense had not been occupied by a military officer. Sá Carneiro knew that to achieve his objectives he would have to further the political gains of the AD in the elections for the AR scheduled for October 1980, only ten months away. He therefore paid great attention to improving Portugal's economy. His finance minister, Aníbal Cavaco Silva, a British-trained economist, was able to improve the balance of trade, reduce unemployment, lower inflation, cut income taxes, and raise wages. Many of the AD's bills designed to rectify the excesses of Gonçalves's governments, however, were either vetoed by President Eanes or struck down as unconstitutional by the CR. This left Sá Carneiro even more determined to send the military back to the barracks and not support Eanes's bid for reelection in 1980.

The election for the AR was held on October 5, 1980, the seventieth anniversary of the organization of the provisional government that established the First Republic. The AD received 47.6 percent of the vote and 134 seats (PSD 82, CDS 46, and PPM 6) in the AR; the PS, this time running in a coalition with the ASDI and the UEDS called the Republican and Socialist Front (Frente Repúblicana e Socialista, or FRS), received 27.8 percent and 74 seats; the APU, 16.8 percent and 41 seats; and the UDP, 1.4 percent and 1 seat. The AD was able to increase its majority, whereas the PS held steady at 74 seats. The APU dropped 6 seats, which meant, in effect, that for the first time since 1975 the PCP had lost ground.

Sá Carneiro was again appointed prime minister. His most pressing immediate task was getting a president elected who would be less resistant than Eanes to the AD's program. In order to get around the AD's lack of the requisite two-thirds majority to pass amendments, Sá Carneiro planned to have the constitution revised by referendum. He chose António Soares Carneiro, a lackluster conservative general with a questionable past in Angola, where it was said he ran a detention camp during the waning days of the African wars. His choice met with some opposition within certain quarters of the PSD that thought the party would be better served by supporting a civilian, which would break the tradition of naming military officers to the presidency. Sá Carneiro disregarded these arguments in the knowledge that Soares Carneiro would go along with his plan to revise the constitution and reduce the powers of the presidency, in effect to become Sá Carneiro's Américo Tomás. The PS supported Eanes, although Mário Soares, who had resigned on October 19, 1980, as secretary general of the party, did not. Soares, who harbored his own presidential ambitions, could not bring himself to personally endorse the man who had dismissed him as prime minister and with whom he had had so many differences of opinion. The PCP put forward its own candidate, Carlos Brito, a longtime PCP leader who headed the party's parliamentary group in the AR. At the last moment, Brito withdrew and the PCP threw its support behind Eanes. Other candidates were General Carlos Galvão de Melo, a right-wing air force officer who appealed to the retornado vote; General António Pires Veloso, a right-wing army officer who had been the rallying point for conservative troops during the waning days of the sixth provisional government; Aires Rodrigues, the PS deputy banished by the party in 1976 for breaking parliamentary group discipline and voting against the government's plan; and Otelo, who again appealed to the far Left.

On December 4, during the final days of the campaign, the nation was stunned by the news that Sá Carneiro, Amaro da Costa, and Snu Bonnier, Sá Carneiro's companion, were killed when the light plane in which they were about to fly to a rally in Porto crashed upon takeoff from Lisbon's Portela airport. In the wake of this disaster it was not certain whether the presidential election would actually be held on schedule. The election commission ruled that the election should go forward, and on December 7 over 6 million voters went to the polls. Eanes received 55.9 percent of the vote; Soares Carneiro, 39.8 percent. Eanes was thus elected for a second five-year term.

CONSTITUTIONAL REVISIONS

On December 13, 1980, the PSD chose Francisco Pinto Balsemão to succeed Sá Carneiro as party leader; he was subsequently appointed prime minister by the newly elected Eanes. Balsemão's most important task was to carry out the revisions to the 1976 constitution promised by the AD during the campaign. The AD held steadfast to its objectives of sending the military back to the barracks and making more room in the economy for private initiative.

Although the AD was the most ardent advocate of revision, all political parties sitting in Parliament wanted some changes in the constitution. Even the PCP, which saw the AD program for constitutional revision as a betrayal of the "revolution," wanted to revise certain of its minor articles. The two-thirds majority required to make amendments gave the PS a key role in the revision process, because without socialist support the AD would not have the votes needed to pass a revision law. To assure its backing, the AD signed an agreement with the PS that limited the extent to which such revisions would affect certain economic changes made after 1974; that is, a greater amount of private enterprise would be permitted, whereas key sectors of the economy would remain nationalized. Following the procedure established in the constituent assembly, the major parties submitted drafts for constitutional revision. These proposals were presented to Parliament in the first week of November 1981.

As would be expected, the AD proposal envisioned the most far-reaching changes to the Constitution. It called for major modifications in the articles dealing with the organization of political power, the economy, and the rights and liberties of the citizenry. In the opinion of some observers, the AD proposal went beyond the limits on revision established by Article 290 of the original 1976 document and was, in effect, an entirely new constitution. At the opposite extreme was the PCP's proposal, which called for the fewest changes. The Communists sought only minor alterations and maintained their support for the original version, being especially favorably disposed toward retaining the CR.

Between these two extremes was the PS proposal, which called for major alterations in the powers of the president and the extinction of the CR but sought no significant changes in those articles dealing with economic organization or the rights and liberties of the people. In the PS version the military was not to be placed squarely under government control, as in the AD proposal, but was to be administered through the Superior Council of National Defense set up specifically for this purpose. This council would be presided over by the president and would include the armed services chiefs as well as representatives from the government and Parliament.

Both the AD and the PS proposed that two new organs be created to take over the powers that the 1976 constitution had assigned to the CR. The AD called for the creation of, first, a council of state composed of the president (who would preside without vote), the president of the Supreme Court, the president of the Supreme Military Court, the attorney general, the ombudsman, the presidents of the governments of the autonomous regions of the Azores and Madeira, and five deputies chosen by Parliament and, second, a constitutional tribunal composed of the president of the Supreme Court, two judges appointed by the president, two appointed by Parliament, two elected by the Supreme Court, and two elected by the Supreme Administrative Court. The two bodies proposed by the PS, on the other hand, were, first, a council of the republic composed of the president of the republic (who would preside), the president of the Supreme Court, the ombudsman, the president of the national planning committee of the regional association of the autonomous regions, the president of Parliament, five citizens selected by Parliament, and five chosen by the president and, second, a constitutional tribunal composed of five citizens of recognized merit selected by the president, five nominated by Parliament, and five judges selected by the Supreme Court.

This clear attempt to return to the parties' original desire to have a system built on legislative supremacy provoked anger from President Eanes. Like Charles de Gaulle, he threatened to resign from the presidency if his powers were reduced. He considered the AD and PS proposals for revision to be aimed at creating a pure parliamentary system in which the president would be a mere figurehead. The AD and PS maintained that the revisions were only a reduction in presidential power and not a fundamental alteration of the nature of the system. Eanes was successful, however, in convincing the PS that their proposal for revision went too far and needed to be modified in order to maintain the "dual responsibility" of the prime minister and the government before the president and Parliament, as found in the original document. In exchange, Eanes gave up the power to appoint military chiefs of the general staff.

This truce between Eanes and the political parties resulted in a new accord between the PS and the AD concerning presidential powers. In order to satisfy Eanes's demand that presidential powers be maintained and the AD's strong desire to move toward a more purely parliamentary system, the PS worked out a compromise with respect to the "dual responsibility" clause. Article 194 of the revised constitution would have three sections. The first section would establish the responsibility of the prime minister and his government to Parliament; the second would specify that this responsibility was political in nature; and the third would provide that the prime minister was responsible to the president, but only institutionally. In practice, this meant that although the prime minister was responsible to the president, the president did not have the power to dismiss a prime minister who enjoyed the confidence of the Parliament. The prime minister and government could be dismissed only when the functioning of democratic institutions was threatened and only after consultation with the Council of State.

Although this compromise was not well received by Eanes, who saw it as a bit of legerdemain that obscured a fundamental loss of presidential power in dealing with governments in which the president had lost confidence, there was not much that he could do to stop the revision process. The 1976 constitution, which Eanes had so vigorously defended, stated in Article 286 that the president's veto power did not extend to laws of constitutional revision. Thus, caught between the sword and the wall (*a espada e a parede*), as the Portuguese say, Eanes reluctantly promulgated the revised constitution on September 24, 1982, making it clear while doing so that had he not been prevented by Article 286, he would have vetoed the revision law.

The new text of the constitution thus clearly defined a system in which Parliament was seen as the major instrument of national policymaking. Relative to the autonomous regions, the president was forbidden from suspending regional governments except when initiated by the government and approved by the Council of State. Although the president retained the power to veto legislation, this power was restricted in such a way as to prevent the "pocket veto." The president was given only two options with respect to legislation passed by Parliament: He could either sign it or veto it. The president's veto could be overridden by an absolute majority rather than the two-thirds majority required by the previous text, and the president was obliged to promulgate within eight days vetoed bills overridden by Parliament. The revised version of the constitution, like the original, still designated the president as the commander in chief of the armed forces but granted to a new organ, the Superior Council of National Defense, the power to deal with defense questions and the organization of the armed forces. The president's power to dissolve parliament was also restricted: He was prevented from doing so within six months after the general election, in the last six months of a president's mandate, and during a state of siege or emergency.

In addition to the reduction of presidential powers, the powers already allocated to Parliament were accentuated and reinforced. States of siege and emergency could be declared only if authorized by parliament and were limited to fifteen days instead of thirty. Interim elections were forbidden so that each election would begin a new legislative period that continued for four years. The Permanent Commission of Parliament was permitted to function continually in the interim between a dissolution of the Assembly and the seating of a new legislature. Moreover, Parliament was empowered to elect, by a two-thirds majority, the members of the

Constitutional Tribunal. Finally, the powers of Parliament were somewhat enhanced with respect to the prime minister; a single vote of censure, instead of the two within thirty days previously required, was all that was now necessary to bring down a government.

The revisions also clearly established civilian control over the military. All references to the role of the MFA in the original version were dropped. According to Article 136, the president could appoint only military chiefs nominated by the government. Article 270 also restricted the political activity of members of the armed forces while on active duty. Article 202 gave to the prime minister managerial control over the armed forces. Finally, the Council of the Revolution was abolished and its powers disbursed to the two new organs of government, the Council of State and the Constitutional Tribunal. The Council of State was to advise the president and approve government dismissals, parliamentary dissolution, states of siege or emergency, and declarations of war. The Constitutional Tribunal, composed of six judges and seven members elected by Parliament, was to determine the constitutionality and legality of legislation.

Very few changes were made in the sections of the constitution dealing with fundamental rights and economic organization except that the role of private enterprise in the economic life of the country was given greater constitutional protection. Article 80, which in the original version clearly made socialism and collectivization of the economy basic principles of economic organization, was redrafted such that private, public, and cooperative sectors of the economy were defined as coequal in the economic life of the country. Article 85 was also modified to remove restrictions on private initiative, and Article 89 was redrafted to change language that relegated the private sector to a residual economic category. In addition to these changes, all language referring to the "building of socialism" was purged.

The revised constitution was a major step forward in the realization of the AD's objectives. The military was all but back in the barracks, and the way had been cleared for an expansion of the private sector. The capstone for the first of these objectives came in September 1982 when Frietas do Amaral, AD's minister of defense, introduced a bill that would define in precise terms the relationship between the military and the civilian government. This bill, called the National Defense Law, clearly established the concept of civilian control of the military. Although it designated the president as the commander in chief, the bill defined this role as purely titular, as it is in other Western European systems. The bill made the minister of defense the real head of the military by giving to that office the power to select the chief of the general staff and the chiefs of the three service branches. The law also provided that the minister of defense would be assisted by an advisory body called the Superior Council for National Defense. The bill was passed on October 29 but was vetoed by President Eanes. Eanes claimed that the defense minister had been given too much power over the military, and he expressed fear that the law would politicize the selection of chiefs of staff and general officers. On November 26 the AR overrode Eanes's veto and the bill became law.

THE CENTRAL BLOC

Although the AD had been successful in achieving its two principal objectives—constitutional revision and the assertion of civilian control of the military—the coalition began to disintegrate because of leadership quarrels inside the PSD. Balsemão, a much less abrasive and more conciliatory politician than Sá Carneiro, who got on better with the PS and President Eanes, began to draw fire from the hard-liners (*duros*) within the PSD. The first shots were fired at the party's seventh national congress held in 1981, when Eurico de Melo, Aníbal Cavaco Silva, Améndio de Azevedo, Angelo Correia, and Helena Roseta accused Balsemão of being too soft, especially in his dealings with Eanes. Balsemão was, however, able to survive their fire and was reelected head of the party and continued as prime minister. The following year, at the party's eighth national congress, the duros again opened fire on Balsemão, this time accusing him of mismanaging the economy. Balsemão again survived their salvos. At the same time he began to draw fire from the AD's main alliance partner, the CDS, which demanded that Balsemão make changes in his cabinet, especially by replacing his finance minister, João Salgueiro, with a more decisive individual.

Meanwhile, in the AR, Balsemão was being attacked by Mário Soares, who had recently gained complete control over PS. Unified, the socialists were able to mount an assault on all fronts. They criticized Balsemão's government for failing to improve the economy, they attacked Eanes for not dismissing the government, and they made war on the PCP for attempting to destabilize Portugal's fragile democracy with politically motivated strikes and massive street demonstrations.

Faced with a political war on all fronts, Balsemão decided to declare the local elections scheduled for December 12, 1982, a plebiscite on the AD government and his leadership. Although the AD's lists received only four fewer percentage points than the 1980 vote and the PS increased its margin by only 5 percent, Balsemão interpreted the results to mean that the voters had lost confidence in his government. He resigned two weeks later. The PSD put forward Vitor Crespo, a lackluster party stalwart, as his replacement. The CDS rejected this choice. The PSD suggested Mota Pinto, but he, too, was rejected. As the AD partners could not agree on a new prime minister, President Eanes dissolved the AR and called for fresh elections.

Unable to agree on a combined list of candidates, the PSD, CDS, and PPM declared the AD defunct and went into the election separately. The PS, now unified, mounted a vigorous campaign that brilliantly exploited Soares's charm, charisma, and skills as a press-the-flesh, U.S.-style politician. The PSD was taken into the campaign by Mota Pinto, who replaced Balsemão as party leader. Voting took place on April 25, 1983. The PS won 36.1 percent of the ballots and 101 seats in the AR; PSD, 27.2 percent and 75 seats; CDS, 12.6 percent and 30 seats; and APU, 18.1 percent and 44 seats. The PS regained the votes it had lost to the PSD over the last two elections and once again proved itself as the only party with a broad national constituency, having elected deputies from all of Portugal's electoral districts. For the first time since 1975, the far left UDP failed to win a seat.

Having made it clear during the campaign that the PS would not again attempt to govern from a minority position, Soares invited the PSD to form a coalition government. On June 4, 1983, after more than a month of negotiations, an agreement was reached between the two parties: The Central Bloc (Bloco Central) government came into being with Soares as prime minister and Mota Pinto as deputy prime minister and minister of defense. The Central Bloc was to last for the duration of the legislative term, four years, and the agreement set forth a number of reforms (in the electoral law, agriculture, the economic sections of the constitution, and so on) to be achieved during that time.

The Central Bloc was a fragile affair from the very beginning, however, and no one expected it to endure for the full legislative term. During the first year the government experienced conflicts between ministers appointed by one party and secretaries of state appointed by the other. The PSD was generally unhappy with Soares's appointments and early on began to pressure him for a cabinet reshuffle. In June 1984 Soares introduced a motion of confidence in the AR even though he had a clear majority. The motion was aimed at the PSD, not the opposition, and with it Soares hoped to quell the clamor for a cabinet reshuffle by forcing the PSD back into line. This maneuver was only partially and temporarily successful, as fifteen PSD deputies managed to be absent from the AR in order to avoid voting the party line.

Meanwhile, Mota Pinto was also having difficulties keeping the PSD internally united. The main point of disagreement concerned the upcoming presidential election. Soares had made no secret about his ambition to be Eanes's successor in the Palácio de Belém. This meant that the PSD would have to fall in behind Soares or put up their own candidate, splitting the coalition because their agreement specified that neither side would put up a candidate not agreed to by the other. The PSD was divided: One faction thought the party ought to run its own candidate; another thought they should seek an independent from outside the party; a third favored a military candidate; and a fourth, a civilian. In an attempt to avoid a knock-down-drag-out fight within the party, Mota Pinto introduced a motion at the eleventh national congress to delay the decision until early 1985 and to allow it to be made by the party's political committee and national council without approval from the congress. Although this motion passed, it was strongly opposed by the duros, led by João Mota Amaral, the president of the regional government of the Azores, and Marcelo Rebelo de Sousa, who favored the presidential candidacy of Freitas do Amaral of the CDS.

In February 1985 Mota Pinto chose as his presidential candidate General Firmino Miguel, the deputy chief of staff of the army who, after 1974, had served as Spínola's minister of defense during the first provisional government. But the national council of the party rejected this choice, which precipitated Mota Pinto's resignation as head of the party. He was replaced by Rui Machete. In order to break the deadlock, Machete encouraged the national council of the party to poll the party's rank-and-file in order to find out their presidential candidate preferences. Although the response was low, party members showed support for an independent, and Firmino Miguel's name began to circulate once again as a possible candidate. The disagreements within the party over whom the party should support and the failure of the party to respond favorably to his quid pro quo for becoming a candidate, however, led Firmino Miguel to formally withdraw his name from consideration. The national committee decided to try and resolve the issue at the party's next national congress, scheduled for May.

The debate at this congress, the party's twelfth, centered on the presidential race and a new party leader. Aníbal Cavaco Silva, who served as Sá Carneiro's minister of finance with considerable success, was chosen to head the party. He proposed to the congress the name of Freitas do Amaral, who had agreed not to use the powers of the presidency to favor CDS or to found his own party, if elected. Although the party accepted Cavaco Silva's nominee, Balsemão and others thought the party would be better served by supporting Soares. One month after the congress, on June 13, 1985, Cavaco Silva led the PSD out of the Central Bloc and the government fell.

A CIVILIAN PRESIDENT

With the collapse of the Central Bloc, President Eanes dissolved the AR and scheduled elections for October 6, 1985. In addition to the

PS, PSD, CDS, PCP, and an assortment of parties on the extreme left, a new party contested these elections. The Democratic Renewal party (Partido Renovador Democrático, or PRD) had appeared in April. Led by Hermínio Martinho, a farmer from the Ribatejo, the PRD was the outgrowth of the desire by many disgruntled socialists and left-wing intellectuals who had supported Eanes for president in 1980 to found a party that would provide the Portuguese electorate with an alternative to the four main established parties. The first of these efforts had been the Movement for the Deepening of Democracy (Movimento para o Aprofundamento da Democracia, or MAD), organized by the former prime minister, Maria de Loudres Pintasilgo. Another, which became the precursor of the PRD, was the National Committee for the Reelection of President Eanes (Comissão Nacional de Apoio a Recandidatura do Presidente Eanes, or CNARPE). The PRD offered little to the voters beyond support for Eanes and the need to bring honesty and morality to Portuguese political life.

In the 1985 balloting, the PSD won 29.9 percent of the vote and 88 seats; the PS, 20.8 percent and 57 seats; the PRD, 17.9 percent and 45 seats; the APU, 15.5 percent and 38 seats; and the CDS, 10.0 percent and 22 seats. These elections produced two major surprises. The first was the PRD's eclipse of the APU and the CDS, which made it the third largest party in the AR. The second was the emergence of the PSD as Portugal's leading party. This came about because Cavaco Silva had established his leadership over the party as had no individual since Sá Carneiro. Under his direction, the party had moved to the right and during the campaign was able to put the blame for Portugal's economic woes on the PS. Cavaco also proved to be an excellent campaigner. The APU support fell to a new low, as did that of the CDS, both parties losing voters to the PRD and PSD. The success of the PRD owed much to the implicit connection between the party and the president, whose wife campaigned for PRD candidates (the Constitution barring Eanes from doing so himself).

After the elections, Eanes called upon Cavaco Silva to form a government, which he did without the involvement of other parties. In Cavaco Silva the PSD had finally found a replacement for the fallen Sá Carneiro. Like Sá Carneiro, he was aggressive, hardworking, and dynamic. He shared Sá Carneiro's political vision for Portugal and was supported by the party's duros. In order to achieve his objectives, he knew that it would be necessary for the PSD to capture control of both the AR and the presidency. As the presidential election was right around the corner, he concentrated his energies on that objective first.

Eanes, who was constitutionally forbidden from running for a third consecutive term, sought to find a candidate who would be acceptable to the PRD and who would be willing to stand aside after five years,

Prime Minister Aníbal António Cavaco Silva. Photo courtesy of General Directorate of Social Communication, Lisbon.

when Eanes would again be eligible for reelection. He chose Colonel Manuel de Costa Brás, the head of the High Authority Against Corruption, who, because of his moderate left views, would be an appealing candidate to the center Left and center Right. Colonel Costa Brás agreed to stand if certain conditions were met. One was that President Eanes would publicly support his candidacy, which he agreed to do. A second was that he receive the backing of the PRD. The third was that Maria de Lourdes Pintasilgo, who had announced her intention to seek the presidency some time before, would be convinced to withdraw from the race. Costa Brás's second two conditions were not met. The PRD refused to officially support him because the party was unhappy with Eanes for not consulting with them before choosing Costa Brás. Pintasilgo refused to step aside because she had the backing of some members of the PRD leadership as well as certain influential members of the April 25 Association (Associação de 25 de Abril), a group organized in February 1984 by military officers and led by Major Vasco Lourenço, who had been involved with the golpe of 1974 and sought to defend the "gains" of the revolution. Consequently, Colonel Costa Brás withdrew his name from consideration. With the election only three months away, Eanes was thus left without a personally designated successor.

In the wake of the withdrawal of Costa Brás, Francisco Salgado Zenha, who had served as the PS's parliamentary group president and was the party's number two leader until a quarrel with Soares over the latter's refusal to support Eanes's reelection in 1980, announced his candidacy. Zenha had no trouble getting support from Eanes, with whom he had been close. Eanes saw in Zenha a candidate of the correct political coloration, squarely on the left, who he thought had a reasonably good chance of winning the presidency and who laid down no conditions for his support. Zenha was also backed by some influential members of the PRD.

In the meantime, Mário Soares moved ahead with his bid for the presidency. His strategy was to project himself as a candidate of the center Left and center Right in order to appeal to voters from the right fringes of APU to the left fringes of the PSD. His candidacy was supported by the PS as well as a group of moderate leftists who organized a campaign committee called the Movement for the Support of Soares for the Presidency (Movimento para a Apoio de Soares para Presidência, or MASP). Soares's campaign strategy had two objectives. First, he sought to overcome the negative feeling that the debacle of the Central Bloc had generated within the electorate. Second, because he was convinced that no candidate would win on the initial ballot, he hoped to attract enough votes from the Left (which was going to be divided among himself, Zenha, and Pintasilgo) to get into the second round of balloting.

Pintasilgo steadfastly remained in the race. Although she did not have the backing of a major party, she did get support from the rank and file of the PCP, many of the small parties of the far Left, as well as some members of the PRD. She was not officially supported by the PCP because she was seen as being too far left. For its part, the PCP had its own candidate, Angelo Veloso, whom it eventually put aside in order to support Zenha in the waning weeks of the campaign.

Freitas do Amaral, the candidate of the center Right, had in effect, been preparing his bid for the presidency as long ago as the autumn of 1982, when he resigned from the CDS, supposedly for personal reasons. He received the solid support of the CDS. Once Cavaco Silva, a strong supporter of Freitas do Amaral, won control of the PSD, he could count on that party's backing as well.

The first round of voting took place on January 26, 1986. Freitas do Amaral, won 46.3 percent; Mário Soares, 25.4 percent; Salgado Zenha, 20.9 percent; and Maria de Lourdes Pintasilgo, 7.4 percent. Freitas do Amaral received 90 percent of the ballots of those in the electorate who had voted for the PSD or the CDS in 1985, as well as 30 percent of the PRD. Soares took 90 percent of those who had voted for the PS whereas Zenha got 90 percent of those who had supported APU in 1985. Freitas do Amaral's strong finish was not enough to win the election (for which 50 percent of the vote was required), so a runoff election was set for February 16.

Soares was reasonably confident of victory going into the second round. It was clear that it was going to be very difficult for Freitas do Amaral to increase his support sufficiently to surpass the 50 percent threshold, having received on the first ballot most, if not all, the votes from the Center to the Right. Soares, on the other hand, if he could attract those voters who had cast their ballots for Zenha and Pintasilgo, would be able to go over the 50 percent mark. The greatest threat to this eventuality would be the PCP's refusal to support him because of the party's strong dislike for Soares and his policies. After much internal debate and a special party congress, the PCP decided to back Soares in order to stop Freitas do Amaral, whom the party saw as the personification of the ancien régime and a serious threat to its future existence. Zenha and Pintasilgo also called on their supporters to vote for the candidate of the Left, Soares.

In the second round Mário Soares won 51.3 percent of the vote and Freitas do Amaral 48.7 percent. Although Freitas was able to squeeze 2.4 percent more support than in the first round, principally from voters who had initially abstained and some who switched from the PRD, it was not enough to defeat the temporary alliance of the Left, which threw to Soares 25.9 percent more ballots. With Soares's victory, Portugal had elected a civilian president for the first time since 1926.

PROSPECTS FOR STABILITY

Upon taking office, Soares reaffirmed Cavaco Silva as prime minister. Lacking an absolute majority, Cavaco found it necessary to make bilateral arrangements with the different oppositions in order to govern. The party most receptive to such contacts was the PRD, which was anxious to play a role in governing the country in order to enhance its visibility among the electorate. To make these bilateral agreements, Fernando Nogueira, Cavaco Silva's secretary of state for parliamentary affairs and spokesperson, generally met with Hermínio Martinho, the leader of the PRD, in one of Lisbon's poshest restaurants. Martinho became the principal interlocutor between the government and the AR. Soares was favorably disposed toward this arrangement because he did not want a governmental crisis so soon after parliamentary elections.

In the first several months after the presidential elections, this informal arrangement with the PRD worked smoothly. In late March 1986, however, the PRD parliamentary group participated in a press conference with the PS and PCP parliamentary groups that was devoted to criticizing the government's budget, then being debated in the AR.

CONSOLIDATION OF DEMOCRACY

President Mário Alberto Nobre Lopes Soares. Photo courtesy of General Directorate of Social Communication, Lisbon.

This behavior violated an understanding worked out between Martinho and Nogueira, according to which the PRD would support the budget in exchange for certain modifications they wanted to see made in a number of policy areas. Cavaco Silva responded to this press conference by holding his own in which he accused the opposition parties, the PRD included, of forcing the government to make changes in the budget that would add significantly to the deficit.

Although this event strained the government's special relationship with the PRD, it did not break it. It was still possible to arrange deals on legislation with the parties of the opposition because each, except the PCP, was experiencing internal quarrels and was incapable of mounting a unified challenge to the government and presenting a viable alternative to it.

When Soares won the presidency, he chose Almeida Santos to be his successor as secretary general of PS. But the PS's poor showing in the 1985 election seriously damaged Santos's image as a leader, and a struggle ensued for control of the party. Jaime Gama, who had been Soares's minister of foreign affairs during several governments, opposed Vitor Constáncio, then the president of the Bank of Portugal and the leader of a faction inside the party known as the *bloco renovador* (renovator bloc). This struggle was to preoccupy the party until its national congress set for June. Despite Martinho's leadership, the PRD was in effect marking time while former President Eanes decided whether he was going to join the party and become politically active or remain aloof as its guiding spirit. Eanes was hesitant because the defeat of his candidate, Salgado Zenha, in the presidential race had deflated his confidence. Eanes's role in the PRD would not be decided until the party's national convention was held in October. The CDS was also experiencing leadership difficulties: Adriano Moreira, who had been a colonial minister under Salazar, had gained control of the party after the departure of Freitas do Amaral and was being held responsible for the party's heavy losses in the 1985 elections.

Although the PSD, too, had minor internal problems, Cavaco handily won reelection to the party's presidency at the thirteenth national congress held in May. He successfully integrated the previous supporters of Pinto Balsemão, who had since resigned from political life, and Mota Pinto, who had died suddenly of a heart attack, into the party's highest decisionmaking organs. The only serious issue that manifested itself at the congress had to do with regionalism and involved Mota Amaral and Alberto João Jardim, the presidents of the autonomous regions of the Azores and Madeira, respectively. Mota Amaral had, at the twelfth party congress, received considerable support for the presidency of the party from Balsemão. He also had resisted Sá Carneiro's choice of Soares Carneiro as the party's standard-bearer in the 1980 presidential election. The deep-rooted successionist sentiments on the islands led Amaral and Jardim to form their own tendency within the party.

Firmly in control of his party, Cavaco Silva continued to govern by making ad hoc, informal arrangements with the PRD. Public opinion polls showed that a large majority of the public believed he was doing a "good" to "very good" job as prime minister. At the end of June, however, the relationship between the government and the PRD became strained as Cavaco Silva requested from the AR an authorization to legislate in the area of labor relations, which meant that he could, in effect, pass such legislation without full consideration by Parliament. Although the PRD did not object to the substance of the proposed legislation, it was strongly opposed to the legislative authorization tactic. On June 29, the AR voted down his request. Cavaco Silva responded by meeting with President Soares in order to inform him that he intended to introduce a motion of confidence in his government in the AR. When the vote was taken some days later, the PRD abstained, knowing that if the government fell the PSD would have no trouble winning fresh elections.

In the wake of this victory, Cavaco Silva confidently predicted that his government would survive for the full four-year term of Parliament. He felt certain that his strategy of working individually with the parties of the opposition by allowing them to amend government bills would be successful. Nogueira continued to meet with Martinho in order to arrange agreements on various bills. In July, however, when all seemed to be going well, the government aggravated the island tendency within PSD by appointing General Rocha Vieira as minister of the republic for the Azores. Mota Amaral refused to have General Vieira in the post because he allegedly had been illegally promoted to colonel, having signed his own promotion papers.

The special arrangement between the government and the PRD began to come apart. Cavaco Silva could not get the PRD to support his supplemental budget, and Martinho made it clear that the PRD would not back agrarian reform. Cavaco Silva could see that he was not going to be able to work with the PRD any longer; therefore, he decided to show the public that an incorrigible AR prevented him from going forward with his program of reform. He accused the PRD of bad faith and of entering an alliance with the PCP against the government on the issue of agrarian reform. His agrarian reform bill was in fact defeated in the AR by the PRD and the PCP.

Tension between the government and the opposition parties continued throughout the remainder of the summer and into the autumn. In September the government requested a ruling from the Constitutional Tribunal on the constitutionality of the supplemental budget the AR passed to increase government spending, which is prohibited by the Constitution. For this action, the PS accused the government of needlessly provoking a conflict with the AR. The PS, now led by Constâncio, decided to organize a "shadow government" in order to create the image that the party could put forward a viable alternative. Constâncio hoped that this would dispose President Soares to dismiss Cavaco Silva and appoint a PS government. Soares, however, made no concessions to his former party and continued to stay above the partisan fray, refusing to side with any faction.

In October, the PRD held its national convention. The highlight of the proceeding was former President Eanes's formal affiliation with the party. He was made president, displacing Martinho, who became vice-president. Many supporters of Eanes, however, did not follow him into the party because they were angry about the Costa Brás affair. After the convention, Eanes, who was now directing the party's political strategy, declared that an informal alliance between the PRD and the PSD was still possible if the latter would allow the former to achieve some of its policy objectives. He declared that an alliance with the PS was not likely because the PS saw itself as the only socialist party in Portugal and illegitimate because it was created from the top down, principally as a vehicle for Soares's political ambitions.

In November and December Cavaco Silva still governed by arranging deals with the opposition in the AR, but he found it increasingly difficult to do with Eanes as head of the PRD. In November the AR approved Cavaco Silva's budget but defeated his plan for 1987. Within the PSD pressures were beginning to build to stop working with the PRD. Some argued that to continue to seek arrangements with Eanes's party would be interpreted by the electorate as a sign of weakness. Such a strategy would gradually destroy the image of the government and hurt Cavaco Silva's positive ratings in the opinion polls. Cavaco Silva resisted these pressures because he did not think the time was propitious for an election, opinion polls showing that the citizenry did not want fresh elections. Nor did he think that the PSD could win an absolute majority if an election were held.

By December the working relationship with the PRD was definitely finished. Cavaco Silva accused all parties of the opposition, the PRD included, of obstructing the government. At this point the parties of the opposition, believing that the government had come to the end of its rope, began to position themselves to take power. The PCP proposed a coalition of the Left to Constâncio. He was also approached by the PRD with the suggestion of a PS-PRD coalition. Constâncio rejected both entreaties, saying that the PS had its own calendar for gaining power.

Although his cabinet had, in effect, become a caretaker government, Cavaco Silva hesitated to send the AR a motion of confidence, even though he was certain that the electorate would punish the opposition and return the PSD with a majority. He held out as long as possible in order to entice the opposition into taking action against him rather than the other way around. This he knew would create the image among the electorate that it was the opposition, not the government, that was responsible for the crisis. Cavaco Silva was aided in this strategy by the economy, which was improving almost daily. In an interview, President Soares hinted that elections might be necessary to overcome the deadlock.

The dénouement came in March, when the government learned that a delegation of deputies led by Fernando Amaral, the president of the AR, had scheduled a side trip to Estonia while on an official visit to the Soviet Union. Cavaco Silva ordered Fernando Amaral to cancel the visit because Portugal had not recognized any of the Baltic republics since 1940. Fernando Amaral obeyed but on his return to Portugal criticized the government's decision, saying that the country's second highest personage after the president of the republic ought to be able to officially travel where he pleases. The government responded by pointing out that such trips abroad were expensive and should only be made after ensuring that the travel conformed to the foreign policy of the government. At this point, the PRD introduced a motion of censure, claiming that the government was too conflictual with the AR and incapable of governing effectively. The PS said it would support the motion unless Cavaco Silva came to terms with them on a new governing arrangement. Cavaco Silva, sensing that the time was ripe, refused, saying that forming a new government without elections would be a fraud. The vote of censure passed. Upon his return from a state visit to Brazil, Soares decided to hold fresh elections, satisfied that no alternative government could be arranged among the opposition parties. Supported by the Council of State, Soares dissolved the AR on April 29 and set new elections for July 19, 1987. The parties of the opposition had thus played directly into Cavaco Silva's hands.

Cavaco Silva was confident that the PSD would win the elections. What he did not know, however, was how big the victory would be. Cavaco Silva, who had been a skillful campaigner in 1985, was again able to generate considerable enthusiasm wherever he went on the campaign trail. His stump speeches were brilliant for their ability to transmit to his listeners sympathy, cordiality, strength, and plain speaking. The other parties were not able to match PSD's electoral juggernaut. The PCP rashly decided to rename the APU coalition the Democratic Unitary Coalition (Coligação Democrático e Unitário, or CDU); Constâncio of the PS was unable to shake his image as a party technocrat; Adriano Moreira of the CDS could not dissociate himself from his past connections with the Salazar-Caetano dictatorship; and Eanes of the PRD proved to be a mediocre campaigner who was always viewed as a former president rather than a potential prime minister.

The PSD won with 50.2 percent of the votes and 148 seats in the AR, an absolute majority of 23 seats; the PS finished second with 22.2 percent of the vote and 60 seats; the CDU, 12.1 percent and 31 seats; the PRD, 4.9 percent and 7 seats; and the CDS, 4.4 percent and 4 seats. These elections marked a turning point: The quadripartite party system that had been frozen in place with the first election after the 1974 golpe was shattered as some 2 million Portuguese voters shifted alliances, pushing one party, the PSD, over the 50 percent threshold for the first time since 1974. The PSD attracted some 398,000 voters from the PRD, 259,000 from the CDS, 194,000 from the PS, and 11,000 from the CDU. For the first time, the PSD took votes away from the PCP in its strongholds in the Alentejo and industrial belt around Lisbon. The PRD and CDS were eviscerated and almost disappeared from the political landscape. The principal reason for the PSD's great victory was the desire on the part of Portuguese voters to maintain Cavaco Silva in office with a stable parliamentary majority.

The election of Mário Soares to the presidency in 1986 and Cavaco Silva's victory in 1987 were the beginning of a new cycle in the post-1974 political history of Portugal. The new democratic system was completely civilianized, and for once the citizenry could look forward to four years of stable government.

REFERENCES

Bruneau, Thomas C., and Alex Macleod. *Politics in Contemporary Portugal*. Boulder, CO: Lynne Rienner Publishers, 1986.

Domingos, Emídio da Vieiga. *Portugal Político: Análise das Instituições*. Lisbon: Edições Rolim, 1980.

Expresso (Lisbon), various issues, 1985–1987.

Gallagher, Tom. "Portugal's Bid for Democracy: The Role of the Socialist Party." *West European Politics* 2 (May 1979):198–217.

Gaspar, Jorge, and Nuno Vitorino. *As Eleições de 25 de Abril: Geografia e Imagen dos Partidos*. Lisbon: Livros Horizonte, 1976.

———. *As Eleições Legislativas: Algumas Perspectivas Regionais*. Lisbon: Livros Horizonte, 1978.

Goldey, David B., "Elections and the Consolidation of Portuguese Democracy: 1974–83." *Electoral Studies* 2 (1983):229–240.

Mujal-León, Eusébio M. "The PCP and the Portuguese Revolution." *Problems of Communism* 26 (January–February 1977):21–41.

Opello, Walter C., Jr. "Local Government and Political Culture in a Portuguese Rural County." *Comparative Politics* 13 (May 1978):271–289.

———. "The New Parliament in Portugal." *Legislative Studies Quarterly* 3 (May 1978):309–334.

———. "The Second Portuguese Republic: Politico-Administrative Decentralization Since April 25, 1974." *Iberian Studies* 7 (Autumn 1978):43–48.

———. "Portugal's Parliament: An Organizational Analysis of Legislative Performance." *Legislative Studies Quarterly* 11 (August 1986):291–319.

8
The Economy

Until recently, Portugal's economy was strongly linked to its overseas colonies. The wealth from Brazil, which produced most of the world's sugar during the sixteenth and seventeenth centuries, allowed Portugal to become Europe's richest nation at the time. This monopoly was broken, however, by the development of the sugar industry in the West Indies and the failure of Brazilian producers to adopt new technology. The subsequent economic depression that ensued in Portugal was mitigated somewhat by the discovery of gold in Brazil's Minas Gerais Province during the eighteenth century. Unfortunately, this new source of wealth did not transform Portugal's economy, for it was spent on palaces and churches; Portugal still had to buy manufactured goods from other countries. The ultimate economic beneficiary was thus Great Britain, which by 1750 replaced Portugal as the world's wealthiest nation. Portugal became impoverished and has remained so ever since. During the nineteenth century 60 percent of Portugal's work force remained tied to the land, with manufacturing limited to textiles, leather goods, cork processing, and wine making. The arrival of the First Republic did nothing to improve economic life. In fact, conditions worsened because of corruption and financial irresponsibility. During the sixteen years of the First Republic, inflation was rampant, and the escudo fell to less than one-third of its 1910 value. As was shown in previous chapters, the economic and political crises associated with the First Republic brought to power Salazar, who rebuilt the government and economy along corporatist lines. During this period, Portugal remained dependent upon its colonial holdings for its economic vitality. It was not until April 25, 1974, that Portugal's economy was disconnected from its overseas possessions and reoriented toward Western Europe.

ECONOMIC LIFE UNDER SALAZAR

Salazar managed to balance Portugal's budget relatively quickly by applying his conservative economic policies. During the Great Depression the economy was stable; Portugal did not suffer the unemployment and business failures afflicting the rest of the world. Salazar's New State was neither capitalist nor socialist. The two main characteristics of the economy were extensive state management and a predominantly privately owned sector that controlled the means of production. The leading financiers and industrialists accepted extensive state regulation and management of the economy in exchange for certain monopolistic privileges. During the New State there developed a close and mutually beneficial relationship between high-ranking public officials and Portugal's leading enterprises. It was common for companies to hire former cabinet ministers and other high government functionaries and for private businesses to have government representatives on their boards of directors.

In addition to this sort of involvement, the government exercised extensive control over private investment decisions and the amount of wages paid to workers. Prior authorization by the state was needed to establish or relocate an industrial plant. Moreover, investment in machinery and equipment also required government approval. Essentially, the government licensed industrial investment, which had the effect of strengthening the monopolistic position of existing firms, misallocating capital and deterring foreign investment.

During the 1960s, faced with the challenges of the liberation movements in the African colonies, Salazar decided to open up Portugal's economy to foreign investment in order to spur economic development in the metropole as well as overseas. Faced with growing expenditures on defense, Salazar was forced to seek financial assistance from abroad. Portugal broke its previously held policy of strict autarky when it floated a $20 million bond issue on London's financial market. This was followed by others for the construction of major public works projects in the metropole and in the colonies. The most important of these was the Douro River hydroelectric project and the Salazar (now April 25, 1974) Bridge, the longest suspension bridge in Europe, which connected Lisbon to the growing industrial region of Setúbal. The bridge allowed the construction of a continuous transportation link around the estuary and mouth of the Tejo, greatly accelerating the industrial growth of Lisbon's industrial zone.

In 1963 Salazar appointed Luís Teixeira Pinto to head the Ministry of Finance. Under Teixeira Pinto, legislation was passed that permitted greater foreign investment, increased industrialization, and advances in tourism by liberalizing the licensing system established during the 1930s. This resulted in the creation of a number of privately organized joint ventures, including a steel mill, a shipbuilding complex, a vehicle assembly plant, an oil refinery, a petrochemical plant, a paper mill, and an electronics plant. Construction was also begun on Lisbon's subway.

As foreign investment caused the economy to expand greatly during the 1960s (Portugal's GNP increased at about 6 percent per annum during those years), there were serious problems. First, the economy came to be characterized by a high concentration of ownership in the hands of a relatively small number of families. A plutarchy of some forty families allied by marriage came to dominate the economic life of the country. Through interlocking directorates and the control of banks, these economic dynasties were able to control cement, mining, refining, shipbuilding, textiles, insurance, brewing, petrochemicals, and steel production. They became so powerful that they were able to form their own associations and bargain with the government directly rather than through the corporate institutions set up for this purpose.

The most prominent among these were the Melo, Champalimaud, Espirito Santo, Quina, de Brito, and Pinto Basto families. The Pinto Basto family had important joint ventures with various British and French firms. The Champalimaud family owned the Banco Pinto e Sotto Mayor as well as several insurance companies. The Espirito Santo family had extensive holdings in the African colonies, several banks, and Portugal's largest insurance company, Tranquilidade. The Quinas owned oil wells in Angola; newspapers; textile, fishing, and civil construction firms; and three banks, Borgia e Irmão, Banco Crédito e Industrial, and the Banco do Alentejo. The largest of all was the industrial and financial empire of the Melo family, which, through its holding company, the Companhia União Fabril, owned an estimated 20 percent of Portugal's industrial production and generated about 10 percent of the productive output of the economy. With assets of over $2.4 billion and nearly 42,000 employees, CUF ranked 173d on *Fortune* magazine's listing of the 300 largest industrial companies outside of the United States. The CUF had interests in mining, textiles, chemicals, refining, cellulose, fertilizer, tobacco, and shipbuilding.

A second major problem was that the economy was dualistic: Large-scale, relatively efficient enterprises existed side by side with myriad small, inefficient producers. In fact, despite the presence and domination of the economy by the great families, the main bulk of Portuguese manufacturing was done by numerous small factories and shops that lacked modern machinery and managerial skills. In the 1960s nearly 75 percent of the 40,000 manufacturing firms had four or fewer employees and only 1,112 had more than 100. Fragmentation was common in all areas of industrial production. There were 10,500 producers of food and beverages; 6,777 of textiles, clothing, and footwear; and 5,415 of wood and cork products. Only the largest enterprises produced refined petroleum, petrochemicals, steel, ships, cement, and wood pulp, although in some sectors, giant and small firms existed together. Most of the largest firms were concentrated in the Lisbon-Setúbal and Porto-Braga areas.

Third, Portugal's agricultural sector was characterized by a similar dualism. Of the 12.3 million acres of cropland, nearly 40 percent was held by farmers who owned not more than 2.5 acres, which represented only about 3 percent of all cropland. Of farmers with holdings of over 125 acres, 1 percent held 51 percent of all cropland. Holdings of 10 acres included about 80 percent of all farmers but represented only 15 percent of all cropland. Very large holdings, those over 500 acres made up only 0.3 percent of all farms but accounted for 40 percent of all cropland.

As was discussed in previous chapters, the small farms prevailed in the north and were family owned. The large farms were mainly in the south, where 50 percent of the agricultural work force consisted of wage-earning rural laborers who were without land and housing. In the north, farms were fragmented into an average of six plots each, which meant much lost time going from one parcel to the next. This system of land tenure plus government food subsidies kept food prices low and inhibited the growth of agricultural output. During the 1960s, agricultural production grew by only 1.5 percent per annum. Producers had no economic incentives to increase production, mechanization was hindered by fragmentation, farm credit was short, and there was no effective rural extension service. As a consequence of agricultural inefficiency, Portugal was required to import 50 percent of its food.

Marcello Caetano continued the process of opening up Portugal's economy when he succeeded to the prime ministership. His secretary of state for commerce, Valentim Xavier Pintado, and secretary of state for industry, Rogério Martins, set out to reform the economy by loosening price controls and trade barriers, reducing monopolies, and selectively modernizing plants and equipment using tax incentives and credits. Finance policies were reformed in order to attract more foreign investment. In 1972 the industrial licensing law was abolished and replaced with a new law that allowed tax holidays for new businesses and government financial support for certain kinds of industrial projects. The thrust of these economic policies was toward the removal of the autarky and protectionism built up under Salazar.

Caetano's ability to effect change in the economy was greatly hampered, however, by the government's large military expenditures, the wars in Africa draining away much-needed resources. Nevertheless, economic progress was made during the Caetano years. Industrial production advanced at about 9 percent per year, and real GDP rose at about 7 percent. There was a rapid expansion of exports, a rise in domestic savings, and an increase in fixed capital formation. A number of large industrial projects were launched, the most ambitious being the heavy industry complex at Sines, south of Lisbon.

By the early 1970s the Portuguese economy had been transformed. Total GDP had grown by 120 percent, industrial production was three times higher, the average increase in the GDP was about 9 percent per annum, and worker productivity had grown. The change could be seen by comparing the sector distributions of the work force and the composition of the GDP. Between 1960 and 1973, the share of the labor force in the primary sector (agriculture) dropped from 44 to 25 percent of the work force; the secondary sector (manufacturing) rose from 29 to 36 percent; and the tertiary sector (services) rose from 28 to 35 percent. With respect to the composition of the GDP, the share contributed by the primary sector shrank from 24 percent in 1960 to 13 percent in 1973; the secondary sector's contribution rose from 37 to 51 percent; and the tertiary sector's share remained at about 37 percent. Within the secondary sector, manufacturing increased from 31 to 41 percent.

The greatest change clearly took place in the primary sector. From 1960 to 1973 there was a shift of population off the land equal to a decline of about 500,000 workers. There was not, however, a corresponding increase in the size of the secondary and tertiary work forces because two-thirds of those who left the land took nonagricultural jobs in some other industrialized country of Western Europe, principally France. This exodus of workers resulted in a serious loss of manpower, which was compounded by the troop requirements of the armed forces fighting in Africa. Nonetheless, it had a simultaneous positive effect: The Portuguese who went abroad remitted to Portugal large chunks of their wages. This influx of capital coupled with substantial receipts from tourism kept the government's budget in the black, despite heavy drains on the treasury to cover the expense of maintaining a large army in Africa. Together, remittances and tourism accounted for 42 percent of Portugal's foreign exchange during these years.

THE ECONOMIC EFFECTS OF APRIL 25, 1974

The impact of the golpe on Portugal's economy was immediate and resulted in a dramatic shift of wealth to the working class, which had neither collective bargaining rights nor the right to strike during the New State and which had therefore been grossly underpaid and exploited. When the New State collapsed in 1974, a labor federation dominated by the PCP, which had clandestinely infiltrated the official worker's sindicatos during the waning years of the dictatorship, emerged and demanded to be recognized as Portugal's only legal labor organization. This federation, called the General Confederation of Portuguese Workers (Confederação Geral dos Trabalhadores Portugueses, or CGTP), argued that Portuguese workers would only receive their just rewards if the labor movement remained unified in one organization. The PCP was thus successful in getting the second provisional government to promulgate a law that gave the CGTP complete control over Portugal's union movement. The adoption of the constitution in 1976, which permitted independent unions, allowed socialist members of the CGTP in concert with the PS and PSD to form a rival labor federation called the General Union of Workers (União Geral dos Trabalhadores, or UGT). The CGTP favored confrontation and strikes, whereas the UGT favored collaboration and negotiation.

Within days of the golpe, Portuguese workers who had not received a fair share of Portugal's economic miracle went out on strike in great numbers and organized massive demonstrations for higher wages, shorter working hours, and better working conditions. Managers were purged and businesses seized when the demands of workers were not met. In the countryside, especially in the Alentejo, agricultural workers began to unionize and make demands on large landowners. Shortly after, workers and tenants began to seize land and organize collective farms. When the waves of land seizures finally subsided, more than 6 million acres of land were in the hands of the workers.

The first provisional government, which was sympathetic to these activities, responded by enacting a minimum wage, developing a system of unemployment compensation, providing much-needed social services, and subsidizing prices. It also broke up the holdings of the forty families who had dominated the economy. In May 1974 all banks of issue were nationalized, and in June the government took over all firms engaged in mining national resources. Later, in response to worker demands for further nationalization, petroleum, steel, tobacco, munitions, and electrical production was taken over. In the months that followed additional banks were nationalized, as were insurance companies, transportation, and brewing, paper making, fertilizer, cement, and shipbuilding firms. The government responded to the land expropriations in the Alentejo by passing an agrarian reform law that essentially legitimized the seizure of at least some of the land occupied by workers.

Nationalization, land expropriations, loss of markets in the African colonies, and strikes resulted in considerable economic dislocation, which was exacerbated by the worldwide energy crisis and general recession of 1974–1976. The momentum of economic growth that Portugal had been experiencing since the beginning of the 1960s was stopped cold. In 1974 the GDP rose by only 3.9 percent and fell to 3.6 percent the following year. Investment shrank by 37 percent and exports by 21 percent. Industrial production, which had been at 9 percent per year, dropped to 2.4 percent. At the same time, the government's redistributive policies made public consumption jump by 16 percent. This resulted in overconsumption by 1.9 percent and inflation between 14 and 21 percent. Increased consumption coupled with the decline in industrial production led to a depletion of stocks, a massive public debt, and a severe foreign trade imbalance. Despite government efforts, the unemployment rate jumped to 14 percent of the work force.

The government began to experience a severe budget deficit because of nationalization and welfare policies. Public-sector debt increased from $6 million in 1973 to $66 million in 1974, $168 million in 1975, and $282 million in 1976. At the same time, tourism earnings fell from $322 million in 1973 to $258 million in 1974 and $101 million in 1975. Remittances from Portuguese working abroad also declined during these years. In the past remittances and tourism had been sufficient to cover Portugal's foreign trade deficit; in 1973 they accounted for Portugal's $200 million foreign exchange surplus. In 1974 this changed to a $550 million deficit, which rose to $900 million in 1975 and $1.2 billion in 1976. This resulted in heavy borrowing against Portugal's foreign reserves, which were $2.8 billion in 1973. External debt soared from a modest $600 million in 1973 to $3.8 billion in 1977.

The loss of the overseas markets represented by Portugal's colonies contributed to the severe economic disruption. In 1973 exports to the colonies accounted for 15 percent of total exports. In 1976 the figure was only 5 percent of total exports. Before decolonization, Portugal bought 36 percent of all agricultural imports from the colonies, 31 percent of mineral imports, and 33 percent of raw materials. Portugal lost important markets for textiles, canned fish, petrochemicals, rubber products, iron and steel, and capital goods. Decolonization also resulted in the swelling of the Portuguese population by about 800,000 individuals who were repatriated from Angola and Mozambique. The government granted to returnees cash subsidies, accommodations, and settlements, all of which drew down the treasury. The influx of such a large number of retornados exacerbated the unemployment rate, as did the demobilization of the armed forces.

Since 1976 Portuguese governments have attempted to put the economy on an even keel. During the first constitutional government, Prime Minister Mário Soares placed a 15 percent ceiling on wage increases, imposed limits on the right to strike, restricted welfare benefits to 50 percent of a worker's base pay, increased taxes, placed quotas on imports, and raised prices on goods and services. The Soares government also moved to evict farm workers from illegally seized latifúndios.

The AR passed an agrarian reform law, called the Barreto Law (Lei Barreto) after the minister of agriculture who wrote it. The law had different provisions for different regions of the country to take into account Portugal's contrasting land tenure systems. In the north the law permitted private ownership to continue, but farmers were encouraged to consolidate their holdings into cooperatives in order to increase output. In the south private ownership was permitted only for farmers who held 74 acres or less. All others were eligible for expropriation according to a complicated point system that took into account the farm's soil quality, amount of capital equipment, livestock, and output. In some cases this new law required the return of land that did not qualify for expropriation and the compensation of owners for assets lost to expropriation.

The Soares government also passed a law delimiting the boundary between the public and private sectors of the economy and devalued the escudo by 15 percent. When this devaluation proved insufficient, the government decided to subject the escudo to a 1 percent a month depreciation until the trade imbalance came into line. To bring down high inflation, the government reduced spending. Prices were raised and credit rationing was instituted. These measures were only marginally effective as 1977 was a disastrous year for Portuguese agriculture. Output of every major crop fell because of poor weather, bad management, and turmoil in the Alentejo connected to the land expropriations. This increased food imports, which added significantly to the balance of payments problem. In order to cope, the government had to sell off $500 million worth of its gold reserves and seek foreign loans, which were provided by West Germany ($250 million), Switzerland ($50 million), the International Settlement Bank in Basel ($500 million), and the United States ($300 million). Portugal also sought a loan of $750 million from the International Monetary Fund. The IMF loan was the most difficult to obtain because it came with stiff conditions: The escudo had to be devalued 25 percent, public spending cut 20 percent, taxes increased by 38 percent, and the current account deficit reduced from $1.5 billion to $800 million within one year.

These stipulations were so harsh that the Soares government lost a vote of confidence in Parliament and collapsed. The PS-CDS coalition government that followed continued to negotiate with the IMF but also tried to borrow $300 million from a private consortium. This loan, coupled with increases in water rates, transportation costs, and electricity and food prices, allowed Portugal to procure the IMF loan under less stringent conditions: The deficit needed to be reduced to $1 billion in the first year and the escudo would be devalued only 6 percent. Together, the two loans allowed the Portuguese to convert their international debts into loans with longer maturities, which made it easier to deal with domestic economic problems. In August 1978 the situation was further alleviated by the procurement of $525 million from private lenders.

Under the conditions laid down by the IMF, Portugal's deficit was cut to $780 million; inflation declined from 27 to 22 percent in 1978. Unfortunately, unemployment remained between 10 and 15 percent. During 1978 the third constitutional government returned more expropriated firms and farms to their owners and raised prices on transportation and gasoline.

By the end of the 1970s much had been accomplished to improve the economy after the excesses of 1974–1976. Tourism began to recover, and remittances from immigrants began to flow into the country. The devaluation of the escudo spurred exports by 25 percent, and imports increased by only 5 percent. Foreign reserves climbed to $2 billion. Portugal's debt service obligation fell to a manageable $800 million. The cost of these achievements, however, was felt most heavily by Portuguese workers, whose private consumption increased only 2.5 percent and whose real wages fell to pre-1974 levels.

ECONOMIC INTEGRATION WITH EUROPE

The response by Western European countries to the Revolution of the Carnations was an outpouring of loans and technical assistance from governments and international agencies wishing to see democracy established in Portugal. Most support came from the European Free Trade Association (EFTA), of which Portugal was a founding member, and the European Economic Community, which Portugal eventually joined.

The EFTA responded to April 25, 1974, with words of encouragement and eventually financial and technical support. Norway was the first EFTA country to give Portugal bilateral aid and pressed the other EFTA members to do likewise. In May 1975 Bent Rabaeus, EFTA's secretary general, visited Lisbon to determine what could be done for the Portuguese economy. After consultations with various entities, including the Confederation of Portuguese Industry (Confederação de Indústria Portuguesa, or CIP), Rabaeus proposed that EFTA form an industrial development fund to promote investment in Portugal. The purpose of the fund would be to help salvage the private sector. In addition to the development fund, the EFTA proposed (1) giving concessions to infant industries; (2) lengthening the tariff reduction timetable; (3) granting Portugal favorable terms on agricultural exports; and (4) providing technical assistance.

Before these proposals were acted upon, however, individual member states of EFTA began to provide aid. Norway sent technicians to help the Portuguese fishing industry organize and equip plants for freezing and refrigerating fish and establish an institute of maritime environment and aquatic pollution. The Norwegians also provided technical assistance in the areas of housing, health, education, tourism, and finance and extended to Portugal a line of credit for the purchase of Norwegian goods. Sweden followed Norway's lead by establishing a program to support education and sending funds to build housing and improve communications and public transport. The Swedes also provided assistance for the reintegration of the 800,000 retornados. Switzerland helped by underwriting the construction of urban transportation lines in Lisbon and Porto and by instituting a two-year program of railroad modernization. In addition, the Swiss provided aid in the tourism sector, especially hotel management.

In November 1975 the EFTA Council of Ministers decided to permit Portugal to deviate from their previously arranged tariff reduction schedule in order to help overcome serious economic difficulties. Although this measure and the bilateral efforts of the member states were helpful to Portugal, the greatest amount of assistance came from EFTA's Development Fund for Portugal, created in November 1975. This fund contained $100 million, which was used to restructure and develop Portugal's industrial sector, especially small and medium enterprises. All of these monies were spent on projects that encouraged regional industrial development, facilitated economic diversification, and enhanced export performance. This aid succeeded in creating 1,800 new jobs and securing some 20,000 jobs previously threatened. Loans were made to a wide variety of industries: poultry feeding plants, textile mills, fiberglass boatbuilding plants, cement companies, pulp mills, and asbestos producers.

Although Portugal was not a member of the EEC, it did have a special free trade agreement with the EEC that had been necessitated by the accession to the EEC of EFTA members Great Britain and Denmark. The EEC encouraged the agreement because a full 25 percent of Portuguese exports went to these two new member countries. Under the arrangement, certain Portuguese commodities and products such as cork, textiles, and clothing were allowed into the EEC with reduced duties. The Portuguese were also permitted to apply tariffs to a number of industrial products entering Portugal from the EEC.

An aspect of the special free trade agreement was a clause that permitted the contracting parties to extend relations between Portugal and the EEC into areas not covered by the initial arrangement. The Portuguese used this clause to legitimize their request for full membership in the EEC. In June 1974 Prime Minister Palma Carlos and Mário Soares, then foreign minister, went to Brussels in order to request economic aid and closer ties between Portugal and the EEC. Following this visit, the EEC Commission announced that it was willing to aid Portugal in order to support democracy and enhance economic and social development. In October 1974 the EEC granted Portugal an emergency aid package, and in June 1976 the Council of Ministers authorized the commission to open negotiations with Portugal for an expansion of the 1973 agreement.

These negotiations resulted in additional protocols to the 1973 agreement, which provided 200 million units of account (European currency units, or ECU) in the form of loans by the European Investment Bank. These loans were restricted to financing small and medium enterprises, the improvement of infrastructure, and the development of agriculture and fishing. The protocols also allowed a slower pace in tariff reductions and the restoration up to 20 percent of import duties on petrochemicals, metallurgicals, electrical machinery, machine tools, and textiles to protect these industries from EEC imports.

On March 28, 1977, the Portuguese government officially applied for EEC membership. The application stressed the importance of the EEC for the consolidation of Portugal's nascent democracy and was supported by all the major Portuguese political parties, except the PCP. Within the EEC itself, however, there was reluctance to admit Portugal. Some members felt that the EEC needed to resolve some of its own internal problems before admitting new members; others proposed an intermediate status between association (which Portugal already had) and full membership that would involve no commitments by the EEC to Portugal but would bring Portugal into the network of economic activities of the community. The difference in levels of development between Portugal and the EEC was a major concern because of the strain this would put on the EEC development funds and the problems it would cause in the area of agriculture.

From the beginning, the principal reason that was given for admitting Portugal was political: Membership would strengthen democracy. In February 1977, Mário Soares, then prime minister, traveled to the capitals of the EEC states in order to persuade them to admit his country. France favored the admission of Spain and Greece—but not Portugal—because of the higher level of economic development of those countries. Italy, on the other hand, favored admitting all three because it wanted to expand the Mediterranean tier of the community and thereby counteract the weight of the northern Europeans. When Soares's tour was finished, the EEC Commission agreed to accept Portugal's application.

Negotiations between Portugal and the EEC were, however, long and arduous not only because of the poor state of the Portuguese economy but also because of developments within the EEC. One of these was the admission of Greece in 1981. As a Mediterranean country, Greece was concerned about agricultural competition from Portugal and Spain (which had applied some three months after Portugal). Greece became a major stumbling block by insisting that the EEC pump into the Greek economy a new infusion of development funds in exchange for their vote for Portugal and Spain's admission. The EEC finally agreed to loans and subsidies worth about $4 billion in order to permit Greek products to compete favorably with products from Spain and Portugal. The finances of the EEC presented another problem. The principal source of income, the value-added tax, had not been enough to cover the expenses of the community. The admission of Portugal, as well as Greece and Spain, would require the expenditure of large sums of money to upgrade the economies of these less-developed members, sums the EEC did not have. Despite these problems, Portugal and the EEC signed a treaty of accession on June 12, 1985, which set the date for formal admission on January 1, 1986, and specified a five- to ten-year period of transition.

Since accession to the EEC, the Portuguese economy has been experiencing a miniboom generated by substantial grants from the EEC's regional development fund, which have totaled $1.7 billion since 1986; direct foreign investment of about $1.5 billion primarily from U.S. and Japanese companies that see Portugal as a gateway to the EEC's unified market (which will come into being on January 1, 1993); and political stability, which has allowed time for the economic policies of the Cavaco Silva government to have their intended effect. Inflation fell from 24 percent in 1984 to 9 percent in 1988; unemployment was reduced from 8 percent in 1984 to just under 5 percent in 1988, the lowest rate in the EEC; real wages rose by 4 percent per annum from 1986 to 1989; and the budget deficit was reduced to only 7 percent over revenues. Privatization of industries nationalized after 1974 is well under way; the Lisbon shipyard has begun to fill orders again for ship repair; the tourist industry is robust; traditional exports of textiles, footwear, cork, paper products, and ceramics are doing well; and new industries, such as electrical appliances and molded plastics, are extremely competitive.

Despite these improvements, many of the structural problems remain. The agricultural sector is still too inefficient; the fishing industry is still not modernized; the industrial sector is still technologically backward; tourism is too concentrated in Lisbon, the Algarve, and on Madeira; the commercial sector is fragmented into an excessive number of retail establishments; the rail and road network is still grossly inadequate. These structural problems must be overcome if the Portuguese are ever to enjoy the standard of living found in the rest of the EEC.

REFERENCES

Baklanoff, Eric N. *The Economic Transformation of Spain and Portugal.* New York: Praeger Publishers, 1978.
Bermeo, Nancy Gina. *The Revolution Within the Revolution: Workers' Control in Rural Portugal.* Princeton, N.J.: Princeton University Press, 1986.

Macedo, Jorge Braga de, and Simon Serfaty (eds.). *Portugal Since the Revolution: Economic and Political Perspectives.* Boulder, Colo.: Westview Press, 1981.

Morrison, Rodney J. *Portugal: Revolutionary Change in an Open Economy.* Boston: Auburn House, 1981.

Pitta e Cunha, Paulo de. "Portugal and the European Economic Community," in Lawrence S. Graham and Douglas L. Wheeler (eds.), *In Search of Modern Portugal: The Revolution and Its Consequences.* Madison: University of Wisconsin Press, 1983, pp. 321–338.

Portugal: Plano de Desenvolvimento Regional, 1989–93. Lisbon: Ministério do Planeamento e da Administração do Território, March 1989.

Sanders, Thomas G. "Portugal and the European Community." *USFI Reports,* no. 21. Indianapolis: Universities Field Staff International Inc., 1985.

9
Portugal and the Wider World

Portuguese relations with foreign powers have reflected to a considerable degree the geographical and historical isolation of Portugal on the southwestern edge of the Iberian peninsula. Historically, Portugal has formed alliances to differentiate itself from Spain. This accounts for the 600-year-old alliance with Great Britain as well as Portugal's participation on the side of France in World War I, which involved sending an expeditionary force to Flanders. Beyond these alliances, Portugal has kept bilateral and multilateral relations to a minimum and limited them almost exclusively to Western nations, practically ignoring the Third World and Communist states. During the New State, Portuguese foreign policy had one fundamental objective: the maintenance of Portugal's colonial empire. In 1960 that empire included Angola, Mozambique, Portuguese Guinea, the Cape Verde Islands, São Tomé and Príncipe, and São João de Ajuda in Africa; Goa, Damão, Diu, Dadra, and Nagar-Aveli in India; Macão; and the eastern half of the island of Timor in Asia. The Portuguese defended their hegemony over these territories by claiming that by their presence they were carrying out a nonracial, Christian, civilizing mission and that their possessions were not colonies but "overseas provinces" of Portugal. The New State clung to these possessions for a variety of economic, social, and historical reasons. The most important was the role that overseas possessions have played in Portugal's national identity and image of itself as a country that had created a racially and culturally diverse community scattered across the globe and held together by bonds of Portuguese language and culture. All of this suddenly changed on April 25, 1974.

DECOLONIZATION

Although there was considerable agreement among Portugal's new elites that the colonial empire had to be abandoned, there was disagreement, especially between Spínola and the MFA, on how this should be done. Spínola advocated a Lusitanian community that would encompass Portugal, the former colonies as autonomous provinces, and Brazil. The MFA favored complete and immediate independence. Despite Spínola's desire to substitute a commonwealth for the colonial empire, Mário Soares, then minister of foreign affairs, opened unilateral negotiations with the leaders of the liberation movements in Angola, Mozambique, and Guinea-Bissau and with the indigenous leaders in the other colonies in order to arrange the independence of each. Faced with this fait accompli, Spínola agreed to recognize the right of the colonies to their independence.

In May 1974 Soares met with Aristides Pereira, the secretary general of the PAIGC in Dakar, Senegal in order to work out a timetable for the independence of Guinea-Bissau. After further negotiating sessions in London and Algiers, Portugal granted independence on September 10, 1974. Since then Portugal has maintained a fairly close relationship to the new country and has given it modest amounts of technical and economic assistance.

Because of their unusual historical and demographic circumstances (a mixed African-Portuguese population was transported to the uninhabited islands from the African mainland) and their extreme poverty, the Cape Verde islands saw no liberation movement before April 25, 1974. The PAIGC always considered itself the party that represented Cape Verdean nationalist aspirations. This situation changed abruptly with the formation of two groups opposed to the PAIGC's goal of unifying the Cape Verdes with Guinea-Bissau. From December 30, 1974, until June 30, 1975, the Portuguese shared a transitional government with the PAIGC. In July 1975 the Cape Verdes were granted independence.

In Mozambique various groups had sprung up in the waning days of the war before April 25, 1974. These included the Revolutionary Committee for Mozambique (Comité Revolucionário para Moçambique, or COREMO), a small group of FRELIMO dissidents; a white settler group called the Front for Independence and Continuity with the West (Frente para Independência e Continuidade com o Ocidente, or FICO), which advocated a unilateral declaration of independence under the white minority; and the United Group of Mozambique (Grupo Unido de Moçambique, or GUMO), a semiofficial multiracial group that favored independence but had close ties to Portugal. These groups were never very successful in generating support for themselves; therefore, the Portuguese government took FRELIMO to be the legitimate representative of the Mozambican people. Talks with FRELIMO for Mozambique's independence were opened on May 12, 1974. Further talks in September resulted in a cease-fire and Portuguese recognition of Mozambique's right to independence. On September 15 a transitional government comprising Portuguese and FRELIMO representatives took office in Mozambique. On June 25, 1975, Mozambique was granted full independence.

In São Tomé and Príncipe a movement for independence called the Movement for the Liberation of São Tomé and Príncipe (Movimento para a Libertação de São Tomé e Príncipe, or MLSTP), which operated from Gabon, had been in existence long before the golpe made independence possible. After negotiations with the MLSTP in Algeria in November 1974, Portugal granted independence to São Tomé and Príncipe in summer 1975.

Negotiations for the independence of Angola were complicated by the presence of three rival independence movements: MPLA, FNLA, and UNITA. Some of Portugal's new elites favored a position of neutrality with respect to these groups whereas others preferred direct negotiations with one group over another. The policy of strict neutrality prevailed, and independence was set for November 11, 1975. On that day no central government existed; the Portuguese therefore handed independence over to the Angolan "people." This was followed by an announcement by the FNLA and UNITA that they were forming a coalitional government in order to drive the MPLA from its stronghold, Luanda. The FNLA and UNITA called their part of Angola the Democratic People's Republic of Angola; the MPLA called its part the People's Republic of Angola. In order to defend themselves from the FNLA and UNITA, the MPLA asked for and received Cuban military support. Gradually, the FNLA dissipated, but UNITA continued to wage war against the MPLA, ultimately receiving military and diplomatic support from the United States and South Africa. This civil war continued until June 1989, when a cease-fire was arranged and negotiations for a peaceful settlement were initiated by an eight-member group of African leaders headed by President Kenneth Kaunda of Zambia.

The loss of Portugal's possessions in India actually began in 1961 when Indian troops invaded Goa, Damão, Diu, Dadra, and Nagar-Aveli. Salazar never forgave India, with whom he broke diplomatic relations. In September 1974 Portugal and India signed an agreement in which Portugal relinquished all claims to these possessions, recognized India's right to them, and reestablished diplomatic relations.

As in the Cape Verdes, independence movements did not appear in Timor until the Portuguese announced that Timor would be decolonized. Three major groups formed: The Timorese Democratic Union (União Democrática Timorense, or UDT), which favored a Western-style democracy and the retention of close ties with Portugal; the Revolutionary Front for Independent East Timor (Frente Revolucionário para Timor do Leste Independente, or FRETLIN), which was leftist and advocated total independence; and the Timorese Popular Democratic Association (Associação Popular Democrática Timorense, or APODETI), which wanted Timor to become an autonomous province of Indonesia. In addition to these three main groups, two minor groups appeared. One was the Timorese Social Democratic Association (Associação Social Democrática Timorense, or ASDT), which favored eventual independence only after a five-year transitional period. The other was the Democratic Association for the Integration of East Timor with Australia (Associação Democrática para a Integração de Timor de Leste no Austrália, or ADITLA), which favored unification with Australia.

In early October 1974, the Portuguese government announced that total independence for Timor was not possible because most Timorese wanted to retain ties to Portugal. Decolonization was put on hold pending the result of a referendum on the question, which was to be held in March 1975. This referendum was cancelled because the Portuguese had in the meantime decided to open negotiations with the three major groups: FRETLIN, UDT, and APODETI. Because of APODETI's participation, FRETLIN boycotted the talks, and Portugal negotiated a timetable for independence with the remaining two groups. In August 1975, two months after an agreement had been reached, the UDT attempted to seize power unilaterally, and Timor erupted in civil war. In the fighting that ensued, FRETLIN succeeded in pushing APODETI and UDT forces to the border of West Timor, which is Indonesian territory. The Portuguese abandoned Timor in the midst of these hostilities, leaving the Timorese to their own devices.

In late October, the UDT and APODETI, who had joined forces, enlisted the aid of Indonesia. These combined forces drove FRETLIN back to Dili, the capital city. While in retreat, FRETLIN declared Timor to be independent. In response the UDT and APODETI declared Timor to be part of Indonesia, a claim the Indonesians initially rejected. Later, in December, Indonesia invaded Timor and captured Dili from FRETLIN, which retreated to the mountains to wage a guerrilla war against Indonesia. Portugal broke diplomatic relations with Indonesia and went before the UN to demand that Indonesia withdraw its forces. The Indonesians have refused to pull out; though many East Timorese cling to their Portuguese heritage, for all intents and purposes East Timor has become a part of Indonesia.

Macão, which comprises a peninsula and two small islands across the bay from Hong Kong, existed as a Portuguese colony only at the sufferance of the People's Republic of China (PRC), which claimed the colony but, unlike India, did not force its claim with troops. After April 25, 1974, Portugal recognized the PRC and indicated a willingness to return Macão to China. The PRC did not initially demonstrate an interest in changing Macão's status because it would force a consideration of the question of Hong Kong, China's window to the outside world. In January 1976, after eight months of negotiations, an agreement was reached that changed Macão's status from colony to Chinese territory temporarily under Portuguese administration. Since the recently negotiated return of Hong Kong to the PRC, the Chinese and Portuguese are working on a similar agreement for the eventual reintegration of Macão with the mainland.

RELATIONS WITH SELECTED COUNTRIES

Great Britain

Perhaps Portugal's oldest ally is Great Britain. In 1386 Portugal and England signed the Treaty of Windsor; reinforced by additional Anglo-Portuguese treaties, it remains in effect today and makes the alliance the longest in the history of Western interstate relations. For centuries the British have had a close economic relationship to Portugal, having invested in Portuguese wine (especially port wine) making, transportation, and telephone systems. Relations during the New State dictatorship were generally correct, although the British were increasingly unhappy with Portugal's persistent desire to maintain its colonial empire. When the Indian government seized the Portuguese colonies in India, Britain refused Portugal permission to use British air bases to fly troops to its beleaguered possessions. Portugal's support of Rhodesia's unilateral declaration of independence in 1964 and Britain's blockade of the port of Beira to prevent petroleum shipments from reaching Ian Smith's rebel regime strained the "oldest alliance" almost to the breaking point. Since 1974, however, the Anglo-Portuguese alliance has been free of problems. Trade continues, as does mutual cooperation within the frameworks of NATO and, since 1986, the EEC.

Brazil

Historically, Portugal's closest international relationship has been with its former colony, Brazil. Although Brazil has been independent since 1822, its economic, cultural, linguistic, and religious ties to Portugal are much stronger than the usual ties between former colony and metropol. Bilateral agreements between Brazil and Portugal have provided for yearly joint consultations between their foreign ministers; Brazilians living in Portugal have been granted Portuguese citizenship, which includes, after five years of residence, the right to vote in Portuguese elections and hold political office. Brazil also extends similar rights to Portuguese living in Brazil.

Spain

Portugal's and Spain's entrance into the EEC on the same day, in joint ceremonies in Lisbon and Madrid, raised "the Spanish question" to the top of Portugal's foreign policy agenda for the first time in a good while. Portugal's relations with Spain have traditionally been marked by mistrust, defiance, and fear. These attitudes are the result of Portugal's long history of resistance to Castilian, and later Spanish, attempts to control the entire Iberian peninsula. Portugal's fear of losing its autonomy and identity as a nation-state and being absorbed by Spain was heightened with the loss of its African colonial empire, which the Portuguese saw as a counterweight to their large neighbor. Membership in the EEC with Spain conjures up in the Portuguese collective memory the Battle of Aljubarrota (whose 600th anniversary was celebrated in 1985), when a small Portuguese army, aided by English archers, defeated a large, well-equipped Castilian force and maintained the autonomy of the kingdom of Portugal. It also stirs up memories of the sixty years between 1580 and 1640 when the Portuguese were ruled by the Habsburgs and Portugal became another segment of the sprawling Spanish empire. This "Spanish captivity" crystallized Portuguese nationalism and has become the chief point of reference for Portugal's attitude toward Spain. The last war between Spain and Portugal was fought in 1801 when the Spanish, who were allied with the French, invaded Portugal. This war resulted in the loss of a portion of Portuguese territory called Olivença, long claimed by Spain. During Spain's civil war, Salazar sided with Franco against the Spanish republicans, whom he saw as a threat to his New State regime. In World War II Portugal remained neutral and supported the neutrality of the Spanish, who, had they joined the fighting, would have surely done so on the side of the Axis. In 1939 Portugal and Spain signed the Iberian Pact, which pledged peace and friendship between the two nations and contained an agreement to remain neutral.

Now that Portugal has joined the EEC it will have to harmonize its foreign policy with that of the EEC in general and that of Spain in particular. Portugal and Spain will, for the first time in their histories, have to work in concert. The prospect of working together has, however, brought to the surface the many differences between them that have been dormant during the long centuries of mutual antipathy, and has renewed Portuguese fears of Spanish domination.

The differences between the countries fall into two broad categories, military and economic. With respect to military differences, the problem is Portugal's worry that NATO will favor the militarily stronger Spain, which joined the alliance in 1982. This fear first manifested itself with respect to the question of how the military command structures of both countries were going to be integrated into that of NATO. The Spanish advocated a universal Iberian command headed by a Spanish general. The Portuguese, for the historical reasons outlined above, found this arrangement unacceptable. They believed Portugal should defend the Iberian Atlantic and thus should remain within the Supreme Allied Command, Atlantic (SACLANT), headquartered outside of Lisbon, and Spain should be placed under the Supreme Allied Command, Europe (SACEUR). Under this arrangement Portugal's role in NATO would be to assist in the defense of the Atlantic whereas Spain's would be to help defend continental Europe. After considerable debate, Portugal's position prevailed, and two separate command structures on the peninsula were created.

With respect to economic differences, the Portuguese fear that the much larger, efficient, and advanced Spanish economy will invade and destroy Portugal's weak and inefficient one. In their dealings with the Spanish, the Portuguese have thus sought to negotiate to their own advantage in fishing, trade, and direct foreign investment, areas the Portuguese contend have largely benefited Spain's economic interests. This was clearly the case with regard to fishing. Spain has one of the largest fishing fleets in the world and for twenty years enjoyed exorbitant fishing rights in Portuguese waters. Granted by Caetano in 1969 as a quid pro quo for Spanish diplomatic support for Portugal's colonial policy, these rights threatened to deplete Portuguese fisheries and eliminate their much smaller and inefficient fleet. The dispute over Spanish fishing rights, which had been festering for some time, came to a head during EEC accession negotiations because the EEC's common fisheries policy allocates fishing rights of member states according to bilateral agreements in force before membership. Portugal fought tooth and nail to reverse Spain's privileged access to its territorial waters.

In 1981 Portugal and Spain set up a committee to study the problem and work out a joint fishing policy on a yearly basis until accession to the EEC. In 1982 the Balsemão government refused to ratify the committee's plan for that year, saying that Spain still benefited too much from its access to Portuguese waters. The Portuguese government stopped issuing licenses to Spanish fishermen, thus denying them legal access to Portugal's exclusive economic zone, the territorial sea 200 miles from the shore. The government hoped to use licenses as a bargaining chip to keep the Spanish out of Portuguese waters. The Spanish, however, refused to budge, holding out for the same number of licenses. In the end, Portugal, in exchange for concessions in the area of trade, capitulated and allowed Spain generous access to its territorial sea, excluding the waters of the continental shelf.

The economies of Portugal and Spain have been highly protected with respect to each other. Portugal's trade with Germany and France, for example, has been much higher than that with Spain, which was abnormally low for neighboring countries. Portugal's major complaint was that Spain had not lowered its tariffs as much as Portugal had done in the negotiations with the EEC. During the negotiations on fishing, however, Portugal's concessions highlighted the differences between Portugal and Spain's economic strengths plus Spain's more advantageous location. By treating Spain as if it were already a member of the EEC, Portugal was able to apply to Spanish imports the same duties it could to other members of the EEC; Spain, in turn, would have to apply to Portuguese imports the same duties that the rest of the EEC would apply.

With respect to direct foreign investment, Portugal's fear was that foreign investors would look at the Iberian peninsula as a single, unified market and, therefore, might decide to supply the Portuguese market by locating their factories in Spain. Spain would thus receive the great bulk of such investment, to the detriment of the Portuguese economy. Although it is true that Spain has received greater amounts of direct foreign investment than has Portugal, the Portuguese, as was mentioned in the preceding chapter, have been successful in attracting a considerable amount of U.S. and Japanese investment. Thus, Portuguese fears in this regard have not been realized.

Portugal's political relations with Spain have ebbed and flowed since 1974. In 1977 Mário Soares, as prime minister, signed a treaty of friendship and cooperation with Spain that superceded the Iberian Pact signed by Salazar and Franco in 1939. The treaty set up the Luso-Hispanic Council, which meets annually to discuss and settle bilateral issues and promote cooperation between the countries. Since then, the question of a unified Iberian command, a heavy trade imbalance in favor of Spain, and the tendency of the Spanish to locate their nuclear power plants in areas near the Portuguese border have aggravated relations. In order to overcome the deterioration of relations and establish mutual respect, since 1983 Portuguese and Spanish prime ministers have periodically held summit meetings.

Africa

After 1974, Portugal's withdrawal from Africa was precipitous and irreversible. Within eighteen months, Angola, Mozambique, and Guinea-Bissau were independent. Portugal's turn toward Europe has drawn the attention of Portugese policymakers away from Africa. In addition, there is considerable debate among Portuguese policymakers about what the country's role in Africa ought to be. Nonetheless, successive Portuguese governments have tried to counteract Soviet influence in the former colonies, facilitate agreements between them and South Africa, and support their sovereignty as newly independent states.

Of the three former colonies, Portugal maintains the best relations with Guinea-Bissau. Its leaders have turned toward Portugal in order to counteract the influence of the French-speaking countries that surround Guinea-Bissau and to ensure the survival of its Portuguese-based national and cultural identity. Portugal's relations with Mozambique, although initially strained, have been improving since independence. Mozambique has pressured Lisbon to curb the activities of private individuals who have been seeking restitution for property nationalized after independence and to stop the military activities of the Mozambican National Resistance (Resistência Nacional de Moçambique, or RENEMO), which has been waging a guerrilla war against the FRELIMO government and terrorizing the population. In response, in 1984 Portugal helped arrange the Nkomati Accord between South Africa and Mozambique in which the former agreed to cease supporting RENEMO and the latter agreed not to give aid and comfort to the African National Congress (ANC). The Portuguese also facilitated the Cape Town Treaty of May 2, 1984, concerning the sale of power to South Africa from the Cabora Bassa hydroelectric project, whose financial liability the Portuguese government had assumed. The Portuguese have also provided limited military training.

Relations with Angola have remained tense since independence. Angola has accused the Portuguese of opposing the MPLA, Cuban-backed government because UNITA has been permitted to maintain an office in downtown Lisbon. The Angolan government was also aggravated by the numerous visits to Portugal of former State President P. W. Botha of South Africa and by the Portuguese role in getting the Nkomati Accord signed.

In general, Portugal's African policy toward the former colonies has been characterized by lack of a clear plan of action and the scarcity of economic means to carry one out. Portugal's persistent economic problems have prevented all but an extremely modest level of developmental aid. There are presently about 20,000 expatriate Portuguese technicians (*cooperantes*) working in the former colonies. Their presence, as well as the presence in South Africa of some 600,000 Portuguese immigrants who are fueling RENEMO and lent support to the South African government's activities in southern Angola, ensure that Portugal will be enmeshed in Africa for some time to come.

United States

Relations between Portugal and the United States have been structured principally by the military-strategic interests of Washington. During

World War II, the United States sought to induce Portugal to maintain its official neutrality and to stop exporting wolfram (tungsten), an important ingredient in the manufacture of munitions, to Germany. Lisbon eventually agreed to cease exports, but only when it was clear that the Allies were going to win the war. In 1943, in order to ingratiate Portugal to the eventual victors, Salazar allowed the British to build an air base on the island of Terceira in the Azores. The United States, also given permission to use the Azores, began constructing an air base at Lajes. The base was built by the Pan-American World Airways corporation so that Salazar could tell Hitler that its purpose was commercial and not military. Since that time, the Lajes base has been at the center of Portuguese-U.S. relations.

After the war, Lajes was turned over to Portugal; its use by the U.S. Air Force has since been regulated by a series of treaties. The first, signed in 1946, ran for eighteen months; the second, signed in 1948, ran for three years. When the third treaty was negotiated in 1951, the United States began to compensate Portugal for its use rights by giving Lisbon substantial economic and military aid. The military aid, which included training, has resulted in the equipment of Portugal's army, navy, and air force with mostly U.S. war matériel, especially heavy weapons such as tanks, artillery pieces, aircraft, and ships.

Political relations between Portugal and the United States from the end of the war until the early 1960s were generally correct and friendly. Throughout this period Portugal was seen as a model of peace and tranquillity, even if not democratic. Satisfied that Lisbon was squarely in the Western camp, Washington did not place Portugal high on its foreign policy agenda. During this period the United States supported Portugal in the United Nations when the question of its African colonies was raised. The Portuguese argued that Angola, Mozambique, and Portuguese Guinea were of no concern to the United Nations because they did not fall under the rubric of "non-self-governing" territories; that is, they were not colonies but merely overseas provinces of Portugal. The United States backed this position, saying that it was up to each member state to decide for itself if it had such territories.

The onset of the wars for independence in Portugal's African colonies brought about a change in U.S. policy toward Portugal's overseas possessions. The Kennedy administration, which was more sympathetic to liberation movements than was Eisenhower's, instructed its ambassador to the United Nations, Adlai Stevenson, to remind Portugal of its obligations under the UN Charter. The United States even voted with the Soviet Union against Portugal's intransigence on several occasions. Portugal argued that it was the innocent target of international communism and the last bulwark in the defense of Western civilization. In order to get the United States to stop its tacit support of the liberation movements, the Portuguese more than hinted that the Lajes base treaty would not be renegotiated when it expired. Faced with this threat, the Kennedy administration modified its policy and began to abstain on or veto all major UN resolutions condemning Portuguese colonialism. This change of policy was a clear result of the importance the Lajes facility had for U.S. security. It also reflected a growing fear that too much pressure on Portugal would incline the Portuguese to withdraw from NATO, which the United States feared might be interpreted by the Soviet Union as a sign that the Western alliance was disintegrating. Throughout this period, the United States continued to send military aid to Portugal, countering criticisms of this practice with the argument that such aid was intended to allow Portugal to meet its NATO obligations. Although the Portuguese were forbidden from using U.S.-supplied equipment in the colonies, they did anyway.

When the MFA brought down the Salazar-Caetano regime, the United States became alarmed by the flow of events and concerned about the emergence of a pro-Soviet regime. Portugal was immediately catapulted to the top of the United States' foreign policy agenda. The secretary of state at the time, Henry Kissinger, had a pervasive fear that the Communists were poised to take over Portugal. In order to counteract this possibility, the United States channeled covert financial aid to the pro-Western democratic political parties through the socialist, social democratic, and Christian democratic parties of Western Europe. President Costa Gomes assured Washington that a Communist takeover was not possible, that Portugal would remain in NATO, and that the United States would continue to be permitted to use the Lajes facility. Gradually, the U.S. ambassador to Portugal, Frank C. Carlucci, a career diplomat, and others in the Department of State were able to convince Kissinger that Mário Soares, who had become the spokesperson for the pro-West democratic parties, was not a latter-day Kerensky and deserved U.S. support. Portugal was thus given over $20 million in aid, and the United States declared its support for Soares.

When the crisis of 1974–1975 passed and it became clear that Portugal would join the club of Western European democracies, Portugal's place on the U.S. foreign policy agenda returned to its previously low level. The key concern for the United States continues to be the Lajes facility. Recently, the Portuguese, angered when Congress cut the $207 million in aid they were expecting under the 1983 treaty to $117 million, requested that the agreement be renegotiated. A promise of a substantial shipment of surplus military equipment did not persuade them to change their minds, nor did a trip to Lisbon by Secretary of Defense Carlucci.

After 500 years, Portugal has finally cast off its imperial mission and rejoined Europe. Portuguese foreign policy makers now seek to define a new international mission for Portugal that capitalizes on the country's Euro-Atlanticity, that is, its position on the western edge of the European landmass and its historical oceanic mission. Since 1974 Portuguese foreign policy makers have been striving to create for Portugal a new international geostrategic role as a bridge between Europe and Africa, Latin America, and Asia.

REFERENCES

Ferreira, José Medeiros. "International Ramifications of the Portuguese Revolution," in Lawrence S. Graham and Douglas L. Wheeler (eds.), *In Search of Modern Portugal: The Revolution and Its Consequences.* Madison: University of Wisconsin Press, 1983, pp. 287–295.

Keefe, Eugene K., et al. *Area Handbook for Portugal.* Washington, D.C.: U.S. Government Printing Office, 1977.

Maxwell, Kenneth (ed.). *Portugal in the 1980's: Dilemmas of Democratic Consolidation.* Westport, Conn.: Greenwood Press, 1986.

Minter, William. *Portuguese Africa and the West.* New York: Monthly Review Press, 1972.

Szulc, Tad. "Lisbon and Washington: Behind the Portuguese Revolution," *Foreign Policy* 21 (Winter 1975–1976):3–62.

10
Whither Portugal?

The central theme of this book is that Portugal's appearance as one of Western Europe's first nation-states and its early acquisition of a seaborne empire exaggerated the power and prestige of its monarchy and retarded its progress toward modern democratic government. For generations, although culturally and geographically Western European, Portugal defined itself as the core of a racially diverse global community that embraced European and non-European peoples and cultures. Thus throughout its long history, Portugal was *in* but not *of* Western Europe. In the nineteenth century, with the advent of liberalism, Portugal began to be transformed from a monarchy to a pluralist democracy of the Western European type. This transformation finally ended with the Revolution of the Carnations, but at the time it was not clear what Portugal's political future would be. During the first decade after April 25, 1974, governments rose and fell with alarming frequency; the country experienced the psychological trauma brought on by the close of its oceanic mission; the economy was a shambles; corruption was rampant; and social life was in turmoil. Political leadership seemed unable to solve the economic and social problems unleashed by the golpe. Indeed, the situation was so desperate during those early years that speculation was rife about when the military would intervene as they had during so many previous crises.

By the beginning of the second decade of democracy, the seemingly intractable economic and social problems of a few years before had begun to ease and Portugal's nascent democracy appeared to be out of danger. The Second Republic began to consolidate and institutionalize itself. Accession to the EEC began to have a salutary affect on the economy. Political stability was finally achieved. There is no reason to expect that the future will be anything but a continuation of this progress.

In the political realm, we can expect to see efforts by the political leadership to deradicalize the constitutional framework established in 1976. Recently, the constitution was revised for a second time, the result of an agreement worked out between the PSD and PS, the two major parties in Parliament. These revisions, which were passed by the AR in June 1989, eliminated the language that declared irreversible the nationalizations undertaken in the aftermath of April 25, 1974. This change will permit the privatization of nationalized enterprises by a simple majority vote of the AR instead of the two-thirds majority required by revisions made to this section of the constitution in 1982. The constitutional revisions also created a new category of laws called "organic laws," which can be introduced by the government or one-fifth of the deputies in the AR and must be passed by two-thirds of the deputies. Organic laws would include any law concerning the electoral system or the organization and functioning of any organ of the government, such as the Constitutional Tribunal having to do with a state of emergency or the armed forces. In future, there will be further efforts to reduce the ideological baggage of the 1976 constitution and to streamline its procedural aspects.

The government will also be further decentralized. Portugal is under pressure from the EEC to put into place regional governments on the mainland. Although called for in the 1976 constitution and reaffirmed in the 1989 revisions, such governments have not been created for a host of complicated political and technical reasons. Eventually, this new level of government—between the national and local levels—will become a reality. At the same time there will probably be an evolution toward greater independence of the already extant autonomous regions of the Azores and Madeira. This will come about as the result of powerful separatist tendencies that first appeared on the islands during 1974 and 1975 when it seemed that Portugal would likely have a Communist government. In those years, the desire to separate was given voice by two movements, the Madeiran Liberation Front (Frente de Libertação Madeirense, or FLAMA) and the Azorean Liberation Front (Frente de Libertação Açoriana, or FLA) which sabotaged government facilities and, in the case of the latter, actively sought to detach the Azores from Portugal and seek to become a protectorate of the United States.

Separatist desires have resurfaced recently in acts of defiance against Lisbon by the presidents of the regional governments. In one incident in 1987, Joaquim Mota Amaral, the president of the regional government of the Azores, insisted that the Azorean flag be flown on the same level as Portugal's national colors. This provoked considerable consternation among the military, who saw Amaral's actions as a clear threat to the integrity of the national territory. More recently, João Alberto Jardim, the president of the regional government of Madeira, defied Lisbon by refusing to proclaim a three-day period of national mourning to remember Samora Machel, the president of Mozambique, who had died in a plane crash. Jardim has also defied Lisbon by inviting P. W. Botha, the former state president of South Africa, to Madeira for a "private" visit.

The desire for separation is fueled by a number of factors that, if they continue, could become a threat to the future physical boundaries of Portugal. First, Lisbon has long neglected the economies of the islands; consequently, they are among the poorest parts of Portugal. Second, there are a large number of Azoreans living in the United States and Canada who spur on separatist activities. Finally, these tendencies have been rekindled by the regionalization policy of the EEC, which the leaders of the islands see as an opportunity to lever greater autonomy from Lisbon.

In the 1991 presidential election, Mário Soares, who has proven to be a very popular president, was supported by the PSD and the PS. He won his second term handily, receiving some 70 percent of the votes.

Elections for parliament will also be held in 1991. If 1989's local elections are a harbinger of the future, it now appears very likely that the PSD will lose its absolute majority in parliament. The most likely scenario is that the PSD will continue to be the largest party in parliament but will have to govern either in formal coalition with the PS or CDS or by seeking support from CDS or PS, depending upon the issues. The next most likely scenario would see the PS as the largest party but without an absolute majority, which would mean that it would have to rely on the PSD or the CDS in order to govern. In either case, the 1990s will probably see a slight shift to the left in government policy as a result of the greater political weight of the PS. This shift will not entail, however, a reversal of efforts to deradicalize the constitution and privatize the economy.

In the economic realm, the future will see greater and greater integration of the Portuguese economy into that of the EEC. There are two possibilities: One is that the economy will come to resemble that of California, that is, it will be based essentially on diversified industry and agriculture. The other is that it will approximate the economy of Florida, that is, one overly dependent upon tourism and the production of a relatively narrow range of agricultural products. In order for the California future to become a reality, Portugal's manufacturing sector will have to be transformed from one of old, inefficient factories making products already overproduced in the EEC—steel, ships, textiles, food, and shoes—to one that produces manufactured goods that are in greater demand. At the same time the agricultural sector will have to be consolidated and mechanized. This sector will have to shed the last vestiges of peasant farming and become commercialized.

The real crunch will come on January 1, 1993, when the EEC is scheduled to become a single, unified market without commercial or trade barriers between member states. In 1993 Portugal's industry and agriculture will be instantly faced with competition from the highly advanced firms of Germany, France, Great Britain, and Italy without the benefit of protective tariffs or EEC aid. Although it is too early to say whether the unified market will devastate Portugal's indigenous industrial and agricultural sectors, there is considerable fear that its economy may face troubled times.

One thing is certain, however: Portugal has finally completed the transition to a democratic government. We can be sure that Portugal will not revert to monarchy or authoritarianism. The only road is forward to greater pluralism, decentralization, individual freedom, and integration into the broader European community.

REFERENCES

Ferreira, José Medeiros. *Portugal: Os Próximos 20 Anos*. Lisbon: Fundação Calouste Gulbenkian, 1988.

Gallagher, Tom. "Portugal's Atlantic Territories: The Separatist Challenge." *World Today* 39 (September 1979):353–359.

Portugal Outlook: A Political and Economic Update, no. 1. New York: Camões Center for the Study of the Portuguese-Speaking World, Columbia University, 1990.

Acronyms

ACN	National Civic Association (Associação Cívica Nacional)
AD	Democratic Alliance (Aliança Democrática)
ADITLA	Democratic Association for the Integration of East Timor with Australia (Associação Democrática para a Integração de Timor de Leste no Austrália)
ADS	Democratic Social Action (Acção Democrática Social)
ANC	African National Congress
ANP	National Popular Action (Acção Nacional Popular)
APODETI	Timorese Popular Democratic Association (Associação Popular Democrática Timorense)
APU	United Peoples' Action (Acção Povo Unido)
AR	Assembly of the Republic (Assembleia da República)
ASD	Social Democrat Action (Acção Social Democrata)
ASDI	Independent Social Democrat Association (Associação Social Democrata Independente)
ASDT	Timorese Social Democratic Association (Associação Social Democrática Timorense)
BR	Revolutionary Brigades (Brigadas Revolucionárias)
CADC	Academic Center of Christian Democracy (Centro Académico de Democracia Cristã)
CDE	Democratic Electoral Committee (Comissão Democrática Eleitoral)
CDS	Christian Democratic party of the Social Democratic Center (Partido do Centro Democrático Social)
CDU	Democratic Unitary Coalition (Coligação Democrático Unitário)
CEM	Monarchy Electoral Committee (Comissão Eleitoral Monarquica)
CEUD	Electoral Committee for Democratic Unity (Comissão Eleitoral para a Unidade Democrática)
CGTP	General Confederation of Portuguese Workers (Confederação Geral dos Trabalhadores Portugueses)
CIP	Confederation of Portuguese Industry (Confederação de Indústria Portuguesa)

CNARPE	National Committee for the Reelection of President Eanes (Comissão Nacional de Apoio a Recandidatura do Presidente Eanes)
COPCON	Continental Operations Command (Comando Operacional do Continente)
COREMO	Revolutionary Committee for Mozambique (Comité Revolucionário para Moçambique)
CR	Council of the Revolution (Conselho da Revolução)
CUF	United Fiber Company (Companhia União Fabril)
DGS	General Directorate of Security (Direcção-Geral de Segurança)
ECU	European currency unit
EEC	European Economic Community
EFTA	European Free Trade Association
EPL	Portuguese Liberation Army (Exército Português de Libertação)
FICO	Front for Independence and Continuity with the West (Frente para Independência e Continuidade com o Occidente)
FLA	Azorean Liberation Front (Frente de Libertação Açoriana)
FLAMA	Madeiran Liberation Front (Frente de Libertação Madeirense)
FNLA	National Front for the Liberation of Angola (Frente Nacional de Libertação de Angola)
FPLN	Patriotic National Liberation Front (Frente Patriótico de Libertação Nacional)
FRELIMO	Front for the Liberation of Mozambique (Frente de Libertação de Moçambique)
FRETLIN	Revolutionary Front for Independent East Timor (Frente Revolucionário para Timor do Leste Independente)
FRS	Republican and Socialist Front (Frente Repúblicana e Socialista)
FSP	Popular Socialist Front (Frente Socialista Popular)
FUR	United Revolutionary Front (Frente Unido Revolucionário)
GDP	gross domestic product
GNR	Republican National Guard (Guarda Nacional Repúblicana)
GUMO	United Group of Mozambique (Grupo Unido de Moçambique)
IMF	International Monetary Fund
JMLN	Military Junta of National Liberation (Junta Militar de Libertação Nacional)
JSN	Board of National Salvation (Junta de Salvação Nacional)
MAD	Movement for the Deepening of Democracy (Movimento para o Aprofundamento da Democracia)
MASP	Movement for the Support of Soares for the Presidency (Movimento para a Apoio de Soares para Presidência)
MDLP	Democratic Liberation Movement of Portugal (Movimento Democrático de Libertação de Portugal)
MDP	Portugueses Democratic Movement (Movimento Democrático Português)
MFA	Armed Forces Movement (Movimento das Forças Armadas)
MLSTP	Movement for the Liberation of São Tomé and Príncipe (Movimento para a Libertação de São Tomé e Príncipe)
MND	National Democratic Movement (Movimento Nacional Democrático)

MNI	Independent National Movement (Movimento Nacional Independente)
MPLA	Popular Movement for the Liberation of Angola (Movimento Popular de Libertação de Angola)
MSP	Popular Socialist Movement (Movimento Popular Socialista)
MUD	Movement of Democratic Unity (Movimento de Unidade Democrática)
NATO	North Atlantic Treaty Organization
PAIGC	African Independence party of Guinea and the Cape Verde Islands (Partido Africano de Independência para a Guiné e Cabo Verde)
PBS	Public Broadcasting Service
PCP	Portuguese Communist party (Partido Comunista Português)
PIDE	International Police for the Defense of the State (Polícia Internacional e do Defesa do Estado)
POUS	Unified Socialist Workers' party (Partido Operário Unificado Socialista)
PPD	People's Democratic party (Partido Popular Democrático)
PPM	Popular Monarchist party (Partido Popular Monárquico)
PRC	People's Republic of China
PRD	Democratic Renewal party (Partido Renovador Democrático)
PRE	Republican Evolutionist party (Partido Repúblicano Evolucionista)
PRP	Portuguese Republican party (Partido Repúblicano Português)
PS	Portuguese Socialist party (Partido Socialista)
PSD	Social Democrat party (Partido Social-Democrata)
PSP	Public Security Police (Polícia de Segurança Pública)
RENEMO	Mozambican National Resistance (Resistência Nacional de Moçambique)
SACEUR	Supreme Allied Command, Europe
SACLANT	Supreme Allied Command, Atlantic
SEDES	Society for Economic and Social Development (Sociadade para o Desenvolvimento Económico e Social)
SUV	Soldiers United Will Win (Soldados Unidos Vencerão)
UDP	Popular Democratic Union (União Democrática Popular)
UDT	Timorese Democratic Union (União Democrática Timorense)
UEDS	Leftist Union for Social Democracy (União de Esquerda para a Democracia Social)
UGT	General Union of Workers (União Geral dos Trabalhadores)
UN	National Union (União Nacional)
UNITA	National Union for the Total Independence of Angola (União Nacional para a Independência Total de Angola)
UNR	Republican National Union (União Nacional Repúblicana)
UPC	collective farms (Unidades da Produção Colectiva)
UR	Republican Union (União Repúblicana)

About the Book and Author

Two basic processes—industrialization and the emergence of the nation-state—have marked the evolution of many modern societies, particularly in Western Europe. Industrialization broadened the class structure of societies. With the new classes came demands for political power and influence, demands that were vigorously resisted by the ruling monarchies and landowning aristocracies. And with these demands came upheaval and, eventually, new forms of democratic social and political organization.

In Portugal's transition from absolutist monarchy to pluralist democracy can be found an example of these transformative processes at work. Yet the experience of this nation has been largely neglected in discussions of Western European politics.

With *Portugal: From Monarchy to Pluralist Democracy*, Walter C. Opello, Jr., brings the transformation of Portugal into sharp focus and, in doing so, offers interesting insights into the problems of forming a democratic regime. This profile traces Portugal's transition to democracy within the broader context of its historical development as a nation-state, documenting the effects of absolutism, imperialism, centralization, class and regional cleavages, and late industrialization on the Portuguese people, their polity, economy, and society. Exploring the themes that have shaped the development of Portugal's democratic structures, Professor Opello also assesses the future viability of these structures in light of the country's nondemocratic legacies.

Walter C. Opello, Jr., is professor and chair of political science at the State University of New York at Oswego. His works also include *Portugal's Political Development* (Westview).

Index

Abortion, 25, 27
Abrilada, 50
Absolutism, 46–48, 50, 51
Absolutists. *See* Absolutism
Academic Center of Christian Democracy (Centro Académico de Democracia Cristã; CADC), 62
ACN. *See* National Civic Association
Açorianas, 16
Action Française, 64
AD. *See* Democratic Alliance
Additional Acts (Actos Adicionais), 52
ADITLA. *See* Democratic Association for the Integration of East Timor with Australia
Administration, 47, 66, 101
ADS. *See* Democratic Social Action
Afonso II, 39, 46
Afonso III, 39, 40, 46
Afonso IV, 39, 40
Afonso V, 33, 41
Afonso VI, 46
Afonso, Jorge, 33
Afonso, José, 85
African Independence Party of Guinea and the Cape Verde Islands (Partido Africano de Independência para a Guiné e Cabo Verde; PAIGC), 81, 141

African National Congress (ANC), 148
Agrarian reform, 15, 99, 104–105, 123, 133–134
Agriculture. *See* Agrarian reform; Economy
Al-Andulus, 38
Albuquerque, Afonso d', 43
Alcazar Quivir, 44
Alcobaça (Cistercian Monastery), 10, 34
Alcoforada, Sister Mariana, 31
Aldeamentos (strategic hamlets), 82
Alentejanos, 15
Alentejo (region), 15
Alfama (Lisbon), 13
Alfonso VI, 37
Alfonso VII, 37, 38
Algarve (province and district), 15, 39
Aljubarrota (battle of), 29, 40, 145
Allies (World War I), 57
Allies (World War II), 71, 149
Almada (town), 13
Almeida, António José de, 56
Almeida, Dinis de, 83, 96
Almohad empire, 39
Alms-shires (*almoxarifados*), 47
Alms-sheriff (*almoxarife*), 47
Alto Alentejo (Upper Alentejo), 15
Alto Douro (Upper Douro), 7
Alves, Vitor, 84, 88, 96

Amaral, Diogo Freitas do, 89, 113, 116, 119, 120, 122
Amaral, Fernando, 124
Amaral, João Mota, 116, 122, 123, 153
ANC. *See* African National Congress
Andrade, Gomes Freira de, 49
Anglicans, 27
Angola, 57, 91, 140, 141, 142, 147, 148, 149
Angra do Heroísmo (district), 5, 16
ANP. *See* National Popular Action (Acção Nacional Popular)
Anticlericism, 25
António, Prior of Crato, 44, 45
Antunes, Ernesto Augusto de Melo, 88, 89, 95, 96
APODETI. *See* Timorese Popular Democratic Association
A Portuguesa (national anthem), 33
April 25 Association, 118
APU. *See* United People's Action
AR. *See* Assembly of the Republic
Arabs, 43
Aragon, 38
Architecture. *See* Arts
Armed Forces Movement (Movimento das Forças Armadas; MFA), 83–87, 88, 90, 92–93, 98, 150
Arriaga, Kaúlza de, 83
Arriaga, Manuel de, 57
Arthurian Legend, 29
Arts
  architecture, 34
  crafts, 35–36
  music, 29, 32–33
  painting, 33–34
  poetry, 29, 30
  prose, 29–32
  sculpture, 34–35
  theater, 30
ASD. *See* Social Democrat Action
ASDI. *See* Independent Social Democrat Association
ASDT. *See* Timorese Social Democrat Association

Assembly of the Armed Forces, 93, 95
Assembly of the Republic (Assembleia da República; AR), 100. *See also* Parliament
Assimilado (assimilated one) 80, 82
Association of Socialist Culture-Workers' Brotherhood (Associação de Cultura Socialista-Fraterndade Operária), 105
Asturias, 1, 6, 37
Atlantic Gothic. *See* Manueline architecture
Autonomous regions (Azores, Madeira), 101, 102, 112
Aveiro (city), 8, 43
Aveiro (district), 5, 8
Avenida de Liberdade (Lisbon), 12
Avis, house of, 29, 40, 44
Axis, 145
Azevedo, Améndio de, 114
Azevedo, José Baptista Pinheiro, 87, 96, 98
Azorean Liberation Front (Frente de Libertação Açoriana; FLA), 153
Azores (archipelago), 16
Azuleijos. *See* Tiles

Bairro Alto (Upper Quarter, Lisbon), 13
Baixa (downtown, Lisbon), 11, 12
Baixo Alentejo (Lower Alentejo), 15
Bakongo, 82
Balsemão, Francisco Pinto, 79, 109, 114, 115, 116, 122
Banco Crédito e Industrial, 129
Banco do Alentejano, 129
Banco Pinto e Sotto Mayor, 129
Baptists, 27
Barbieri, Nuno, 92
Barcelos (town), 6
Barreio (town), 13
Barreno, Maria Isabel, 32
Barreto, António, 104, 107
Barreto Law (Lei Barreto), 133
Barros, João de, 30

INDEX

Basto, Pinto family, 129
Bathalha Monastery, 10, 34
Battle of Aljubarrota. *See* Aljubarrota
Beatriz, 40
Beira Alta (Upper Beira, province), 8
Beira Baixa (Lower Beira, province), 8, 9
Beira Litoral (Coastal Beira, province) 8, 9
Beires, Sacramento, 71
Beja (district), 5, 15
Belém (city), 13(& photo), 14(photo)
Berbers, 19
Beresford, William Carr, 48, 49
Bloco Renovador (Renovator bloc), 121
Board of National Salvation (Junta de Salvação Nacional; JSN), 87–91
Bocage, Manuel Maria Barbosa du, 31
Bomtempo, João Domingos, 33
Bonnier, Snu, 109
Borges, Sá, 96
Borgia e Irmão (bank), 129
Botha, P. W., 148, 154
BR. *See* Revolutionary Brigades
Braga (district), 5, 6
Braga, Teófilo, 31, 54
Bragança, house of, 46
Branco, Aresta, 56
Braque, Georges, 34
Brás, Manuel de Costa, 118, 123
Brazil
  discovery of, 43
  relations with, 144
Brethren, 27
Brito, Carlos, 109
Brito, de (family), 129
Bucelas (wine region), 9
Bureaucracy, 47
Buiça, Manuel, 54
Burgundy, house of, 37
Business seizures, 132

Cabeçadas, José Mendes, 59, 72
Cabinet. *See* Council of Ministers

Cabo de São Vicente (Cape Saint Vincent), 15
Cabora Bassa (hydroelectric project), 82, 148
Cabral, Amílcar, 81
Cabral, Luís, 81
Cabral, Pedro Alvares, 43
Caciques (patrons), 24, 69
CADC. *See* Academic Center of Christian Democracy
Cadetes, 69
Caetano, Marcello José das Neves Alves, 78(photo)
  early life, 76, 77
  prime minister, 77–80, 81, 85, 130
Caetano, Maria de Jesus, 63
Caixas de Providências (social assistance institutions), 67
Calatravans (knights), 21, 39, 40
Caldo verde (soup), 6
Camacho, Brito, 56
Camões, Luís de, 30, 41
Campinos, Jorge, 96
Cancioneiros (songbooks), 29
Cantigas (songs), 29
Canton, 43
Cão, Diogo, 42
Cape Boador, 42
Cape of Good Hope, 43
Cape Town Treaty, 148
Cape Verde Islands, 91, 140, 141
Caravela (caravel), 41
Cardoso, Amadeus da Soua, 34
Cardoso, Lopes, 96, 104, 105
Carlos, Adelino da Palma, 89, 136
Carlos I, 54
Carlucci, Frank C., 150
Carmo, Isabel do, 76, 98
Carmo, Marques do, 96
Carmona, Oscar Fragosa, 59, 60, 64, 72, 73
Carneiro, António Soares, 109
Carneiro, Francisco Sá, 79, 93, 98, 106, 107, 114, 117
  deputy prime minister, 89
  killed, 109

leader of PSD, 89
  prime minister, 108, 109, 116
Cartaxo (wine region), 14
Carthaginians, 18
Carvalho, João de Sousa, 33
Carvalho, Otelo Saraiva de, 84
  commander of COPCON, 90, 91, 95, 96
  operations officer for MFA, 85
  presidential candidate, 103, 109
Carvalho e Melo, Sebastião José de. See Pombal, Marquês de
Casa da India (India House), 30
Casa São Marco, 73
Casas do povo (community centers), 68, 78
Casas dos pescadores (fishermen's centers), 68
Cascais (town), 13
Castelo Branco (district), 5, 9
Castelo São Jorge (Lisbon), 13
Castenhada, Fernão Lopes de, 30
Castile, 38, 40, 41
Castros (hilltop forts), 18, 19
Catholic party, 62, 63
Catholic University, 28
CDE. See Democratic Electoral Committee
CDS. See Social Democratic Center party
CDU. See Democratic Unitary Coalition
Celts, 18
Celtiberians. See Celts
Censorship, 32, 70, 87
CEM. See Monarchy Electoral Committee
Central Bloc (Bloco Central), 115, 116, 119
Centralization, 48
Cereal cultivation/production, 53
Cerejeira, Manuel Gonçalves, 62
CEUD. See Electoral Committee for Democratic Unity
Ceuta (Morocco), 41
Ceylon, 43

Cézanne, Paul, 34
CGTP. See General Confederation of Portuguese Workers
Chailly, Comte de, 31
Champalimaud, Miguel, 92
Champalimaud family, 129
Chamusca (wine region), 14
China. See People's Republic of China
Christian Democrats. See Social Democratic Center party
Christian reconquest, 19, 20
Church-state relations, 25–27, 70
CIP. See Confederation of Portuguese Industry
Civil wars, 51, 57, 95
Class system, 20–22, 47–48
Climate, 6, 7, 8, 9, 14, 15, 16
CNARPE. See National Committee for the Reelection of President Eanes
Coelho, Bento, 33
Coimbra (city), 8, 39
Coimbra (district), 5, 8
Coimbra (university), 8
Colares (wine region), 9
Collective farms, 93, 104, 105, 132
Colonial policy, 80–81, 140
Colonial wars, 80–83
Columbus, Christopher, 42
Comarcas (provinces), 47
Communists, 32, 64, 65, 66, 68, 86, 150. See also Portuguese Communist party.
Companhia União Fabril (CUF) See United Fiber Company
Concelhos (counties), 66, 102
Concordat of 1940, 26, 70
Confederation of Portuguese Industry (CIP), 135
Congo River, 43
Congregationalists, 27
Congress of Vienna, 50
Constâncio, Vitor, 121, 123, 124, 125
Constituent assembly, 93, 98

INDEX 165

Constitutional monarchy. *See* Liberalism
Constitutional revisions, 110–113, 152–153
Constitutional Tribunal, 111, 113, 123, 153
Constitutions
  Carta Constitucional, 50–51, 52, 64
  1822, 49–50, 52
  1838, 52
  1911, 54–55, 64, 65
  1933, 64–66, 77, 102
  1974, 98–102
Continental Operations Command (Comando Operacional do Continente; COPCON) 90, 91, 92, 95
Contreiras, Almada, 88
Convento de Cristo (Convent of Christ), 14, 34, 35(photo)
Cooperantes (technicians), 148
COPCON. *See* Continental Operations Command
Cordes, João Sinal de, 59, 60
COREMO. *See* Revolutionary Committee for Mozambique
Corporations, 68
Corporative Chamber (Câmara Corporativa), 66, 77
Correia, Angelo, 114
Correia, Gaspar, 30
Correia, Ramiro, 98
Cortes, 44, 45, 49, 50, 51. *See also* Parliament
Corvacho, Eurico, 96
Corvo (Azores), 16
Costa, Adelino Amaro da, 89, 108, 109
Costa, Afonso, 54, 56, 67
Costa, Alfredo, 54
Costa, Alfredo Nobre da, 106
Costa, Almeida e, 96
Costa, Fernando dos Santos, 72
Costa, José da, 87
Costa, José Júlio da, 57, 98
Costa, Manuel Gomes da, 57, 59

Costa, Maria Fátima Velho, 32
Couciero, Henrique Paiva, 57
Council of Ministers (*Conselho de Ministros*), 101
Council of the Revolution (Conselho da Revolução; CR), 93, 101, 108, 110, 113
Council of State, 110, 111, 112, 113, 125
Councilmen (*vereadores*), 66
Coups d'état. *See* Golpes d'estado
Coutinho, Rosa, 87
Couto, Diogo do, 30
CR. *See* Council of the Revolution
Cunha (wedge), 24
Cunha, Correia, 79
Cunha, Joaquim da Luz, 85
Cunhal, Alvaro, 88, 89, 105

Dadra, 91, 140, 142
Damão, 91, 140, 142
Dão (wine region), 8
Décadas, 30
Decentralization, 153
Decolonization, 140–144
Decree-law 353/73, 84
Delgado, Humberto, 74–75
Democratic Alliance (Aliança Democrática; AD), 107, 108, 109, 110, 111, 114, 115
Democratic and Socialist Left (Esquerda Socialista e Democrática), 105
Democratic Association for the Integration of East Timor with Australia (Associação Democrática para a Integração de Timor de Leste no Austrália; ADITLA), 143
Democratic Electoral Committee (Comissão Democrática Eleitoral; CDE), 75, 107
Democratic Liberation Movement of Portugal (Movimento Democrático de Libertação de Portugal; MDLP), 95
Democratic party, 56

Democratic People's Republic of Angola. *See* Angola
Democratic Renewal Party (Partido Renovador Democrático; PRD), 117, 118, 119, 120, 121, 122, 123, 124, 125
Democratic Social Action (Acção Democrática Social; ADS), 75
Democratic Unitary Coalition (Coligação Democrática Unitário; CDU), 125
Deputies, 100
DGS. *See* General Directorate of Security
Dias, Adalberto Sousa, 60
Dias, Bartolomeu, 43
Dinis, 38, 46
Discoveries. *See* Voyages of Discovery
Districts (*distritos*), 5
Diu, 91, 140, 142
Divorce, 25, 26, 27
Dom Henriques. *See* Prince Henry the Navigator
Douro River (Rio Douro), 1, 4, 7
Douro River hydroelectric project, 128
Drake, Sir Francis, 45
Duarte, 29
Duarte, Duke of Bragança, 45. *See also* João IV
Duarte, Nuno, 71, 73
Duros. See Hardliners
Dynastic revolutions, 40, 45, 46

Eanes, António dos Santos Ramalho
 Group of Nine Members, 96, 104(photo)
 presidential candidate, 8, 103
 president of PRD, 122, 123, 124, 125
 president of the republic, 104, 106, 108, 111, 112, 114, 115, 116, 117, 118, 119
 reelected president, 109
Eanes, Gil, 41

Economy
 after April 25, 1974, 131, 132
 agricultural sector, 130, 131
 balance of payments, 105, 108
 before April 25, 1974, 53, 79–80, 127–131, 134
 budget deficits, 53, 60, 79, 133, 138
 concentration of ownership, 129
 effects of unified market on, 154–155
 foreign exchange, 131
 foreign investment in, 128, 129, 138, 147
 foreign loans/aid, 134, 135, 136, 138
 imports, 133, 134, 135
 industrialization, 128, 130, 132, 136
 inflation, 105, 108, 127
 integration with EEC, 135–138, 154
 land expropriations, 104, 132
 manufacturing, 127, 129
 nationalizations, 93, 98, 132, 153
 overseas markets, 133
 privatization of, 113, 138, 153, 154
 state management of, 128, 130
 technical assistance for, 135, 137
 unemployment, 105, 135, 138
 workforce, 131
ECU. *See* European currency unit
Education, 28–29
Edward VII, 12
EEC. *See* European Economic Community
EFTA. *See* European Free Trade Association
Elections
 after April 25, 1974. *See* Elections, constituent; Elections, local; Elections, parliamentary; Elections, presidential
 during First Republic, 54, 56
 during liberal era, 52–53
 during New State, 72, 75, 79

See also Political attitudes; Voting behavior; Voting registration
Elections, constituent, 93-94
Elections, local, 114, 115
Elections, parliamentary
  1976, 102-103
  1979, 108
  1980, 108
  1983, 115
  1985, 117
  1987, 125
Elections, presidential
  1975, 103
  1980, 109
  1986, 119-120
  1991, 154
Electoral Committee for Democratic Unity (Comissão Eleitoral para a Unidade Democrática; CEUD), 75
Electoral constituencies, 89
Electoral system, 93, 100
Elizabeth I, 45
Elvas (town), 15
Emigration, 20, 80
Enlightenment, 25
EPL. *See* Portuguese Liberation Army
Espirito Santo family, 129
Estado Novo. *See* New State
Estremadura (province), 9
Estremoz (town), 15
European currency units (ECU), 137
European Economic Community (EEC), 135, 136, 137, 138, 144, 145, 146, 147, 152, 153, 154
European Free Trade Association, 135, 136
European Investment Bank, 137
Évora (district), 5, 15
Exports, 53, 133, 136, 138
Expresso (newspapers), 79

Fado, 33
Faial (Azores), 16
Faria, Leite de, 89
Farinha, Pinheiro, 96
Faro (district), 5
Fátima, 14, 26
Ferdinand II (León), 38
Ferdinand II (Spain), 49, 50
Fernandes, Vasco, 33
Fernando, 40
Ferreira, Casanova, 85
Ferreira, Madeiros, 107
FICO. *See* Front for Independence and Continuity with the West
Fifth Division, 82, 83, 85
Figueierdo, Mário de, 62
Figueira da Foz (town), 8
Fireside Chats (*conversas en família*), 78
First constitutional government, 92-93, 119
First provisional government, 80, 117
First Republic, 23, 53-58, 62
FLA. *See* Azorean Liberation Front
FLAMA. *See* Madeiran Liberation Front
FNLA. *See* National Front for the Liberation of Angola
Foreign relations, 140-151
FPLN. *See* Patriotic National Liberation Front
France, 137, 140, 147, 155
Franco, António Sousa, 107
Franco, Francisco, 147
Franco, João, 54
Freemasonry. *See* Masons
Freguesias (parishes), 66
Freitas, José Vicente, 60, 73
FRELIMO. *See* Front for the Liberation of Mozambique
French Revolution, 45
FRETLIN. *See* Revolutionary Front for Independent East Timor
Front for Independence and Continuity with the West (Frente para Independência e Continuidade com o Occidente; FICO), 141
Front for the Liberation of Mozambique (Frente de Libertação de Moçambique; FRELIMO), 82, 141, 142, 148

FRS. *See* Republican and Socialist Front
FSP. *See* Popular Socialist Front
Funchal (city), 16
Funchal (district), 5
FUR. *See* United Revolutionary Front

Galicia, 18, 37, 38
Galvão, Henrique, 73–74
Gama, Jaime, 121
Gama, Vasco da, 30, 43
Gambia River, 41
Garção, Pedro António Correia, 31
Garrett, Visconde de Almeida, 31
Gaspacho, 15
Gaulle, Charles de, 111
GDP. *See* Gross domestic product
General Confederation of Portuguese Workers (Confederação Geral dos Trabalhadores Portugueses; CGTP), 131, 132
General Directorate of Security (Direcção-Geral de Segurança; DGS), 79, 87. *See also* International Police for the Defense of the State
General Union of Workers (União Geral dos Trabalhadores; UGT), 132
Generation of 1870, 31
Geraldes, Geraldo, 38
Germany, 147, 149, 155
GNP. *See* Gross national product
GNR. *See* Republican National Guard
Goa, 91, 140, 142
Golpes d'estado
   April 25, 1974, 83–87
   May 28, 1922, 57–58
   October 5, 1910, 54
Gomes, Francisco de Costa, 84, 85, 87, 91, 92, 95, 96, 103, 150
Gomes Mário de Azevedo, 72, 75
Gomes, Rico Luís, 73
Gomes, Varela, 74, 92, 98
Gonçalves, Nuno, 33
Gonçalves, Pacheco, 89

Gonçalves, Vasco, 88, 89, 90, 91, 92, 93, 95, 96, 98, 108
Gouveira, André de, 28
Government, 98–102. *See also* Administration; Constitutional revisions; Constitutions; Local authorities; New State
Graciosa (Azores), 16
"Grandola, Vila Morena" (protest song), 85
Granjo, António, 57
Great Britain, 140, 144, 155
Great Depression, 127–128
Greece, 137, 138
Greeks, 18
Grêmios (guilds), 67
Gross domestic product (GDP), 130, 131, 132
Gross national product (GNP), 129
Group of Nine, 95–96, 98, 103
Guarda (city), 8
Guarda (district), 5, 8
Guimarães, 6, 37, 38
Guinea-Bissau, 81, 83, 141, 147, 148. *See also* Portuguese Guinea
GUMO. *See* United Group of Mozambique
Gypsies, 19

Hardliners (*duros*), 114, 117
Henri, Count, 37
Henrique, 44
Henriques, Afonso, 37, 38, 39
Herculano, Alexandre, 31
High Authority Against Corruption, 118
Historicals (Históricos), 52, 53, 54
Hitler, Adolf, 149
Holy Alliance, 50
Holy See, 25, 70
Hong Kong, 126
Horta (district), 5, 16
Horta, Maria Teresa, 32
Hospitalers (knights), 21, 39
"Hot Summer of 1975," 94
Human rights, 99

INDEX

Iberian Pact, 145, 147
Iberian Union, 44–46
Igreja da Santa Engrácia (Church of Saint Engrácia), 34
Igreja das Clerigos (Clerics' Church), 7
IMF. *See* International Monetary Fund
Independent National Movement (Movimento Nacional Independente; MNI), 74
Independent Social Democratic Association (Associação Social Democrata Independente; ASDI), 107
India, 142
Indígenas (natives), 180
Indonesia, 143
Infantes, 69
Inquirições (inquiries), 46
Inquisition, 27, 28
Institute for Agrarian Reorganization, 104
Integralismo Lusitano (Lusitanian Integralism), 64
International Monetary Fund (IMF), 105, 134, 135
International Police for the Defense of the State (Polícia Internacional e do Defesa do Estado; PIDE), 70, 73, 75, 79
International Settlement Bank, 134
Isabelle, Marie-Françoise, 42

Jacobins. *See* Liberalism
Japan, 43, 138
Jardim, Alberto João, 122, 153, 154
Jesuits, 28
Jews, 27, 43
JMLN. *See* Military Junta of National Liberation
João I, 30, 40
João II, 41, 42, 44
João III, 44, 45
João IV, 45, 46
João V, 47
João VI, 48, 49, 50
João, master of the Order of Aviz. *See* João I
John XXIII, Pope, 76
John of Gaunt, 40
José I, 47, 48
JSN. *See* Board of National Salvation
Juan I, 40
Junot, General, 48
Junqueiro, Abílio, 31
Junta (board), 66, 68

Kaunda, Kenneth, 142
Keil, Alfredo, 33
Kennedy administration, 149, 150
Khrushchev, Nikita, 73
Kissinger, Henry, 150

Labor Statute of 1933, 67
Lajes air force base, 16, 149, 150
Land Occupations/expropriations, 90, 92, 104, 132, 134
Latifúndios (large estates), 21, 23, 53
Latifundistas (owners of large estates), 22
League of Nations, 60
Leal, Francisco Cunha, 61, 72, 75
"Left Alternative," 95
Leftist Union for Social Democracy (UEDS), 105
Legislature. *See* Parliament
Leiria (district), 5, 8, 9
Leo XIII, Pope, 63
León, 37, 38
Lettres Portugaises (Portuguese Letters), 31
Liberalism, 23, 48, 49, 50, 51
Liberals. *See* Liberalism
Liceus (high schools), 29
Lisboa (district) 5, 9. *See also* Lisbon
Lisbon, 10–14, 38, 40, 43, 47, 48
Liszt, Franz, 33
Literacy, 28
Local authorities (*autarquias locais*), 101, 102
Local government. *See* Local authorities

Lopes, Fernão, 29, 30
Lopes, Higino Craveiro, 73
Lourenço, Vasco, 84, 96, 118
Luís, brother of Manuel I, 44
Luís, Philipe, 54
Luisa, Queen to João IV, 46
Lusitanian integralists, 63–64
Lusitanians, 18, 19
Lusitos, 69
Luso-Hispanic Council, 147
Luso-romans, 19

Mação, 140, 143, 144
Machado, Bernardo, 59
Machel, Samora, 153
Machete, Rui, 116
MAD. See Movement for the Deepening of Democracy
Madeira (archipelago), 16
Madeira (wine), 16
Madeiran Liberation Front (Frente de Libertção Madeirense; FLAMA), 153
Mafra (palace and monastery), 10, 34
Maia, Salgueiro, 86
Malabar Coast, 43
Manuel I, 30, 34, 43, 44, 47
Manuel II, 54, 55(photo), 71
MASP. See Movement for the Support of Soares for the Presidency
Manueline Architecture, 34
Mapa Côr de rosa (rose-colored map), 53
Maranos. See New Christians
Maria da Glória. See Maria II
Maria I, 48
Maria II, 50
Marques, Jaime Silveiro, 87
Marques, Marcelino, 84
Martinho, Hermínio, 117, 120, 121, 123
Martins, Joaquim, 32
Martins, José Ignácio da Costa, 88
Martins, Rogério, 130
"Marvelous generation," 41
Masons, 48

Matos, Norton de, 72, 73, 79
Maurras, Charles, 64
Maylays, 43
May 28 Movement, 57–58, 59, 74
Mayor (*presidente*), 66
Mbundu, 82
MDLP. See Democratic Liberation Movement of Portugal
MDP. See Portuguese Democratic Movement
Media, 32
Meireles, Manuel Quintão, 73
Mekong Delta, 43
Melo, Carlos Galvão de, 87, 109
Melo, Eurico de, 114
Melo, Francisco Manuel de, 30
Melo e Castro, Guilherme de, 78, 79
Melo family, 129
Meseta, 4, 7, 9
Methodists, 27
Methuen Treaty, 46
MFA. See Armed Forces Movement
Miguel, Frimino, 89, 116
Miguel I, 50, 51
Milicianos (conscripted officers), 84
Military Junta of National Liberation, 72
Minas Gerais (Brazil), 127
Minho (province), 5–6, 8
Minho River (Rio Minho), 6
Minhotos, 6
Minifúndios (small farms), 6, 23
MLSTP. See Movement for the Liberation of São Tomé and Príncipe
MND. See National Democratic Movement
MNI. See Independent National Movement
Modigliani, Amadeo, 34
Moghul empire, 43
Molaccas, 43
Mombassa, 43
Monarchist Cause, 71, 75
Monarchists, 59. See also Monarchist Cause; Monarchy Electoral Committee

Monarchy Electoral Committee (Comissão Eleitoral Monarquica; CEM), 75
Mondego River (Rio Mondego), 8
Mondlane, Eduardo, 82
Monsanto (village), 9
Moreira, Adriano, 122, 125
Morocco, 44
Moslems, 4, 19, 20, 37, 38, 39, 40, 41, 44
Mosteiro dos Jerónimos (Monastery of Jerome), 13
Mota, Joaquim Magalhães, 79, 89, 96, 107
Movement for the Deepening of Democracy (Movimento para o Aprofundamento da Democracia; MAD), 117
Movement for the Liberation of São Tomé and Príncipe (Movimento para a Libertação de São Tomé e Príncipe; MLSTP), 142
Movement for the Support of Soares for the Presidency (Movimento para a Apoio de Soares para Presidência; MASP), 119
Movement of Democratic Unity (Movimento de Unidade Democrática; MUD), 72
Mozambican National Resistance (Resistência Nacional de Moçambique; RENEMO), 148
Mozambique, 57, 82, 83, 91, 140, 141, 142, 147, 148, 149
MPLA. *See* Popular Movement for the Liberation of Angola
MSP. *See* Popular Socialist Movement
MUD. *See* Movement of Democratic Unity
Mulattoes, 82
Municipal Assembly (assembleia municipal), 102
Municipal Chamber (*Câmara Municipal*), 102
Muscat, 43
Mussolini, Benito, 57

Nagar-Aveli, 140, 142
Napoleon. *See* Napoleonic Wars
Napoleonic Wars, 48, 49
National Academy of Music, 33
National anthem, 33
National Assembly, 65, 66. *See also* Parliament
National Civic Association (Associação Cívica Nacional; ACN), 73
National Committee for the Reelection of President Eanes (Comissão Nacional de Apoio a Recandidatura do Presidente Eanes; CNARPE), 117
National Defense Law, 113
National Democratic Movement (Movimento Nacional Democrático; MND), 73
National Front for the Liberation of Angola (Frente Nacional de Libertação de Angola; FNLA), 82, 91, 142
National Political Council, 64
National Popular Action (Acção Nacional Popular; ANP), 79, 87, 89, 106. *See also* National Union
National Union (União Nacional; UN), 69 71
National Union for the Total Independence of Angola (União Nacional para a Independência Total de Angola; UNITA), 82, 91, 142, 148
NATO. *See* North Atlantic Treaty Organization
Nazaré (town), 10
Neto, Diogo, 87
Neves, Jaime, 96
New Christians (*Maranos*), 27
Newspapers, 32
New State (*Estado Novo*)
  Catholic Church, 26, 70
  censorship during, 32, 70
  collaborative agencies, 69
  constitution of, 64–66

Corporative Chamber of, 66
downfall of, 77–97
economic life during, 127–133
foreign policy of, 140, 144, 145, 146
formation of, 64
labor statute of, 67
local government during, 66
opposition to, 71–76, 80
organizations of, 68–70
parliament of, 65–66
school curriculum during, 70
Nkomati Accord, 148
Nogueira, Fernando, 120, 121, 123
North Atlantic Treaty Organization (NATO), 144, 145, 146, 150
Norway, 135
Novas Cartas Portugueses (New Portuguese Letters), 32

Obidos, Josefa de, 33
O Crime do Padre Amaro (The Sin of Father Amaro), 31
Olivares, Duke of, 45
Oliveira, Alvaro Augusto Viega de, 96
Oliveira, Júlio Domingos, 64
Olivença, 145
O'Neill, Alexandre, 32
O Primo Basílo (Cousin Basílo), 31
Ordens (professional orders), 68
Order of Avis, 40
Order of the Tower and Sword, 64
Organic laws, 153
Ormuz, 43
Ortigão, José, 31
Os Lusíadas, 30
Ourique, 38
Ovimbundo, 82

Pacem in Terris, 76
Paço Episcopal (Bishop's Palace), 7
Padrão dos Descobrimentos (Monument of the Discoveries), 35, 42(photo)

PAIGC. *See* African Independence Party of Guinea and the Cape Verde Islands
Palácio da Pena (Pena Palace), 10
Palácio Nacional (National Palace), 10
Pan American World Airways Corporation, 149
Parish assembly (assembleia de freguesia), 102
Parliament, 50, 52, 55, 65, 100, 112
Parliamentary groups (grupos parlamentar), 100
Parque Eduardo VII (Edward VII Park), 12
Pato, Octávio, 103
Patriotic National Liberation Front (Frente Patriótico de Libertação Nacional; FPLN), 75
Patronage. *See* Patron-client networks
Patron-client networks, 25
PBS, 32
PCP. *See* Portuguese Communist Party
Pedro, Emperor of Brazil, 49, 50
Pedro I, 40
Pedro II, 46
Pedro IV, 51
Penal colonies. *See* Prisons
Pentecostals, 27
People's Assemblies, 94, 95
People's Democratic party (Partido Popular Democrático; PPD), 89. *See also* Social Democrat party
People's Republic of China (PRC), 143, 144
Peregrinaçam (Pilgrimages), 30
Pereira, Aristides, 141
Pereira, Carmalinda, 105
Pereira, Nun'Alvares, 40
Pereira, Pedro Teotónio, 67
Peres, Fernando, 37
Persian Gulf, 43
Pessoa, Fernando, 31–32
Philip II, 44, 45
Philip III, 45
Philip IV, 45

Philipa of Lancaster, 40
Phoenecians, 10, 18
Pico (Azores), 16
Pico Ruivo (Madeira), 16
PIDE. *See* International Police for the Defense of the State
Pintado, Valentim Xavier, 89, 130
Pintasilgo, Maria de Loudres, 106, 107, 117, 118, 119, 120
Pinto, Carlos Mota, 106, 115, 116, 122
Pinto, Fernão Mendes, 30
Pinto, Luís Teixeira, 128
Pinto, Pereira, 88
Pinto, Serpa, 53
Political attitudes, 23–24
Political parties
  after April 25, 1974, 88–89, 95, 102–109, 114–126
  during First Republic, 53–58
  during New State, 65–66, 71–76, 78–79
  during nineteenth century, 51–53
  See also Democratic Renewal party, Popular Democratic Union, Portuguese Communist party, Portuguese Socialist party, Social Democrat party, Social Democratic Center party
Pombal, Marquês de, 11, 34, 47–48
Pombaline (architecture), 34
Ponta Delgada (district), 5, 16
Ponta de Sagres (Sagres Point), 15, 41
Ponte 25 de Abril (April 25 Bridge), 13, 128
Popular Democratic Union (União Democrática Popular; UDP), 94, 102, 103, 115
Popular Monarchist party (Partido Popular Monárquico; PPM), 94, 107, 115
Popular Movement for the Liberation of Angola (Movimento Popular de Libertação de Angola; MPLA), 82, 91, 142, 148

Popular Socialist Front (Frente Socialista Popular; FSP), 105
Popular Socialist Movement (Movimento Popular Socialista; MPS), 105
Population, 20
Portalegre (district), 5, 15
Porto (city), 7
Porto (district), 5
Porto Santo (Holy Port), 16
Portucalense, 1, 6, 37, 38
Portugal e o Futuro (Portugal and the Future), 84
Portuguese (language), 29, 39
Portuguese Communist Party (Partido Communista Português; PCP), 24, 88, 94, 102, 103, 105, 106, 109, 110, 114, 117, 119, 120, 121, 123, 124, 125, 131, 132, 137
Portuguese Democratic Movement (Movimento Democrático Português; MDP), 107
Portuguese Guinea, 82, 140, 149. *See also* Guinea-Bissau
Portuguese India, 142
Portuguese Legion (Legião Portuguesa), 69, 74, 87
Portuguese Liberation Army (Exército Português de Libertação; EPL), 95
Portuguese Republican party (Partido Republicano Português; PRP), 55–56
Portuguese Socialist party (Partido Socialista; PS), 24, 94, 102, 103, 105, 106, 109, 110, 111, 114, 115, 117, 119, 120, 121, 123, 124, 125, 132, 153, 154
Portuguese-Spanish armada, 45
Portuguese Youth (Mocidade Portuguesa), 69
POUS. *See* Unified Socialist Workers' party
PPD. *See* People's Democratic party
  See also Social Democrat party
PPM. *See* Popular Monarchist party

Praça de Restauradores (Lisbon), 12
Praça do Comêrcio (Lisbon), 11, 12, 13
PRC. See People's Republic of China
PRD. See Democratic Renewal party
PRE. See Republican Evolutionists party
Prester John, 41
Prince Henry the Navigator, 15, 41
Prisons, 70
Privatizations, 113, 138, 153, 154
Proctors (*procuradores*), 66
Progressives (Progressistas), 52
Promessas (vows), 27
Protestants, 27
Provinces, 12, 47
PRP. See Portuguese Republican party
PS. See Portuguese Socialist party
PSD. See Social Democrat party
PSP. See Public Security Police
Public Security Police (Polícia de Segurança Pública; PSP), 69–70
Purges. See Saneamentos

Quadragesimo Anno, 63
Quadruple Alliance, 51
Queiroga, Fernando, 72
Queiros, Eça de, 31
Queluz (what light) palace, 10
Quental, Antero de, 31
Quijo da Serra (mountain cheese), 8
Quina family, 129

Rabaeus, Bent, 135
Radio, 32
Rádio Renascença, 85
Reconquest, Christian, 38–40
Reformation, 27
Reformers, 107
Regenerators (Regeneradores), 52, 53, 54
Regionalization. See Decentralization
Rego, Raúl, 89
Regulatory commissions, 68
Religious practice, 27

RENEMO. See Mozambican National Resistance
Republican and Socialist Alliance, 71
Republican and Socialist Front (Frente Repúblicana e Socialista; FRS), 108
Republican Evolutionist party (Partido Repúblicano Evolucionista; PRE), 56
Republicanism, 26, 53, 54, 59, 60, 73. See also Republican Evolutionist party; Republican National Union; Republican Union
Republican National Guard (Guarda Nacional Repúblicana; GNR), 70, 86
Republican National Union (União Nacional Repúblicana; UNR), 56
Republicans. See Republicanism
Republican Union (União Repúblicana; UR), 56
Rerum Novarum, 63
Retornados (returned colonial settlers), 92, 95, 109, 133, 136
Revolutionary Brigades (Brigadas Revolucionárias), 76, 98
Revolutionary Committee for Mozambique (Comité Revolucionário para Moçambique; COREMO), 141
Revolutionary Front for Independent East Timor (Frente Revolucionário para Timor do Leste Independente; FRETLIN), 142, 143
Revolution of the Carnations, 86
Rhodes, Cecil, 53
Ria (lagoon), 8
Ribatejo, 14
Ribeiro, José, 61
Roberto, Holden, 82
Rodrigues, Aires, 105, 109
Romanceiros (ballads), 29
Romarias (pilgrimages), 6
Rosa, Tomás, 96

INDEX 175

Rosa, Walter, 96
Roseta, Helena, 114
Rossio (Lisbon), 12
Rotativism (rotativismo), 52–53, 54
Royal Commissions. *See Inquirições*
"Royal fifth," 42

SACEUR. *See* Supreme Allied Command, Europe
SACLANT. *See* Supreme Allied Command Atlantic
Sado River (Rio Sado), 18
Saint Thomas. *See* Thomist philosophy
Salazar, António de Oliveira, 62(photo)
 early life, 61–63
 finance minister, 60–61
 incapacitated, 69
 prime minister, 64–65
 See also New State
Salazar, Maria António, 63
Salazar, Maria de Resgate, 61
Salazar, Micas, 63
Salazar Bridge. *See* Ponte 25 de Abril
Salgueiro, João, 114
Saloio (region), 9
Saloios (hicks), 9
Sancho I, 39
Sancho II, 39
Saneamentos (purges), 87, 88
Santa Comba Dão, 61
Santa Liberdade. *See Santa Maria*
Santa Maria (Azores), 16
Santa Maria (cruise ship), 74
Santarém (district), 5, 14
Santos, Almeida, 96, 121
Santos, António Machado, 57
Santos, Eugénio dos, 12, 48
São João de Ajuda, 140
São Jorge (Azores), 16
São Mamede, 38
São Miguel (Azores), 16
São Tomé e Príncipe, 91, 140, 142
Savimbi, Jonas, 82
Scarlatti, Domenico, 33
Schools. *See* Education

Sebastião, 44
SEDES. *See* Society for Economic and Social Development
Segueira, Domingos António, 33
Seixal (town), 13
Selvagens (Rugged Islands), 16
Sena, Jorge de, 32
Senghor, Léopold, 81
Septemberists, 51
Serpa (town), 15
Serra, Manuel, 74, 105
Serra da Cabreira, 5
Serra da Estrela, 4, 8
Serra de Barroso, 5
Serra de Monchique, 5, 15
Serra de Sintra, 10
Serra do Caldeirão, 5, 15
Serra do Gerês, 5
Serra do Marão, 5
Setúbal (city), 16
Setúbal (district), 5, 9
Shantytowns (*bairros de lata*), 13
Silva, Aníbal Cavaco, 118(photo)
 finance minister, 108
 leader of PSD, 114, 116, 119, 122
 prime minister, 117, 120, 121, 123, 124, 125
Silva, António Maria da, 58, 59
Silves, Diogo de, 16, 41
Sindicatos (unions), 64–68, 131–132
Sinédrio, 48
Sines (industrial complex), 130
Sintra (town), 10
Slave trade, 46
Soares, Mário Alberto Nobre Lopes, 121(photo)
 foreign minister, 89, 90, 136, 141, 147
 opposition leader, 75
 presidential candidate, 119, 120
 president of the republic, 120, 121, 122, 123, 124, 125, 133, 137, 154
 prime minister, 103–106, 115
 secretary-general of PS, 88, 93, 109, 114

Social Democrat Action (Acção Social Democrata; ASD), 107
Social Democratic Center party (Partido do Centro Democrático Social; CDS), 24, 89, 94, 102, 103, 104, 106, 114, 115, 116, 117, 119, 122, 125, 154
Social Democrat party (Partido Social Democrata; PSD), 24, 89, 94, 102, 103, 104, 105, 106, 107, 109, 114, 115, 116, 117, 119, 122, 123, 124, 125, 132, 153, 154
Socialism. *See* Socialists
Socialists, 53. *See also* Portuguese Socialist party
Society for Economic and Social Development (Sociadade para o Desenvolvimento Económico e Social; SEDES), 76, 89
Soldiers United Will Win (Soldados Unidos Vencerão; SUV), 96
Sorel, Georges, 63, 64
Sousa, António Rebelo de, 107
Sousa, Marcelo Rebelo de, 116
South Africa, 148
Soutocico, 10(photo)
Soviet Union, 149, 150
Spain, 137, 138, 140, 145–147
Spínola, António de
　attempted golpe, 92–93
　chief of the general staff, 84, 85
　in exile, 95
　governor-general of Portuguese Guinea, 81
　head of the JSN, 87, 88
　interim president of the republic, 87
　return to Portugal, 98
　struggles with MFA, 89–91, 140, 141
Stalin, Joseph, 73
Stevenson, Adlai, 149
Strikes, 67, 71, 89, 132
Sumatra, 43
Superior Council of National Defense, 110, 112, 114

Supreme Allied Command, Atlantic (SACLANT), 146
Supreme Allied Command, Europe (SACEUR), 146
SUV. *See* Soldiers United Will Win
Swabians, 19
Sweden, 136
Switzerland, 136

Tagus River (Rio Tejo), 4, 7, 9, 11, 13
Tarik, 19
Tarrafal (penal colony), 70
Teatro Nacional de Dona Maria II (National Theater of Dona Maria II), 34
Technical University of Lisbon, 28
Telenovelas, 32
Teles, Eleanor, 40
Television, 32
Templar (knights), 14, 21, 39
Temple of Diana (Évora), 34
Terceira (Azores), 16
Teresa, 37, 38
Terrafria (cold land), 7
Terraquente (hot land), 7
Terras, 47
Thomist philosophy, 63
Tiles (*azuleijos*), 35–36
Timor, 43, 140, 142, 143
Timorese Democratic Union (União Democrática Timorense; UDT), 142, 143
Timorese Popular Democratic Association (Associação Popular Democrática Timorense; APODETI), 143
Timorese Social Democratic Association (Associação Social Democrática Timorense; ASDT), 143
Tomar (town), 14
Tomás, Américo, 74, 76, 79, 85, 86, 109
Topography, 4, 5, 6, 7, 8, 9, 10, 14, 15, 16
Torre de Belém, 13

Tourism, 10, 15, 16, 131, 133, 135, 136, 138
Tranquilidade (insurance company), 129
Trásmontanos, 7
Trás-os-Montes (province), 5, 6–7, 50
Treaty of Windsor, 40, 144
Tripeiros (tripe eaters), 7
Turks, 43

UDP. *See* Popular Democratic Union
UDT. *See* Timorese Democratic Union
UEDS. *See* Leftist Union for Social Democracy
UGT. *See* General Union of Workers
Ultimatum of 1890, 53
Ultras, 78, 79, 81, 83
UN. *See* National Union
Unified Market of 1992, 138, 154155
Unified Socialist Workers' party (Partido Operário Unificado Socialista; POUS), 105
Unionists. *See* Republican Union
Unions. *See* Sindicatos
UNITA. *See* National Union for the Total Independence of Angola
United Fiber Company (Companhia União Fabril), 92, 93, 129
United Group of Mozambique (Grupo Unido do Moçambique; GUMO), 141
United Nations, 149
United Peoples' Action (Acção Povo Unido; APU), 107, 115, 117, 119, 125
United Revolutionary Front (Frente Unido Revolucionário), 95
United States, 148–150
Universities. *See* Education
University of Coimbra, 8, 28
University of Lisbon, 28
UNR. *See* Republican National Union
UPC. *See* Collective farms

UR. *See* Republican Union
Urban-rural cleavage, 23–24

Vandals, 19
Vanguardistas, 69
Vatican. *See* Church-state relations
Veloso, Angelo, 119
Veloso, António Pires, 96, 109
Veto power, 112
Viana do Castelo (district), 5
Vicente, Gil, 30, 33
Vieira, Rocha, 123
Vila Francada, 50
Vila Franca de Xira, 50
Vila Nova de Gaia, 7
Vila Real (district), 5
Vila Real (town), 50
Vimieiro, 61
Vinho da mesa (table wine), 14
Vinho Verde (green wine), 6
Vintistas (Twentiests), 51
Viriato, 18
Viseu (district), 5, 8
Visigoths, 19
Vote of no confidence, 101
Voting behavior, 23–24, 27
Voting registration, 100
Voyages of Discovery, 21, 25, 30, 41–44

War of the Brothers, 51, 60
War with Castile, 40
Wards (bairros), 66
Weimar Republic, 64
Wellington, Duke of, 48
Wolfram (tungsten), 149
Women, 25, 32

Zaire River. *See* Congo River
Zarco, João Gonçalves, 16, 41
Zenha, Francisco Salgado, 89, 96, 118, 119, 120, 122
Zurara, Gomes Eanes de, 30